Environmental Evasion

Environmental Evasion

The Literary, Critical, and Cultural Politics of "Nature's Nation"

Lloyd Willis

Published by State University of New York Press, Albany

Printed in the United States of America

For information, contact State University of New York Press, Albany, NY
www.sunypress.edu

Production by Kelli W. LeRoux
Marketing by Michael Campochiaro

Library of Congress Cataloging-in-Publication Data

Willis, Lloyd, 1978–
Environmental evasion : the literary, critical, and cultural politics of "Nature's Nation" / Lloyd Willis.
p. cm.
Includes bibliographical references and index.
ISBN 978-1-4384-3281-6 (alk. paper)
1. American literature—History and criticism. 2. Environmentalism in literature. 3. Human ecology in literature. 4. Environmental policy in literature. 5. Environmental literature—History and criticism. I. Title.

PS169.E25W55 2010
810.9'36—dc22 2010005119

10 9 8 7 6 5 4 3 2 1

To Windy, Hailey, Owen, and Aiden

Contents

Acknowledgments ix

Introduction
American Literature and Environmental Politics 1
Historicizing Environmental Politics 4
The Unique Problem of Environmental Politics 8

Chapter 1
Ralph Waldo Emerson, Henry David Thoreau, and the Formation of American Literature's Core Environmental Values 19
Emerson's Redefinition of Nature 21
The Consequences of Emerson's Abstract and Imperialist Nature 25

Chapter 2
James Fenimore Cooper, American Canon Formation, and American Literature's Erasure of Environmental Anxiety 37
Removing Cooper from History and Delegitimizing His Environmental Politics 38
Recontextualizing Cooper and Restoring His Environmental Politics 43

Chapter 3
Henry Wadsworth Longfellow, United States National Literature, and the American Canon's Erasure of Material Nature 55
Longfellow's Literary Manifestoes 56
Longfellow and the Nineteenth-Century American Literature Debates 58
Longfellow's Un-Emersonian Nature 62
The Nation's Shifting Sense of Nature and Longfellow's Hedge Against the Future 64
Erasing Longfellow and Naturalizing American Literary Personality in the Early Twentieth Century 67

Chapter 4
Willa Cather and John Steinbeck, Environmental Schizophrenia, and Monstrous Ecology 75
The Unavoidability of Environmental Politics in Willa Cather's World 76
Environmental Desire and Environmental Schizophrenia 80
Cather's Canonically Modulated Environmental Schizophrenia 82
Steinbeck, Ecology, and American Culture 89
Steinbeck and Monstrosity 92
Steinbeck's Monstrous Ecology 94

Chapter 5
Zora Neale Hurston, the Power of Harlem, and the Promise of Florida 103
Hurston, Harlem, and Power 104
Creating a Floridian Blackspace 109

Afterword
Ernest Hemingway and American Literature's Legacy of Environmental Disengagement 125
The Circular Trajectory of Environmental Openness in *In Our Time* 127
Bad Faith in *Green Hills of Africa* 130

Notes 135

Works Cited 167

Index 185

Acknowledgments

Environmental Evasion would not be what it is without the tremendous efforts of the friends and colleagues who have supported me along the way. Stephanie Smith has tirelessly supported this project from the beginning, as have Sid Dobrin and Phil Wegner, and Jack Davis deserves credit for most of what I know about environmental history. I owe a debt of gratitude to my wonderful friend, James McDougall, who has always been willing to help me work through my own confusion, and this project, like all of my academic work, is a testament to the devotion of Bill Atwill, the professor who sacrificed amounts of time and energy, which I now begrudge my own students, to teach me how to think and write during my years as an undergraduate.

I must also thank everyone in the Lander University community who has helped me complete this book. Two grants from the Lander Foundation provided me with course relief in 2007 and 2008 that helped me finish two rounds of revisions. My colleagues in the English department willingly accepted the burden that fell upon them when my teaching load was reduced, and my work was made much easier by the reference librarians, Adam Haigh and Michael Berry, who always did whatever it took to provide the materials I needed.

Early versions of chapter 3 and chapter 4 have been published in the *Journal of American Culture* and *American Transcendental Quarterly*, respectively.

Finally, I must thank my parents, Danny and Sybil Willis, for support that has been so steady that I have always taken it for granted; my brothers and sister, whose support has been equally unwavering; and especially my wife and children. Windy and I married a year before I completed my BA, and she went with me to Florida so that I could continue my education in Gainesville. No one has made greater sacrifices to support my career than she has, and there are no words that can adequately express my gratitude for everything she has done for me. I began writing this book when our daughter, Hailey, was a newborn. I took it through its first round of wholesale revisions while watching my first son, Owen, take his first steps. By the time this book goes into print, Aiden, my second son, will be a toddler. I will always associate this book with the most wonderful times of my life: the Summer of 2004 when neither Windy nor I had to teach, which allowed us to spend our time doing nothing but loving each other and our beautiful daughter; the years we spent perfecting the art of road trips to Florida beaches—first on our own and then with Hailey; the frenzied years in South Carolina that forged us into a tightly knit, self-sufficient family of five.

Introduction

American Literature and Environmental Politics

"I think I liked the old Lou and Oscar better, and they probably feel the same about me. I even, if you can keep a secret,"—Carl leaned forward and touched her arm, smiling,—"I even think I liked the old country better. This is all very splendid in its way, but there was something about this country when it was a wild old beast that has haunted me all these years. Now, when I come back to all this milk and honey, I feel like the old German song, 'Wo bist du, wo bist du, mein geliebtest Land?'—Do you ever feel like that, I wonder?"

"Yes, sometimes, when I think about father and mother and those who are gone; so many of our old neighbors." Alexandra paused and looked up thoughtfully at the stars.

—Willa Cather, *O Pioneers!*

He watched even the last puny marks of man—cabin, clearing, the small and irregular fields which a year ago were jungle and in which the skeleton stalks of this year's cotton stood almost as tall and rank as the old cane had stood, as if man had had to marry his planting to the wilderness in order to conquer it—fall away and vanish. The twin banks marched with wilderness as he remembered it. . . . There was some of it left, although now it was two hundred miles from Jefferson when once it had been thirty. He had watched it, not being conquered, destroyed, so much as retreating since its purpose was served now and its time an outmoded time, retreating southward through this inverted-apex, this ∇-shaped section of earth between hills and River until what was left of it seemed now to be gathering and for the time arrested in one tremendous density of brooding and inscrutable impenetrability at the ultimate funneling tip.

—William Faulkner, *Go Down, Moses*

> This is not said in criticism of one system or the other but I do wonder whether there will come a time when we can no longer afford our wastefulness—chemical wastes in the rivers, metal wastes everywhere, and atomic wastes buried deep in the earth or sunk in the sea. When an Indian village became to deep in its own filth, the inhabitants moved. And we have no place to move.
>
> —John Steinbeck, *Travels with Charley*

> A continent ages quickly once we come. The natives live in harmony with it. But the foreigner destroys, cuts down the trees, drains the water, so that the water supply is altered and in a short time the soil, once the sod is turned over, is cropped out and, next, it starts to blow away as it has blown away in every old country and as I had seen it start to blow in Canada. The earth gets tired of being exploited. A country wears out quickly unless man puts back in it all his residue and that of all his beasts. When he quits using beasts and uses machines, the earth defeats him quickly. The machine can't reproduce, nor does it fertilize the soil, and it eats what he cannot raise. A country was made to be as we found it. We are the intruders and after we are dead we may have ruined it but it will still be there and we don't know what the next changes are. I suppose they all end up like Mongolia.
>
> Our people went to America because that was the place to go then. It had been a good country and we had made a bloody mess of it and I would go, now, somewhere else as we had always had the right to go somewhere else and as we had always gone. . . . Now I would go somewhere else. We always went in the old days and there were still good places to go.
>
> —Ernest Hemingway, *Green Hills of Africa*

I became interested in American literature's environmental politics when I noticed what seemed like environmental sentiments in Willa Cather's *O Pioneers!* and *My Ántonia*. I was struck by the way Cather punctured the tale of Alexandra Bergson's triumph over the prairie that killed her father with Carl Linstrum's blunt claim that he preferred the old, wild prairie. I was intrigued by her decision to undermine Jim Burden's credibility in *My Ántonia* by accusing him of being a romantic boy who made his fortune in oil and timber before having him suggest a deep affinity for the fading native prairie in the process of telling Ántonia Shimerda's story. Each novel seemed to present a faint, plaintive lamentation for the prairie that was being turned into a grid of agricultural production, but I associated environmentalist sentiment with another era, and the environmental lamentation was so subtle—so buried within layers of narration, expressed in such tentative voices—that I was not sure how to account for it.

Reading William Faulkner and Ernest Hemingway and John Steinbeck provided some answers. Like Cather, each of them recognized environmental change as an unavoidable part of the modern world. Faulkner saw it in Mississippi and wrote about it in *Go Down, Moses*; Hemingway witnessed it in Michigan and Africa and wrote about it in pieces such as *In Our Time* and *Green Hills of Africa*. Steinbeck witnessed environmental change in California, in the Gulf of California, and throughout the American heartland, and he bears witness to it all in texts such as *Cannery Row*, *Sea of Cortez*, *Travels with Charley*, *America and Americans*, and a whole host of articles and essays that he published throughout his career.

Faulkner, Hemingway, and Steinbeck show that Cather was not alone in her awareness of environmental change, and, along with Cather, they show that authors we do not automatically remember as "nature writers" were attuned to such matters. In the different ways they approach these issues, they also suggest that environmental change was a politically charged issue that had to be approached with great care. Cather approached it obliquely and with great delicacy; Faulkner offered an absolutely gut-wrenching portrayal of environmental ruin in Mississippi's "Big Bottom" in *Go Down, Moses* but refused to wade into politics; Hemingway offered clear testimony to environmental destruction in two continents but found ways to ignore it; Steinbeck, after much apparent wrangling with the issue, made bold statements about it in *Sea of Cortez*, *Travels with Charley*, and *American and Americans*, but he knew enough about how American culture reacted to radicalism in the mid-twentieth century to tread carefully in the footsteps of Tom Joad.

The environmental concerns these authors engage appear in their texts unexpectedly, almost as if they are unwelcome, as if they have forced their ways into the stories without the full permission of the authors themselves. Rather than serving as the guiding principles of the works in which they appear, these environmental problems are simply issues that could not be avoided. Cather, it seems, could not write a novel about the prairie without lamenting the loss of the place's original qualities; Hemingway could not write about Africa without mentioning the destructive impact of Western incursion; Steinbeck could not write about Monterey, California, without thinking about the ecological impact of the Pacific sardine industry.

When I set out to write this book, my purpose was to interrogate the oddity of these tense, halting encounters with environmental change in early-twentieth-century American literature. I wanted to understand why these authors were writing about environmental change in such complex and often conflicted ways. I wanted to understand why they approached the subject with such delicacy, and I wanted to understand how these engagements with environmental problems fit into the broader story of American literature.

To satisfy these curiosities, I have had to move from the twentieth century and the writings of those like Cather, Steinbeck, and their contemporaries to the early nineteenth century and the writings of those such as James Fenimore Cooper, Henry Wadsworth Longfellow, Ralph Waldo Emerson, and Henry David Thoreau. I have also had to dig quite extensively into the history of American environmental politics, which I have encountered in the recent work of historians such as William Cronon and Carolyn Merchant and in the writings of those, like Jeremy Belknap, Timothy Dwight, Marquis de Chastellux, George Perkins Marsh, John Muir, Gifford Pinchot, and Theodore Roosevelt, who shaped this history. In the grand scale, my conclusion is quite simple: environmental change—or environmental destruction, depending upon how one wishes to characterize it—has been recognized as a problem since the colonial period, but it has not been given a place in the story the nation prefers to tell about its relationship with the natural world.

The preferred explanation of the relationship between American culture and the North American environment is the one Perry Miller identifies in "The Romantic Dilemma in American Nationalism and the Concept of Nature," where he explains that the United States has always been imagined as "Nature's Nation" in relatively unproblematic terms (201). The nation's uniqueness, magnificence, and strength have been staked on the glory of its natural world from the beginning, and the body of literature that critics have shaped into a national canon since the late nineteenth century has preserved those authors, such as Emerson and Thoreau, who investigate the wonder and complexity of the natural world while marginalizing those, such as Cooper and Longfellow, who express anxiety about the consequences of the nation's environmental destructiveness.

Thus, the early twentieth century posed an intricate series of problems for authors who were bothered by American culture's environmental destructiveness. The prevailing aesthetics of the age held no place for the overt criticism of environmental destruction, and, despite early-twentieth-century conservation efforts, the nation was largely committed to maintaining its faith in the illimitability and indestructibility of its unique natural environment.

Historicizing Environmental Politics

When I began this project, I could not account for the faint environmentalist sentiments in Willa Cather's novels because I understood environmentalism as it is casually portrayed in popular discourse (and in the rare historical study such as Kirkpatrick Sale's *Green Revolutions*): as a unique phenomenon of the late twentieth century. Defined in that way, environmentalism is an unprecedented movement whose origins are marked by the publication of Rachel Carson's *Silent Spring* in 1962, the passage of the Wilderness Act in 1964, the celebration of Earth Day in 1970, and the constant media coverage of environmental crises such as the Love Canal incident in the late 1970s and the Exxon Valdez oil spill in the 1989.

From the perspective of that historical frame, any discussion of environmentalist sentiment in literature written before the 1960s can seem like an unfair imposition of our own concerns upon the past. The problem, however, is not the critical method but the imperfect understanding of environmentalism's history that seems to persist quite stubbornly—in popular and academic discourse alike—even after the burgeoning of ecocriticism and its related subdiscipline, environmental history.

As is the case with all historical narratives, the story of environmentalism's history is an exercise in periodization, and the events of the 1960s and 1970s, which seem to bear all the marks of pure originary moment, are best viewed as the markers of a periodic break in the history of environmental politics, not its absolute beginning. Historians of environmental politics have consistently shown this to be the case since the early 1980s. They agree, almost unanimously, that environmental politics should be understood as a long tradition that existed well before the nineteenth century.[1]

In New England, for instance, records of resource depletion, environmental anxieties, and conservation measures date back to the colonial period. Environmental historians have made it quite clear that the general pattern of colonial settlement produced almost immediate firewood shortages and then serious deforestation, which led, in turn, to depleted populations of game animals and exhausted soils.

The statistics the William Cronon and Carolyn Merchant present in their classic studies of environmental history offer the same shock value as those in *Silent Spring* or any of the World Watch reports or Al Gore's *An Inconvenient Truth*: colonies were experiencing firewood shortages within ten to fifteen years of settlement; Boston was experiencing wood shortages by 1683; populations of wild turkey and white-tailed deer were noticeably reduced by 1700 while beaver (and their attendant fur trade) had already generally vanished in New England; by 1800 the deer, elk, bear, and lynx had all gone the way of the beaver; by 1850, Rhode Island, Massachusetts, Vermont, and New Hampshire were all 30 to 50 percent deforested; and through all of this—the deforestation, the exhaustion of game animals—nonintensive agricultural practices were exhausting the region's soils to such an extent that a major portion of the population would bolt to the newly opened lands of formerly Iroquois and British territory in New York during the opening decades of the nineteenth century.[2]

The colonists and the citizens of the new nation surely took these changes in stride—that is largely what we do today, after all, even when the changes are observed with scientific precision and presented in film—but to imagine that these people were oblivious or unconcerned is inaccurate. The record here is just as compelling as the evidence of environmental change: the British government was taking steps to reserve all timber in Massachusetts for the Royal Navy as early as 1691, and in 1694 Massachusetts responded to the depletion of wild game by instituting hunting seasons for white-tailed deer (Cronon, 110, 101).[3]

By the middle of the eighteenth century, European and American observers were wringing their hands over the wastefulness of the American approach to nature. Peter Kalm, a Swedish naturalist who traveled extensively from Pennsylvania to Canada from 1748 to 1751, was appalled by the "carelessness" with which the American colonists treated "the grain fields, the meadows, the forests, [and] the cattle" (308). He perceived a particularly "hostile" attitude among Americans toward their "woods" and cites example after example of reckless agricultural practices that "will do for a time; but . . . will afterwards have bad consequences, as everyone may clearly see" (308, 307).

By the dawning of the nineteenth century, American and European observers were certain that the North American environment was experiencing major changes—even climatic changes—due to European involvement with the continent. Even the rare individuals, like Noah Webster, who vehemently rejected the notion that human impact could effect climate change eventually found their stance more and more difficult to maintain (Webster denied climate change in a series of publications between 1799 and 1806, but his confidence in his own claims noticeably declined over time) (Jehlen 51–54).

For most, these environmental changes were welcome—the winters seemed shorter and milder; the place seemed more capable of sustaining "civilized" life—but ambivalence and anxiety often ran throughout even the most optimistic descriptions of the situation. In a fashion that is similar to the later writings of Jeremy Belknap and Timothy Dwight, Marquis de Chastellux expresses profound optimism about climate change in his *Travels in North-America in the Years 1780, 1781 and 1782*, but his optimism is tempered by cautionary tales that make it sound as if the American environment may be teetering on the edge of disaster. He does not hesitate to suggest that a particular "climate may . . . be rendered more salubrious by draining some morasses in the neighbourhood" (275), but he still hints that the fate of imperial nations depends upon how environmental modification is managed:

> Nothing is more essential than the manner in which we proceed in the clearing of a country, for the salubrity of the air, nay even the order of the seasons, may depend on the access which we allow the winds, and the direction we may give them. It is a generally received opinion at Rome, that the air is less healthy since the felling of a large forest situated between that city and Ostia, which defended it from the winds known in Italy by the names of the Scirocco and the Libico. It is believed in Spain also, that the excessive droughts, of which the Castilians complain more and more, are occasioned by the cutting down of the woods, which used to attract and break the clouds in their passage. (232–33)

Having situated the history of environmental modification in this way, Chastellux explains that he feels compelled to "fix the attention of the learned in this country" upon the situation in Virginia, where environmental changes will have to be guided by the most judicious of hands. "The greatest part of Virginia," Chastellux writes,

> is very low and flat, and so divided by creeks and great rivers, that it appears absolutely redeemed from the sea, and an entire new creation; it is consequently very swampy, and can be dried only by the cutting down a great quantity of wood; but as on the other hand it can never be so drained as not still to abound with mephitical exhalations; and of what ever nature these exhalations may be, whether partaking of fixed or inflammable air, it is certain that vegetation absorbs them equally, and that trees are the most proper to accomplish this object. *It appears equally dangerous either to cut down or to preserve a great quantity of wood; so that the best manner of proceeding to clear the country, would be to disperse the settlements as much as possible, and to leave some groves of trees standing between them.* (233; emphasis added)

While Belknap and Dwight do not completely match the level of anxiety that is reflected in Chastellux's equation of Rome and Spain with the American colonies, they both offer the type of instruction that Chastellux calls for here. Belknap devotes two volumes of *The History of New Hampshire* (the volumes published in 1784 and 1791) to celebrating the blossoming of New Hampshire civilization and then makes the third volume (published in 1792) into a veritable guidebook for potential settlers, complete with advice on the most effective ways to clear forests and develop farms. Dwight offers similar advice throughout his *Travels in New England and New York* (1821–22) but not without counterbalancing glowing panoramic descriptions of the almost totally cultivated Connecticut River Valley with descriptions of the injudicious use of forest resources, as in the case of Newbury, Connecticut, where, he writes, settlers have "cut down their forest" with such an "improvident hand" that the resulting lack of resources may "hereafter put a final stop to the progress of population." (2:238)

The Unique Problem of Environmental Politics

Kalm, Chastellux, Belknap, and Dwight were actively participating in the environmental politics of their eras. They identified resource depletion as a problem that could limit the growth of the population and the nation, they diagnosed it as a product of wastefulness and laziness, and when they felt that ignorance was the culprit (as is the case with Belknap and Dwight) they provided the information they felt their audiences needed. Despite the pervasive evidence that people of the colonial and early republican periods noticed and worried about environmental change, it is still difficult to grant legitimacy to those thoughts and opinions.

It was difficult for Perry Miller when he wrote "The Romantic Dilemma in American Nationalism and the Concept of Nature." Miller's essay recognizes that the North American environment was monumentally important to nineteenth-century American culture (he argues that it was revered as a place where God spoke, as a place where the nation, not just individuals, could find spiritual guidance and psychic restoration), it recognizes that the march of American civilization threatened the very natural world that it revered, and it recognizes that this tendency to destroy the beloved produced a kind of psychic crisis for the young nation that only artists and writers had any hope of remedying. Nineteenth-century American culture, he explains, felt that it was the special "calling" of American artists—"our Coles, Durands, and Cropseys, our poets and novelists"—to urgently undertake "an accurate recording of scenery" to "fix the fleeting moment of primitive grandeur" because "in America Nature is going down in swift and inexorable defeat. She is being defaced, conquered—actually ravished" (198).

Miller clearly believes that serious environmental changes were taking place in the nineteenth century, and I think that to a lesser or greater extent he believes that artists and authors really did play a role in the shaping the culture's reaction to those changes. His misgivings, though, are apparent in the language he uses. He feels that the impassioned spirit of the nineteenth century, which reacted to environmental change in terms of "inexorable defeat" and ravishment, was overwrought. He casts the situation as a conflict between the civilized and the primitive, and when he applies those terms he feels that any argument against civilization must be specious. He even seems to feel that the whole crisis of American civilization overwriting American nature is made up, an unpleasant product of a Romanticism that allowed the locus of truth, beauty, and virtue to shift from God or the Bible to Nature, and that this elevation of Nature is what made nature's effacement a problem in the first place. Miller was all the more confident in his interpretation of this crisis as artificial because he knew, beyond the shadow a doubt, that "on the whole . . . the founders had no qualms about doing harm to nature by thrusting civilization upon it" (198).

The problem with environmentalism is not just the persistent sense that it is historically limited—it is easy enough to unearth the longer tradition that extends well beyond the nineteenth century. The problem for us, as it was for Miller, is that environmentalism is an anomalous form of politics because it moves against the grain of virtually every element of the modern Western episteme: it refuses to accept economic gain and national expansionism as unquestionable pursuits, it asks people to stop acting as atomized individuals and make sacrifices in the pursuit of goals as impersonal and abstract as saving the planet, and from time to time it asks that people subvert human interests for the good of the nonhuman.

These environmentalist demands can seem like trite, innocuous platitudes, but when they are taken seriously and inserted into literary, cultural, and political fields that are dedicated to nationalism, rationalism, democratic idealism, and material progress, they are more likely to seem incongruous and threatening, in some ways as Bartleby's "I prefer not to" is incongruous within and threatening to the office culture of nineteenth-century Wall Street. Bartleby's protest is entirely subversive, but it is deeply personal—it is an expression of Bartleby's own grievances, and, since he won't explain his actions, it attracts no followers. In the end, for all its revolutionary potential, it goes down as a severe case of individual petulance or belligerence that engendered nothing—no followers, no movement, no change.

When environmentalist demands emerge forcefully, in ways that suggest they are meant to be taken seriously, they carry Bartleby's incongruity, but they are all the more threatening because they articulate the grievance. They refuse to remain silent; they demand that the surrounding world shift and re-center its thinking around a new way of understanding the relationship between human existence and the world that supports it, and they call for communal action against the status quo.

Because it recognizes a flaw in the established system, because it demands an epistemological shift, and because it contains a call to action, environmentalism is less the fringe, hysterical, phenomenon that its detractors find it to be than it is an example of what the French philosopher Alain Badiou defines, in works such as *Being and Event*, *Saint Paul*, and *Ethics*, as a truth event. In these treatises, Badiou argues that truth is not an a priori construct but a thing produced by an event or rupture that arises unexpectedly from within an established situation. In this theory, every established situation contains a void—an unknowable, unspeakable aspect of its own being—and truth happens in the rare, unexpected moments when the void is recognized, given a name, and acted upon in a way that inspires a chain of future actions performed in the spirit of the original event.

The important thing about Badiou's idea of truth for our work here is that it points out the inherent radicalism that environmentalism possesses *as a truth event*, and it provides us with a way to explain the irregularity of environmentalism's extended historical narrative. By virtue of what it points out and what it asks people to do, environmentalism cannot help but be radical; it cannot help but challenge the current situation, and, like all truth events, all odds are stacked against its success. To be viable, to make any difference, truth events must exist beyond the fleeting moments when they articulate the previously unrecognized problem of a given situation. They must break through the inertia of the status quo, which Badiou refers to as the "instituted knowledges" or dominant ideologies of any given situation, and survive the forces that are invested in *not changing*. In the United States, the radicalism of environmental politics is particularly pronounced because the "instituted knowledges" it must displace are myths (that the continent is an empty, virgin space created by God to be redeemed or developed by the white race), misperceptions (that the continent is illimitable and its nature indestructible), and beliefs (commitments to technological progress, national expansion, and the development of wealth) that have been so woven into the national identity that opposing them can seem like opposing "Americanness" itself.[4]

Thus, it has been profoundly difficult for environmental politics to gain ground in American culture. We can create lists of writers and thinkers who have presented environmentalist ideas from the colonial era to the middle of the twentieth century (it is not exhaustive or authoritative, but my list includes Peter Kalm, Marquis de Chastellux, Jeremy Belknap, Timothy Dwight, James Fenimore Cooper, Susan Fenimore Cooper, George Perkins

Marsh, John Muir, Gifford Pinchot, Willa Cather, Ernest Hemingway, William Faulkner, Aldo Leopold, and John Steinbeck), but in many ways the story that such lists tell is one of starts, stops, and restarts rather than a steady historical progression toward a consistent, well-defined program of environmental politics. It is a history of ruptures that named the void in the American situation but that did not spark subsequent truth events so that what appears to be chronological progress toward the environmental politics we know today is often not progress or historical continuity but an arrangement of figures on a timeline independently arriving at the same realizations again and again.

From this perspective, Kalm and Chastellux named the void—the limitedness and fragility of the nation's nature—at the heart of the eighteenth century's understanding of the natural world, but it went nowhere. No secondary figures immediately appeared to carry their message forward. So, when James Fenimore Cooper expressed his concerns about the state of the environment in the early decades of the nineteenth century, he was largely restarting the debate, not continuing the one that had begun earlier. In almost every instance—in the case of Marsh and Muir and Leopold—this pattern repeated itself until, it seems, writers such as Cather and Steinbeck began to feel that pointing out the unsustainability of American culture's relationship with nature was either futile or not worth the risk they would incur as the bearers of a radical message.[5]

Environmental Evasion is certainly not a book about Alain Badiou or his philosophy of truth, but Badiou's work has shaped how I think about environmental politics. It has brought me to feel that the story of American environmental politics, from the beginning, has been a negotiation of *what could be said* about the relationship between the nation and the natural world upon which it has been built and what writers and activists *have been allowed to say* by a national culture dominated by ideologies that place it in direct opposition to environmental activism, and Badiou's work has helped me recognize that these same tensions exist in American literature and the critical conversations that have grown up around it.

In American literary studies, just as in American culture writ large, "instituted knowledges" have pushed back against environmental politics for decades. From the late nineteenth century to the last decades of the twentieth century, literary studies eschewed politics altogether and promoted aesthetics that often withheld from view the authors and texts that engaged literary politics. The first wave of American Studies contributed to the nation's mythologizing of the natural world as a virgin land (with Henry Nash Smith's *Virgin Land* in 1950) while also making any discussion of nature a discussion of literary genres (the pastoral) or literary devices (myths, symbols, and archetypes).

When environmental politics have entered literary criticism, they have been met with charges of "presentism," a term that seems designed to carry a burden of shame parallel to plagiarism. The two most prominent examples of this are Leo Marx's *Machine in the Garden* (1964) and Annette Kolody's *The Lay of the Land* (1975). Many would include *Machine in the Garden* with the other "master texts" of "cold war" American Studies because it tacitly accepts the thesis of *Virgin Land*, it uses the same white and male canon, it omits the same women and people of color of the master texts, and it recasts American literature into molds of archetypal pastoralism, but Marx does depart from the established order in one way: he suggests that white Americans of the nineteenth and early twentieth centuries were *bothered* by technology's intrusion into their virginal, pastoral gardens.[6] In the opinion of his critics, however, Marx's text is flawed because of problems inherent to the "Myth/Symbol" school of Americanist criticism and because (and here is the more damaging problem) they feel the technological anxieties Marx focuses upon in the book are really the concerns of his own era, not those of the nineteenth-century authors he studies in the book. For Bruck Kucklick, who famously desconstructed *Machine in the Garden* in "Myth and Symbol in American Studies" (1972), the damning flaw is presentism, the "notorious" error of historians that causes them to "read their interest back into the past, and misconstrue an individual's thought so that it is relevant for the present" and eventually "extract from an author what is significant for us," rather than what really was significant to the author (77).

When Annette Kolody published *The Lay of the Land*, she was met with a similar reception. Kolodny's book, of course, argues that North American environmental destruction is the unfortunate result of the way nature has been gendered since the beginning of European colonization. She argues that by turning the "new" land into a female virgin land Europeans placed North American nature into the category of the exploited and exploitable. Surely, the groundbreaking nature of her study can bear part of the blame for the stiff resistance it met—it was, after all, the first book to seriously challenge the commitment of American Studies to "virgin land" mythology—but one fleeting line in the book's preface, the line that says the project's "*original impetus*" is a "growing distress at what we have done to our continent," seems to have also played a role in the book's reception (ix). In her *New World, New Earth* (1979), Cecelia Tichi applied to Kolodny's book the same logic that Kuklick had used against Marx years earlier: in her opinion, *The Lay of the Land* is irredeemably damaged by its confession of environmentalist motivations, and Kolodny's tendency to recognize environmentalist sentiments in pre-contemporary authors is nothing more than another case of "mistaking palpable present effects for past intentions" (xvii).

In the 1980s and 1990s, American Studies concluded a major phrase of challenging the guiding assumptions of "cold war" criticism; revised its relationship to history; entered a deeply introspective moment; and finally grew silent on issues relating to either the environment or environmental politics. When environmental topics reappeared in literary criticism in the mid-1990s, they appeared as the special purview of the emerging field of ecocriticism, but, during those early years, even this critical field that operated under explicitly environmentalist motivations bore the signs of institutional resistances to environmental politics. When Cheryl Glotfelty first envisioned this new type of literary criticism, she was motivated by "the most pressing contemporary issue of all, namely, the global environmental crisis," but the criticism that ensued tended to focus on interdisciplinarity rather than politics (xv). It investigated the science and philosophical implications (holistic worldviews, metaphors of connectivity) of ecology and often converted these concepts into a new interpretive matrix that critics could use to dive beneath the surface of texts in search of ecological truths while almost unconsciously maintaining the idea that environmentalism is no more than a contemporary concern that can motivate criticism but not be the subject of it.

My purpose is not to undermine ecocriticism; as an undergraduate mentored in the 1990s by one of the people who was involved in its development, I was virtually reared on it, and I have been engaged with ecocriticism ever since. My purpose is merely to identify the degree to which environmental politics is, and has been, an anomaly in American Studies and its related critical fields. In these critical fields—even those most sympathetic to environmentalism—what has been said about environmental politics has been limited by the power of instituted knowledges that, in this case, include longstanding commitments to modernist aesthetics that devalue some of the texts that are most involved in environmental politics, related critical methods that focus on aesthetics and the creation of national mythologies, and a general resistance to political criticism that is further exacerbated by commonly held assumptions about the presentism of environmental politics. For all of these reasons, it was more natural for environmentally motivated scholars to turn toward interdisciplinarity—toward ecology and its related concerns—than it was for them to turn their lines of inquiry toward the very forms of politics that were explicitly motivating their work.

While it originated in my curiosities about the environmental commitments of early-twentieth-century authors, the story I have to tell in this book is much broader. *Environmental Evasion* is an attempt to explain the forces that have regulated environmental discourse in American literature since the early nineteenth century, to identify what has been omitted or silenced in the process of regulating this discourse, and to then resituate the work of early-twentieth-century writers such as Willa Cather and John Steinbeck in the matrix of literary, cultural, and environmental politics that was under construction well before they began their literary careers.

As one might expect in such an examination of the center and periphery of American literature's environmental politics, *Environmental Evasion* begins with a reassessment of American literature's most privileged environmental thinkers, Ralph Waldo Emerson and Henry David Thoreau. Chapter 1 argues that while Emerson and Thoreau both offer rich and varied interpretations of nature they unwittingly empower American imperialism and develop ways of evading the environmental destruction that this imperialism always leaves in its wake. Moreover, while their canonization—brought about in the broad shift in values that was guided by critics from Cornelius Mathews and Margaret Fuller to Mark Twain, George Santayana, Van Wyck Brooks, D. H. Lawrence, and Leslie Fiedler—has affected American literature's relationship with the natural world in two ways: it has limited the terms of subsequent environmental discourse in American literature, and it has marginalized the much different environmental visions of other authors such as James Fenimore Cooper and Henry Wadsworth Longfellow.

Chapter 2 and chapter 3 are attempts to recover the environmental politics of James Fenimore Cooper, the first commercially successful American novelist, and Henry Wadsworth Longfellow, the nineteenth century's most popular, most widely read American poet. Thus, chapter 2 argues that despite his devaluation in a critical tradition that stretches from Mark Twain to Leslie Fiedler Cooper's Leatherstocking series constitutes a significant intervention into American culture's vision of the natural world by breaking from a federalist rhetoric of environmental inexhaustibility that was pervasive in the early republic. Rather than continuing a tradition of federalist optimism practiced by those such as William Cooper (his father) and Timothy Dwight, Cooper argues that the United States is expanding into a limited environment, that the dominant capitalist culture of the United States is environmentally ruinous and unsustainable, that the continent has always already been a contested space rather than a virgin void, and that language and science are mechanisms of a Euro-American imperialism that was much more complex than the squatters, squires, and outcasts that populate Cooper's romances.

Chapter 3 argues that Henry Wadsworth Longfellow defined nature as a terrestrial rather than abstract phenomenon that could provide a basis for American exceptionality in a new transnationalist American literature. Longfellow's poetic project, as he defines it in three manifestoes published between 1823 and 1839, was to create a transnational American literature that based its exceptionality upon the uniqueness of the North American continent. Longfellow promoted his plan for an environmentally determined national literature through the 1850s, with the help of other powerful critics like James Russell Lowell, against Young Americans such as Cornelius Mathews who were vehemently promoting a drastically different American literature rooted in nativist patriotism. Longfellow attempted to fulfill his vision of an environmentally determined national literature in *Evangeline* and *The Song of Hiawatha*. Longfellow's plan for the development of a legitimate American literature depended upon the continued existence of a pristine and culturally significant North American environment, but his plan waned along with his critical reputation. By the time Santayana and Brooks formulated their vision of "American Literature" in the early twentieth century, any lingering notion of an environmentally determined or transnationalist American literature had vanished, and American Literature had become the product of an inclusive Whitmanian personality that was clothed in naturalistic rhetoric but freed from any dependence upon material nature itself.

Environmental Evasion's final two chapters and its afterword return to the twentieth century. While I could have extended my argument into other authors—particularly William Faulkner—I have limited the primary focus of these chapters to Willa Cather and John Steinbeck, Zora Neale Hurston, and Ernest Hemingway. Cather and Steinbeck are unique because they were in tune with the period's emerging ecological sciences, Hurston is unique because she was able to depart wholly from established methods of writing about the natural world, and Hemingway is remarkable because his extreme denial of environmental catastrophe seems to represent the culmination of American literature's evasive environmental politics.

Chapter 4, then, argues that Willa Cather and John Steinbeck, who recognized American culture as an environmentally destructive force, reacted to environmental crisis with an Emersonian environmental vision that suited the expectations of critical and national audiences that they believed would not tolerate any declaration of an unequivocally environmentalist position. As Emerson does in the nineteenth century, Cather and Steinbeck's fictional characters—and in some instances the authors themselves—fix their environmental gazes upon metonyms of environmental health and viability. Cather's characters maintain their faith in the permanence and permanent virginity of nature by fixing their environmental gazes upon horizons and vast environmental cycles that metonymically represent the health and availability of whole environmental systems, while Steinbeck and his characters perform the same action as they contemplate whether scientifically preserving small bits of the natural world from beneath the eaves of industry can provide a satisfactory hedge against widespread environmental destruction. Although Cather's refusal of environmental activism may be excused as a function of her general belief that literature should abstain from politics, there were plenty of reasons to stay within the Emersonian paradigm of abstract nature during the early twentieth century. Steinbeck seems to speak for both of them, and for the historical moment in general, in fact, when he suggests that launching a pointed environmentalist attack on American culture would subject anyone—authors included—to the social ostracism and group violence that befalls outcasts and monstrous figures throughout his body of work.

Chapter 5 pursues two goals: it offers a revisionist account of Zora Neale Hurston's relationship with the Harlem Renaissance, and it suggests that her work, read in the context of her letters and biographies, offers one way out of the Emersonian tradition of environmental abstraction. Although she is often portrayed as a central figure in the Harlem Renaissance—as the fun-loving, brash, life-of-the-party Zora—I argue that Hurston resented the system of patronage that she experienced in Harlem and that she viewed the South, and Florida in particular, as a place where the abjection of patronage could be avoided, where an alternative black art community could be formed and sustained, and where a vibrant black life could be practiced without impediment. From Richard Wright to Hazel Carby, Hurston's critics have claimed that she refused to engage the Great Migration and the desperate situation that the South offered to African Americans at the turn of the twentieth century. Against this line of critique, though, I suggest that Hurston's work is a bold act of spatial reterritorialization that uses fiction to reclaim a highly organic and immanently physical natural space within which a rich and vibrant African American life can be practiced without fear, humiliation, or apology.

Environmental Evasion's afterword argues that Ernest Hemingway brings American literature's politics of environmental evasion to its logical fulfillment. Particularly in texts such as *In Our Time* and *Green Hills of Africa*, Hemingway admits the reality of widespread environmental destruction but simultaneously proclaims that there will always be a "last good country" somewhere for those who have the knowledge, desire, and means to pursue it. In all cases and against all logic, he maintains faith in a vision of nature as ahistorical, illimitable, and indestructible along with a type of environmental imperialism that is like Thoreau's environmental imperialism but without Thoreau's claim that the self is the wilderness most worthy of pursuit.

In the end, it can be argued that literature is just not political in the ways that I am politicizing it, or that it should not be, and that American literature's failure to spur along a vigorous and sustained environmental movement from an early date should surprise no one. Cather, after all, argues in "The Novel Demeuble" that politics should be left to activists and their pamphlets rather than authors and their serious works of literature. Such arguments, though, disregard the basic fact that literature cannot help but politicize space—all space, including natural space. Whether or not they want to claim their agency, the stories we tell shape our spatial realities. They have always performed this function, and in American literature various spatial narratives have existed in competition from the moment that European explorers had to choose between casting North America as a wasteland or as a Garden of Eden. To recognize the power of the spatial politics that resides in storytelling or in the narrative, however, it is not necessary to return to the contact period. We need only return to 1962 and contemplate the ways that the story Rachel Carson told in 1962 revealed a new environmental reality that could not be ignored, a new environmental reality that fundamentally changed the way people thought about and experienced the natural world in the last decades of the twentieth century.[7]

Chapter 1

Ralph Waldo Emerson, Henry David Thoreau, and the Formation of American Literature's Core Environmental Values

There may be no figure in American literature who worked harder and had more success at cultivating a public image than Ralph Waldo Emerson.[1] In 1882, the year of Emerson's death, Bronson Alcott published a panegyric—originally presented to Emerson on his birthday in 1865—that describes him as the most influential American thinker of his age and presents "his genius [as] the measure and present expansion of the American mind" (21). Compared to some of the critical assessments that would follow, Alcott's assessment seems modest. In 1885, Oliver Wendell Holmes's biography of Emerson would find it "not irreverent but immanently fitting" to compare him to Jesus Christ (419). In 1907, George Woodberry's biography would go even farther. For Woodberry, the Jesus comparison is fair but insufficient; Emerson, he writes, is "a shining figure as on some Mount of Transfiguration," but he is also "kin with old Ionian philosophers . . . who first brought the light of intellect into this world," just as he is also an archetypal "Bostonian, living in a parish suburb of the city, stamped with peculiarity, the product of tradition, the creature of a local environment" (1).

After Woodberry, critics from George Santayana and Van Wyck Brooks to Harold Bloom established and consistently reaffirmed Emerson's centrality to American literature. Emerson is undoubtedly important, but this critical legacy, which is so committed to preserving his legacy in often hyperbolic terms, does not always allow for a complete understanding of his work, especially where we wish the record told a more flattering picture than it does.

Emerson's reputation as a poet and philosopher of nature is a case in point. The treatment that he grants the natural world in his total body of work is diverse and complex. In essays such as "Nature," "Circles," and "The Method of Nature," Emerson argues that the natural world is controlled by divine design but is nonetheless dynamic and ultimately unknowable. This is particularly clear in "The Method of Nature," which describes nature as an ultimately unobservable stream of perpetual motion (124–25). In poems such as "Hamatreya," "Earth-Song," and the three-part "Woodnotes," he writes of a generally anthropomorphized nature in an observational and spiritually reflective mode that is reminiscent of William Cullen Bryant while claiming a unique relationship between the poet and the natural world and occasionally slipping into a form of environmental apocalypticism that anticipates Robinson Jeffers's lyrics about the continued existence of the natural world after the demise of the human species.

We cannot fully understand the significance of Emerson, though, without acknowledging that there are less positive aspects of his environmental legacy and that these troublesome elements lie right in the heart of his body of work, in his 1836 *Nature*. In this essay, even as he extols nature's ability to heal the soul-squelching effects of the modern world and glorifies wilderness, Emerson abandons the nineteenth century's prevailing definition of nature as a terrestrial, tactile, female-gendered, and immanently destructible natural space. In the place of this common definition of nature, Emerson casts nature as an abstract and masculine intellectual field that contains female nature in the drastically different forms of disembodied, indestructible, and perpetually available essences.

Emerson's redefinition of nature is important because he has been so thoroughly absorbed into mainstream American culture and because he became a central figure of the American literary canon that emerged shortly after his death. For nineteenth-century American culture, Emerson's redefinition of nature was supremely convenient. By granting the culture a way to evade the moral and representational crises that are unavoidable when the destruction of nature is so easy to regard as the rape of a "virgin nature," a "mother nature," or a simultaneously pure and generative "virgin mother" nature, it offered the culture a way to cope with the environmental ravages of its own expansionism and imperialism.

For American literature, Emerson's redefinition has had numerous consequences. As I will explain in the second half of this chapter, his philosophy of nature has troubling implications that reappear in the ominous portions of Thoreau's writing, and as I will explain in the rest of *Environmental Evasion*, it is the philosophy of nature that has shaped American literature's reaction to the natural world. It has endured as the alternative environmental visions of writers such as James Fenimore Cooper and Henry Wadsworth Longfellow have been pushed into obscurity by generations of critics, and it is the philosophical expression of the environmental attitudes that Willa Cather, John Steinbeck, Ernest Hemingway, and Zora Neale Hurston responded to in the twentieth century.[2]

Emerson's Redefinition of Nature

When Emerson wrote about the natural world, he approached the subject with attitudes, interests, and modes of thinking that we already understand quite well. We know that Emerson could be unhinged by the female and feminine; we know that he was obsessed for a time with natural science—a science that developed along with Western imperialism as a method of opening up, pinning down, and bringing order to the wild and unruly natural world—and we know that his mode of thinking empowered American imperialism if it did not openly support it. When this combination of predispositions and interests meet in *Nature*, they render nature abstract and manipulate its gender in such a way that it becomes impervious to the ravages of imperial expansion.[3]

Much of Emerson's broad redefinition of nature appears in *Nature*'s introduction in four fundamental assertions that Emerson presents with his characteristic swiftness and self-confidence. In the space of a paragraph, he asserts that nature is "all that is separate from us, all which Philosophy distinguishes as the NOT ME, that is, both nature and art, all other men and my own body"; he asserts that "Nature, in the common sense, refers to the essences unchanged by man; space, the air, the river, the leaf"; he asserts that since these things are "essences" they remain unchanged as they are combined with human will to produce such things as "a house, a canal, a statue, a picture"; and he asserts that all of "man's" "operations taken together are so insignificant, a little chipping, baking, patching, and washing, that in an impression so grand as that of the world on the human mind, they do not vary the result."

There is nothing inflammatory in these four assertions; there is certainly nothing malicious. They simply seem like Emerson's typical philosophical discourse. The problem, though, is that Emerson mixes the philosophical with the common in such a way that a very physical problem—the state of the natural world in North America—comes to be disregarded because of the philosophical frame that he has applied to it. Framed as it is here—as everything that is "NOT ME"—nature immediately loses the materiality that it possesses when Timothy Dwight laments the improvident destruction of the forest around Newbury, Connecticut, or when James Fenimore Cooper's Natty Bumppo (whom I will discuss in chapter 2) watches the wasteful destruction of forests, fish, and fowl with disgust.

Thus, there is nothing "common" about Emerson's claim that "Nature, in the common sense, refers to the essences unchanged by man." The historical record shows that by the nineteenth century there was very little in Emerson's New England that had remained *un*changed by "man." Since European arrival, the landscape had changed, human, animal, and plant populations had changed, and geological cycles had changed to the point that some thought the climate itself had been changed by European involvement. Certainly, any claim in 1836 that the total sum of human activity had produced an "insignificant" impact on nature would have been disingenuous.

If Emerson had been suggesting that human impact had not changed North America, or if he were really suggesting that nature had not been—or could not be—changed by human impact, we could say that he was wrong. But he is not saying any of those things. Rather, he is demonstrating how to solve the entire problem of a mutable, destructible, finite environment that has always been gendered female; his solution is to remain in the disembodied and consistently masculine realm of the philosophical. When he appeals to the common meaning of nature, he never means "forests, fields, and streams" or anything of the sort.

They are *the essences*, not the *bodies*, of "space, the air, the river, the leaf" that remain unchanged for Emerson, and it is only in this abstract sense that Emerson can claim the impact of humans on the environment has been as "insignificant" as "a little chipping, baking, patching, and washing." What matters, in Emerson's formulation, is not that nature endures in any viable physical sense, but that an "impression" of it endures for "the human mind."

If one part of Emerson's redefinition of nature involves rendering it abstract and placing it in the realm of the philosophical, the other part involves manipulating the gender politics that surround nature and its use. Throughout Emerson's whole body of work, it is men who need nature. They need it to cure them from the feminizing crush of urban life. But the problem, for Emerson, is how to interact with a female thing, and he fixes this problem by simultaneously shifting the gender of both nature and the humans who interact with it.

At every opportunity, he erases the traditional gender assignments of humanity and nature so that when humans interact with the environment the exchange occurs between equals. When he focuses on "essences," for instance, Emerson effectively converts the female body of nature into disembodied abstractions that he generally regards as male. When nature is a disembodied essence, it and the male mind can interact on equal terms in the intellectual realm. In other instances, the gender reversal moves in the other direction. When he describes human impact on the environment—"a little chipping, baking, patching, and washing"—he transforms human environmental impact into women's work that is being performed upon a presumably female body.

When possible, it seems, Emerson prefers human interactions with nature to be platonic same-sexed affairs of intellectual exchange and or women's work, but, because of his anxieties about the state of masculinity in nineteenth-century America, he cannot abandon the notion that American men must reclaim or reassert their masculinities by penetrating nature—not through such feminine activities as "washing" or "patching." Men, Emerson claims, and particularly men "in the streets of cities," need nature to help them "believe and adore" a thoroughly masculine Christian God (8, 9). Nature is "so needful to man," that it is a healing "commodity" capable of restoring mind, body, masculinity, and sense of self:

> To the body and mind which have been cramped by noxious work or company, nature is medicinal and restores their tone. The tradesman, the attorney comes out of the din and craft of the street, and sees the sky and the woods, and is a man again. In their eternal calm, he finds himself. (13)

The shorter "Nature" that Emerson included in his 1844 *Essays, Second Series*, makes it even clearer than it is in *Nature* that this restorative meeting between men (and especially city men) and nature is—or ultimately must be—an act of penetration, not one of "chipping, baking, patching, and washing." In this essay, nature is again explicitly "medicinal," particularly for men threatened by cities that "give not the human senses room enough," but regeneration is available "at the gates of the forest" (312, 311). Here, Emerson writes, the city "man . . . is forced to leave his city estimates of great and small, wise and foolish. The knapsack of custom falls off his back" as he "penetrate[s] bodily this incredible beauty" before regaining a state of embryonic parasitism after penetration: "[W]e nestle in nature, and draw our living as parasites from her roots and grains, and we receive glances from the heavenly bodies, which call us to solitude" (311, 313, 312).

Even when Emerson maintains the standard gendering of human-environmental interactions, he does two things to defuse the situation's sexual tension and the attendant possibility of sexual violence. He infantilizes the masculine figure, and he revises the nation's pervasively terrestrial environmental gaze, which cannot help but focus frequently on environmental change, with a metonymic one that locates environmental health and perpetuity in exceptional specimens and celestial objects that lie beyond the reach of human activity.

Emerson's infantalization of the penetrating masculine figure is obvious in "Nature" in the suggestion that "we nestle in nature, and draw our living as parasites from her roots and grains," but it is also a persistent trope in *Nature*. He writes, for instance, that "the sun illuminates the eye of the man, but shines into the heart of the child," and he claims that "the lover of nature is he whose inward spirit and outward senses are still truly adjusted to each other; who has retained the spirit of infancy even into the era of manhood" (9). For this child of nature, "*intercourse* with heaven and earth" is not sexual, penetrative, or regenerative in any way; it is actually nourishing: it "becomes part of his daily food" (9; emphasis added). Lest anyone should fear that this childhood could be irrecoverably lost, Emerson explains that any man can recapture it by, ironically, penetrating nature as an adult: "In the woods too, a man casts off his years, as the snake his slough, and at what period soever of life, is always a child" (10).

We know that sexuality bothered Emerson, and his vexed relationship with sexuality did not end when he wrote about the natural world. For him, as for mainstream American culture, it has always been problematic that nature is traditionally gendered female—this gendering has always exposed any destruction of the natural world to the charge of metaphorical rape. Emerson evaded this problem by converting human-environmental interactions into nonthreatening homosexual, or fraternal, interactions and by infantilazing the male in such a way that intercourse with nature, even when it involves penetration, is so nonthreatening that it does not reaffirm a man's manhood but restores him to a childlike state.

If for Emerson there is an even better way to evade environmental crisis, it is to elevate the environmental gaze and literally *look over* the problems that threaten material nature and locate the essential qualities of nature in absolutely indestructible and practically immaterial astronomical bodies. Emerson creates this new method of seeing the natural world in the same moments that he champions nature's ability to salvage a threatened masculinity. Throughout *Nature*, Emerson locates nature in woods, horizons, sunrises and sunsets, and the sky in general, and he claims that "all natural objects make a kindred impression, when the mind is open to their influence" (9). Over the course of the essay, however, stars emerge as especially effective signifiers of nature. Nature and all of its medicinal qualities may be found, Emerson writes, by simply "look[ing] at the stars" (8). The mere visual presence of stars, according to Emerson, grants solitude; the "rays" that they emanate "separate between him and vulgar things;" and they offer "the perpetual presence of the sublime" (8). "If . . . stars should appear one night in a thousand years," Emerson continues, "how men would believe and adore; and preserve for many generations the remembrance of the city of God which had been shown!" (8–9). They are "envoys of beauty" that "light the universe with their admonishing smile" and, perhaps most importantly, they "awaken a certain reverence, because though always present, they are always inaccessible" (9).

By creating an environmental gaze that is fixed on astronomical space, Emerson finds a way to see everything he wants to see in nature. This particular gaze presents a natural world that is "uncontained," "immortal," "always present," and "always inaccessible"; it is a natural world entirely beyond the impact of any destructive human agency. With this environmental gaze, Emerson consolidates the qualities that he associates with the natural world into "stars," which function in the essay as discrete and ultimate metonyms for all that his vision of nature encompasses, and he protects this move toward an abstract metonymic nature by suggesting again that the actual presence and viability of nature's material phenomena are not so important as the disembodied "impression" of presence and viability that they offer the human mind. He creates, in other words, a situation in which the continued existence of a signifier of natural health and perpetuity is dispensable so long as the *signification* of natural health and perpetuity endures.

The Consequences of Emerson's Abstract and Imperialist Nature

Emerson's consistent conversion of nature into an abstraction—into a set of symbols that allow the nation to legitimize its destruction of the signified thing—is an act of spatial politics that is not unlike the imperialism that other critics have recognized in his "disembodied discourse" and "rhetorical circumvention," and I believe the consequences of this consistent move toward the abstract are clearest when Emerson is read in the context of Henri Lefebvre and Michel de Certeau's theories of space (Dallal, 50). In the context of spatial theory, Emerson's abstraction of nature does much to threaten the actual existence of physical, terrestrial natural space, and his power as both the crafter of narrative and an institutionally and culturally privileged figure makes Emerson an incredibly important figure in the formation of a national politics of environmental evasion during the nineteenth and early twentieth centuries.

In *The Production of Space*, Henri Lefebvre argues that social space is produced in successive layers upon an originary "natural space" that is the bedrock of all spatial productions. (30). He also understands that natural space, in the late twentieth century, exists under the immanent threat of ultimate destruction or erasure; "[N]ature is resistant, and infinite in its depth," he writes, "but it has been defeated, and now waits only for its ultimate voidance and destruction" (31). Lefebvre argues that the endangerment of natural space is due, in large part, to the destructive technological and industrial modes of spatial practice that have risen to prominence during the twentieth century, but he also understands that these destructive spatial practices are undergirded by methods of abstracting space that should bring Emerson's treatment of space in *Nature* squarely into any question about how nature and space have been theorized in American literature and culture.

Lefebvre understands abstract space as the product of economic and state power. Always "a product of war and violence," he writes, it is produced by both "capitalism and neocapitalism" and "instituted by a state, it is institutional" (285, 53, 285). Lefebvre argues that "*There is a violence intrinsic to abstraction*, and to abstraction's practical (social) use," and he suggests that this violence is manifested in the ways that abstraction "passes for an 'absence'—as distinct from the concrete 'presence' of objects, of things" while its "*modus operandi*," in reality, is always "devastation, destruction (even if such destruction may sometimes herald creation)" (289).

Abstract space, then, is a social, political, and economic production that obliterates that which it removes from the realms of physicality and history. It accomplishes all of these things by transforming the physical, historical space into signs and symbols—two concepts that Lefebvre approaches skeptically. In his formulation, "any space infused with value by a symbol is also a *reduced*—and homogenized—space," and "signs have something lethal about them—not by virtue of 'latent' or so-called unconscious forces, but, on the contrary, by virtue of the forced introduction of abstraction into nature." (288, 289).

Although Lefebvre's central purpose in *The Production of Space* is to complicate what he admits to be a nearly obvious fact—that "*(Social) space is a (social) product*"—his arguments about the production, practice, and experience of social space always recognize that social space happens in or on a physical environment. Natural space is often the first space impacted by political and economic social changes, and in the rise of abstract space it is constantly under threat of being reified into such abstractions as natural resources, commodities, or property. In perhaps the most apocalyptic line of his book, Lefebvre writes that "viewed as an instrument—and not merely as social appearance—abstract space is first of all the locus of nature, the tool that would dominate it and that therefore envisages its (ultimate) destruction" (307).

Lefebvre's work bears on Emerson's treatment of natural space in *Nature*, then, in numerous ways. *The Production of Space* should first of all call into question the neutrality—even placidity—of Emerson's quiet reconfiguration of nature as astronomical space, but it should also foreground the important role that Emerson played in the social, political, and economic processes of his day. In the two passages I have already quoted, nature is removed from physical and historical realms as Emerson associates it with disembodied qualities and concepts: solitude, the sublime, God, beauty, health and healing, masculinity, peace, rest and vigor. Emerson attaches all of these qualities to stars, thus creating signs and symbols that lack any physical referent whatever; he creates an entirely abstract concept of a natural world that lies entirely apart from not only the human realm, but the much broader spheres of the physical and tactile.

As helpful as I believe his work is in uncovering the method and results of Emerson's abstraction of natural space, Lefebvre cannot explain the special importance of Emerson's role in shaping spatial practice in the United States, which I believe lies at the nexus of narrative's unique spatial agency and Emerson's celebrity status. Although Lefebvre seems to imply it (particularly when he discusses the destructive power of signs and symbols), he does not spell out, as Michel de Certeau does in *The Practice of Everyday Life*, that narratives are a particularly powerful agent in the formation and modification of spatial practices. As he works to differentiate between "place," which he defines as a static "configuration" of subjects and objects, and "space," which he defines as the dynamic intersection of "mobile elements," de Certeau argues that narratives perform a function "that constantly transforms places into spaces or spaces into places" (117, 118). Narratives, according to de Certeau, are " 'culturally creative act[s] that "found" spaces just as they register "the loss of space" "where stories are disappearing" (123).[4]

Surprisingly, the act of spatial abstraction that Emerson carries out in *Nature* inverts and darkens de Certeau's claims. Emerson's culturally creative act founds an abstract space that philosophically effaces—and justifies the actual destruction of—a physically defined space upon which (as Lefebvre recognizes) cultures themselves are constructed. This narrative of spatial abstraction possesses a measure of inherent spatial agency, but this agency is tremendously amplified by the enormity of Emerson's celebrity, which is so powerful and so carefully guarded that it approximates the type of institutional power that Lefebvre associates with all processes of spatial abstraction. Emerson cultivated his own celebrity during his lifetime, by the time of his death he had become an icon of Americanness, and in the twentieth century his influence infiltrated fields as diverse as American politics, economics, architecture, and music as his literary-critical reputation underwent successive renewals that prevented him from ever slipping into a period of Melvillean obscurity.

In 1911, shortly after Woodberry's overreaching equation of Emerson with Jesus and "Ionian" philosophers and before Melville's rediscovery, George Santayana argued in "The Genteel Tradition in American Philosophy" that Emerson should be regarded, along with Poe and Hawthorne as one of "the three American writers whose personal endowment was perhaps the finest" (43). In 1915, in *America's Coming of Age*, Van Wyck Brooks proclaimed that he was the chief representative of American Transcendentalism and the figure who paved the way, in the fashion of John the Baptist, for Walt Whitman. In 1941, in *American Renaissance*, F. O. Matthiessen argued that "Emerson's theory of expression" was the foundation upon which all subsequent American literature would be built; it "was that on which Thoreau built, to which Whitman gave expression, and to which Hawthorne and Melville were indebted by being forced to react against its philosophical assumptions" (xii). In 1964, in *Waiting for the End*, Leslie Fiedler presented Emerson as the progenitor of one "of four lines of descent in our verse" (the other lines originate in Longfellow, Poe, and Whitman), without whom it "is impossible to deal with . . . Frost and E. A. Robinson" (196, 209). In 1968, in *American Poets: From the Puritans to the Present*, Hyatt Waggoner reasserted Emerson's centrality by arguing that "without understanding Emerson we cannot possibly begin to understand the later development of our poetry. No other poet, unless it be Whitman, has been so important as Emerson to later poets, including the greatest of them" (91).

Emerson's centrality to American literature and culture has been so firmly entrenched for so long that during the early 1980s questions about the *terms* of his centrality—not the centrality itself—cast the Emerson industry into a sustained attempt to maintain the positive legacy that Emerson had generally enjoyed, virtually uninterrupted, throughout the late nineteenth and early twentieth centuries. In 1980, in "Emerson, Nature, and the Sovereignty of Influence," Donald Pease introduced Emerson to deconstruction—his essay begins with a three-page discussion of Derrida and then argues that Emerson "represses his precursors when he declares originality, despairs of his past when he envisions the future, denies . . . fate when he recovers his freedom" (46). In 1981, in his Yale baccalaureate address, Bartlett Giamatti suggested that "it is Emerson who freed our politics and our politicians from any sense of restraint by extolling self-generated, unaffiliated power as the best foot to place in the small of the back of the man in front of you" (101). In June 1984, John Updike probed what he felt to be the "cloudy center," the "fatally faded" quality that Emerson seemed to have at the waning decades of the twentieth century (112). Over the course of his "Emersonianism," Updike argues that Emerson just no longer inspires new writing; he suggests that we don't find (and have never found) Emerson's idealism as believable as he did himself; he claims that Emerson's "optimistic cosmology must have seemed moonshine. . . . The assertion that nature and our souls are one is a deliberate affront to our common assumptions"; and he claims that "there is an awkwardness . . . in Emerson's present reputation: what we like about him is not what is important, and what *is* important we do not much like. Emerson the prophet of the new American religion seems cranky and dim; what we like is the less ethereal and ministerial Emerson, the wry, observant, shrewd, skeptical man of this world" (112, 117, 118, 128).

Pease's essay appeared in the academic (and a conservative would say radical) journal, *boundary* 2, and although it was eventually published Giamatti's critique was still originally offered in the ephemeral oral genre of the public address. Updike's "Emersonianism," though, appeared in the highbrow but still prominent public forum of the *New Yorker*. And, as if he had heard enough, or as if a family dispute had spilled out into the front yard where the neighbors could see it, it was after Updike's essay that Harold Bloom stepped in to stop the rabble-rousing and restore Emerson's hallowed status with a review in *The New York Review of Books*, entitled "Mr. America," that attacked Emerson's critics while reasserting the basic Emersonian claim that

> Emerson is *the* mind of our climate, *the* principal source of *the* American difference in poetry, criticism and pragmatic post-philosophy. . . . Emerson, by no means *the* greatest American writer . . . is *the* inescapable theorist of all subsequent American writing. From his moment to ours, American authors either are in *his* tradition, or else in a counter-tradition originating in opposition to him. (Section I; emphasis added)

While thus restating the basic tenets of Emersonianism, Bloom describes Giamatti's critique of Emerson as "humanistic" even as he dismisses it as unimportant, he diminishes Updike's claims as little more than "churchwardenly mewings," and he refuses to name Pease even as he attacks his work through a series of unmistakable allusions (Section IV). Pease's deconstructive method is precisely what Bloom attacks when he jeers at "the European modes [of interpretation] . . . currently touching their nadir in a younger rabblement celebrating itself as having repudiated the very idea of an individual reader or an individual critic," and the " 'Marxist literary groups' " and " 'Lacanian theory circles" that he believes to have generated such cockeyed criticism ("Mr. America" section III).

This debate between Bloom, Pease, Giamatti, and Updike was kept alive throughout the 1980s and 1990s in a series of essay collections that sharply defend the institution of positive Emersonianism. Since Bloom's initial reaffirmation of Emerson's cultural centrality, Bloom himself, Lawrence Buell, and Joel Porte and Saundra Morris have published collections of Emerson criticism that maintain his positive institutional status against what they clearly understand to be the rising threat of revisionist scholarship in the vein of Pease, Giamatti, and Updike.[5]

Bloom's "Mr. America" has been republished three times under the title "Emerson: Power at the Crossing"—in a collection of his own essays, in his own collection of Emerson criticism, and in Buell's collection of Emerson scholarship—and where it is not reprinted Porte and Morris repackage his defense in their own words. Although Giamatti's essay is mentioned in Bloom's response and in the opening portions of Porte and Morris's volume (in their joint preface and in Porte's own longer introduction), neither it nor Pease's essay, nor any of the later criticism that has carried their project forward is included in any of these collections—even in their (highly) selective bibliographies of Emerson scholarship. Responses to such reinterpretive work range, in these collections, from silent omission in Buell's volume (where only Bloom's reprinted essay performs any critique of the course of Emerson scholarship) to rebuffs and redirections in Porte's collection. In his introduction, Porte directly engages and works to rebuff Giamatti's claims, and rather than including or acknowledging the criticism that approaches Emerson *from* a postcolonial perspective to reveal Emerson's imperialism, Porte includes an essay by Robert Weisbuch that treats Emerson not as an imperialist but as a postcolonial American who "could not afford Europe because America could not" (193).[6]

By the time Porte and Morris's collection of Emerson scholarship appeared in 1999, the most pressing issue facing the Emerson institution had become postcolonialism and the suggestion, originating forcefully in Eric Cheyfitz's, *The Poetics of Imperialism: Translation and Colonization from* The Tempest *to* Tarzan in 1991, that Emerson's philosophy contains a more or less latent imperialism. To this suggestion Porte responded by again restating the privileged position of Emerson criticism: "Emerson would have nothing to do with an American civilization, so-called, willing to cover its crimes with cries of manifest destiny and America first. . . . [He] was a severe critic of an America capable of invading Mexico, oppressing blacks, and denying women equal rights" (11).

The problem for Porte in this passage, and for Emerson criticism in general, is the difference between Emerson as he was and what we might call—in terms like the ones Derrida uses in *The Post Card*—his textual transmissions. However Emerson might have reacted to American imperialism or racism, or environmentalism, the textual record he left us is an intricate but still powerful assemblage of philosophical, rhetorical, and visual methods of avoiding the very things that he would have regarded as so much unpleasantness. If Emerson had been Thoreau—if he had lived his life in relative obscurity and without a considerable audience for his writing and speaking engagements—his methods of evading these peculiarly American problems might have been transmissions into the void. Because of the national celebrity status Emerson cultivated for himself, though, all of his messages were injected directly into the national scene, and they were all the more powerful because they were coming from him. From the moment they left Emerson their consequences became unruly and unpredictable, they became subject to interpretations and applications that he may not have approved; at the moment of transmission, it became possible to take a comment that Emerson offered in a purely idealistic sense and use it to justify a set of exploitative national policies and attitudes, and considering the nation's intertwined suspicion of the intellectual and its affinity for the practical it should come as no surprise that Emerson's ideas have been applied in a very pragmatic sense to the goals of national power and progress.[7]

The consequences of Emerson's environmental philosophy, and evidence that they live an unruly life beyond his control, are evident even in the work of his closest disciple. Henry David Thoreau might have believed in the necessity of contact with nature even more than his mentor, but he found it more difficult to find a nature capable of restoring the soul and maintaining nineteenth-century masculinity. Like Emerson, he tried to maintain his faith in nature's regenerative capacity by restricting his environmental gaze, but his idealism in this sense proved insufficient. Stepping outside and gazing at the stars, for Thoreau, was not enough.

For Thoreau, as we all know, it was not just nature but a particularly wild manifestation of it that best restored the nineteenth-century's threatened masculinities. As he puts it in *Walden*,

> [O]ur village life would stagnate if it were not for the unexplored forests and meadows which surround it. We need the tonic of wilderness . . . we require that all things be mysterious and unexplorable, that land and sea be infinitely wild . . . we must be refreshed by the sight of inexhaustible vigor, vast and titanic features . . . of Nature. (298)

Almost everything that Thoreau identifies as fundamentally important in this passage—"unexplored forests and meadows," even "wilderness" itself—is either an object of Euro-American fantasy or, by the middle of the nineteenth century, deeply threatened. Even Walden Pond struggled to live up to what Thoreau wants in this passage—scarred by settlement, it was merely a simulacrum of the type of wilderness "we need."

To keep the revitalizing presence of wilderness alive even in the face of its actual demise, Thoreau poses two divergent arguments: locate wilderness in the self, and find wilderness in the corners of the globe where it has not been entirely effaced. In *Walden*, Thoreau argues that the Emersonian inquest is the best method of experiencing wilderness in an age of environmental destruction. In typically epigrammatic fashion, Thoreau writes, "One hastens to southern Africa to chase the giraffe; but surely that is not the game he would be after. How long, pray, would a man hunt giraffes if he could? Snipes and woodcocks also may afford rare sport; but I trust it would be nobler game to shoot one's self" (300). As he advocates this turn into the self, however, Thoreau calls upon the language of imperialism. "Be rather the Mungo Park, the Lewis and Clark and Frobisher, of your own streams and oceans; explore your own higher latitudes," he commands, "be a Columbus to whole new continents and worlds within you, opening new channels, not of trade, but of thought" (300–301).

Despite all the emphasis Thoreau places upon exploring interior wildernesses, his entire discussion is rife with exotic locations (Tierra del Fuego, Africa, China, Japan) and the explorers, such as Mungo Park, who "opened" them to the West. At the very least, the presence of these places and explorers underscores the fact that imperialism was a very real force in Thoreau's world. In *Walden* imperialism offers a secondary but still powerful avenue of nature experience that is entirely different from the inquest that Thoreau simultaneously promotes. Explorers and exploration usually appear in *Walden* as metaphors for this inquest, but Thoreau confesses that actual colonialist adventuring is a real and viable way to come into contact with a curative nature. "It is not worth the while to go round the world to count the cats in Zanzibar," he writes, "Yet do this even till you can do better, and you may perhaps find some 'Symmes' Hole' by which to get at the inside at last" (302).

On his way to discussing exotic manifestations of wilderness in *Walden*'s "Conclusion," Thoreau mentions the wilds of Canada, Ohio, Colorado, and the Yellowstone, but the trajectory of his narrative moves without hesitation toward Tierra del Fuego and the other extracontinental locations that offer "pure" wildernesses. *Walden* itself does not explain why Thoreau would overshoot the American West as he maps the globe's wildest regions, but eight years later, in "Walking" (1862), Thoreau hints that he has consigned natural space in North America to obliteration. In almost the same breath, he touts wildness, wilderness, and fertile soil as the primary sources of national power, he praises more explorers and glorifies the regions they have penetrated, and he unequivocally endorses the logic of imperialism.

Thoreau never explicitly discusses the fate of nature on a national or continental scale, but his comments upon New England land use contain a sense of environmental anxiety that is as representative and expansive as it is particular. He writes, for instance, that

> [a] hundred years ago they sold bark in our streets peeled from our own woods. In the very aspect of those primitive and rugged trees there was, methinks, a tanning principle which hardened and consolidated the fibres of men's thoughts. Ah! Already I shudder for these comparably degenerate days of my native village, when you cannot collect a load of bark of good thickness, and we no longer produce tar and turpentine. (648)

In typical fashion, Thoreau associates environmental health with intellectual health, but his concern with the state of the New England mind should not obscure the fact that he clearly understands the natural environment of New England as "degenerate[d]" in its own right.

The state of environmental degeneration, though, is not the whole story for Thoreau. It is equally disturbing for him that the entire situation is taken as a matter of course. When he returns to the topic of ecological degeneration later in the essay, he writes, "We are accustomed to say in New England that few and fewer pigeons visit us every year. Our forests furnish no mast for them . . . and there is scarcely a twig left for them to perch on" (660–61). In my reading at least, the most compelling element of this passage is its opening, which centers the entire anecdote around the community's response to the disappearance of the pigeons. The objective of the passage, it seems, is not to simply relate an ecological fact but to register the community's apathy. The disappearance of the pigeons is merely a custom that has woven itself into the fabric of the community, and the way Thoreau treats this communal indifference suggests that he understands this attitude as *the* problem facing nature in North America. It seems it is this combination of environmental destruction and communal apathy that causes Thoreau to concede the ultimate destruction of wild nature in North America.

Even though Thoreau seems to acquiesce to the destruction of North American nature, he does not so easily abandon the project of American empire, which he understands to depend upon close contact between nation and nature. All of Thoreau's examples of national strength simultaneously signify imperial power—"Greece, Rome, England"—and he argues that all such enduring empires "have been sustained by the primitive forests which anciently rotted where they stand. They survive as long as the soil is not exhausted" (648). Thoreau is suggesting, of course, that national and imperial strength are constructed with very real natural resources, but he also believes that state power depends upon a "wild source" of a vitality that resides in the nation's soil and forests (644).

With this combined awareness of a compromised North American natural environment and his sense that nations derive their strength from contact with wild nature, Thoreau faces a critical problem: If the destructive and apathetic culture of the United States destroys the vitality of its environment, how will the nation maintain its strength? Thoreau offers two alternatives: inquest or imperialism. In the case of "Walking," the inquest involves finding wilderness where you are. For Thoreau in *Walden* and "Walking," every swamp, bog, and patch of woods, in the right frame of mind, can become a revitalizing wilderness. Life itself, he argues, can be viewed as a "wildness" that "refreshes" ("Walking" 646). "One who pressed forward incessantly and never rested from his labors, who grew fast and made infinite demands on life," he writes, "would always find himself in a new country or wilderness, and surrounded by the raw material of life" (646).

Amid such transcendental arguments, though, lurk subaltern figures and newly colonized regions that offer the promise of contact with real, rather than imagined, wild nature—regions and figures, incidentally, that play no part at all in any of the traditional discussions of Thoreau's work. They raise questions with ugly answers, but they are there in the text nonetheless: Thoreau mentions "the Hottentots" and "our Northern Indians," as well as the archetypal figures of "the African" and "a Tahitian" (644–45). Just as "[o]ne who pressed forward incessantly and never rested from his labors," might generate his own regenerative wildness, it seems that in Thoreau's vision one could just as easily find fulfillment (and probably better fulfillment at that) by following the path of "the African hunter Cummings," whose clothes even bear the odor of close contact with a revivifying wilderness (646, 644).

Every explorer, exotic location, or subjugated population Thoreau mentions can be dismissed as a metaphor for introspective searching, but these places and figures exist in his work alongside a tacit acceptance of a particularly American colonialist logic that makes any such dismissal much more difficult. In a statement that legitimizes, if it does not endorse, the imperialist quest for contact with soil and wilderness, he writes that "[i]t is said to be the task of the American 'to work the virgin soil,' and that 'agriculture here already assumes proportions unknown everywhere else.' I think that *the farmer displaces the Indian even because he redeems the meadow, and so makes himself stronger and in some respects more natu-*

ral" (648; emphasis added). It can be argued in his defense that Thoreau promotes nonimperialist methods as the first and best ways to maintain contact with wild nature (however it is construed), but his allusion to the displacement of Native Americans unmistakably reprises the imperialism that stalks *Walden* and "Walking" in the specters of Cummings, Park, Africa, and Tahiti.

Emerson was the most prominent voice of American environmental philosophy in the nineteenth century, but in recent decades the old pecking order seems to have been reversed.[8] In terms of enduring importance, Thoreau seems to have supplanted his teacher. For Max Oelschlaeger in *The Idea of Wilderness* and Lawrence Buell in *The Environmental Imagination*, Thoreau is an environmental hero because his writing is less anthropocentric than Emerson's, because he is more interested in strict environmental observation than Emerson, and because his emphasis on environmental wholeness is more distinct than Emerson's. For Oelschlaeger, Thoreau is simply "St. Henry" ("Environment and the 21st Century" 13). For Buell, Thoreau's "Walden project" presents "a record and a model of a western sensibility working with and through the constraints of Eurocentric, androcentric, homocentric culture to arrive at an environmentally responsive position" (*Environmental Imagination* 23). For others such as Daniel Botkin in *No Man's Garden*, he is "an icon of environmentalism" who reminds us that "we must return to nature"; he is a figure whose life is "a metaphor for the search for a path to nature-knowledge and a resolution of the questions inherent in humanity's relationship with the rest of the natural world" (xvi).[9]

Oelschlaeger, Buell, and Botkin are correct. Thoreau accomplished everything they claim he accomplished, but this does not change the fact that the environmental philosophies of both Emerson and Thoreau, at least in part, elude what might have been the intentions of their creators. In spite of themselves, perhaps, their environmental philosophies propose a politics of environmental evasion that copes with the reality of environmental loss by continually replacing a material, feminine, finite, and destructible nature with an abstract, masculine construct that is always available somewhere, whether as astronomical metonyms of environmental health or as the object of imperialist pursuit.

While we may *want* to claim that Thoreau's ecological vision is the true environmental legacy of nineteenth-century America, it might be more accurate to suggest that the patterns of environmental evasion practiced by both Emerson and Thoreau had a greater impact on the course of American environmental history throughout the rest of the nineteenth century and through most of the twentieth century. As I will show in the rest of this book, these patterns of environmental evasion became tropes in environmentally engaged literature during the twentieth century, and the magnanimity of Emerson and Thoreau effectively shaded from view the much different environmental visions of authors who, though they may have been described as old, gray, and kind, were never granted the importance of our Emerson, who stands up so favorably with the likes of Jesus, or our Thoreau, who is our inveterate "Saint Henry."

Chapter 2

James Fenimore Cooper, American Canon Formation, and American Literature's Erasure of Environmental Anxiety

During the early 1840s, Horace Greeley was one of Emerson's most important supporters. He made sure that positive reviews of Emerson's work appeared regularly in his *New Yorker* and *New York Tribune*, effectively keeping Emerson's name in circulation even before he seemed to deserve the publicity. During the same period, though, Greeley was at odds with James Fenimore Cooper. In 1842, in fact, he lost a libel suit (with a judgment of two hundred dollars) that Cooper had brought against him.[1]

Emerson's interactions with Greeley moved him toward national fame and recognition; Cooper's interactions with the man, though providing a brief and satisfying legal victory, amounted to one episode in an entire decade of controversy that badly damaged his standing with the American public. Cooper had embroiled himself in a host of libel suits beginning in 1837 (one year after Emerson published *Nature*) after the press attacked him for his role in the Three Mile Point controversy in Cooperstown (in which Cooper forbade public use of a popular tract of land that he owned). The last libel suit was not settled until 1843, just one year before Cooper adopted another unpopular stance by defending the landholders in the 1844 New York anti-rent agitation.

From 1837 until the middle of the nineteenth century, then, Emerson's reputation took flight as Cooper's crumbled. While Emerson received the consistent support of the press even before he could maintain himself through book sales and lecturing, Cooper and the press were openly hostile to each other. Of course, the points of divergence between Emerson and Cooper extend far beyond their relationships with Greeley and the press. In their own writings, these two authors developed different relationships to the natural world that reflected the differences in their relationships with female intellectuals and female audiences. In literary criticism, Emerson became a part of American literature's origin story while Cooper came to live a shadowy half-life as part of what Van Wyck Brooks would describe as the nearly unreadable primordial soup that preceded the beginning of a legitimate national literature in the United States.

In his most enduring body of work, the five novels of the Leatherstocking series, published between 1823 and 1841, James Fenimore Cooper articulates a relationship with the natural world that is fundamentally at odds with Emerson's environmental vision. Rather than treating the natural world as the type of abstract, illimitable, and indestructible space that it becomes in Emerson's *Nature*, Cooper insists that nature in North America is a fundamentally political, physical, and limited space. He argues that the United States is expanding into a limited environment, that its dominant capitalist culture is environmentally ruinous and unsustainable, that the continent has always already been a contested space rather than a virgin void, and that language and science are mechanisms of a Euro-American imperialism that was much more complex than the squatters, squires, and outcasts that populate his romances.

Cooper damaged himself with his libel suits and with his stance on the rent wars, and it did not help that he continued to hold his family's federalist sympathies as the nation turned toward Jeffersonian and then Jacksonian democratic politics. For all of this, though, Cooper endured as a commercially successful and completely *readable* voice who maintained a transnationalist perspective in the face of American nationalism and artistic nativism until he became an example of all that was wrong with American literature for the authors and critics who shaped the twentieth century's modernist aesthetic—beginning with Mark Twain.

Removing Cooper from History and Delegitimizing His Environmental Politics

Mark Twain's 1895 essay, "Fenimore Cooper's Literary Offences," was a harbinger of the even sharper decline Cooper's reputation would undergo in the early twentieth century. In the snarky, sometimes vicious, mode that we expect from Twain, the essay mocks Cooper's style and suggests that his "English [is] a crime against the language," but it also marks a shift away from the historically and politically focused literature that dominated the literary scene of the nineteenth century.[2]

The critical assault on Cooper would become a sustained phenomenon several years later, largely at Harvard where George Santayana exerted his influence upon students such as Van Wyck Brooks and T. S. Eliot, and it would continue through the main line of American literary criticism from D. H. Lawrence to F. O. Matthiessen, Henry Nash Smith, Richard Chase, Leslie Fiedler, and Leo Marx.[3] This critical tradition constructed an ahistorical and apolitical American canon based on what Jane Tompkins has succinctly described as the "modernist demands" of "psychological complexity, moral ambiguity, epistemological sophistication, stylistic density, formal economy," and in the process it drastically devalued Cooper, which has had the secondary effect of silencing the environmental anxieties that are fundamental to his body of work even as it preserved the centrality of Emerson and his philosophy of environmental evasion (xvii).

Santayana and Brooks, as I explained in chapter 1, identified Emerson as one of the few stars in the dark night of nineteenth-century American letters, as a figure who was stunted by his sparse cultural environment but who still managed to lay out the artistic blueprint upon which Whitman would build his career. This privileging of Emerson, though, was accompanied by a thorough deconstruction of American culture as muddle-minded and effeminate.

In "The Genteel Tradition in American Philosophy," the cornerstone of his critique of American culture, Satayana argues that from a time shortly after its beginning the American cultural scene had been hamstrung by the dominance of an intellectual system, derived from bastardized forms of Calvinism and Transcendentalism, that was outdated, weak, passive, and feminine. This "genteel tradition," he argues, was the product of a Calvinism that had lost its convictions and its sense of rigor and a Transcendentalism that had lost its focus on systematic thought (61). It was a lazy, decadent, and "doubly artificial" intellectual foundation, in his opinion, that precluded the development of any legitimate national literature with the exception of a few rare masters whose genius could not be squelched by the meager culture that produced them (61). Beyond Emerson, Santayana respects the work of Poe and Hawthorne because they preferred to be "starved" rather than "retail the genteel tradition," and he reveres Walt Whitman as "the one American writer who has left the genteel tradition entirely behind" (43, 52).

Cooper, of course, was not starved by the nineteenth-century reading public, he did not disdain the femininity of his audience, and he was not ashamed of writing to satisfy it. None of this was lost on Leslie Fiedler, who repeats Santayana's gender bias in *Love and Death in the American Novel* when he states, in a scandalized tone, that "Cooper began his career imitating an English gentlewoman. . . . It is disconcerting to find him impersonating a female" (186).[4] After Santayana's "The Genteel Tradition in American Philosophy" and before Fiedler's *Love and Death in the American Novel*, however, it was Van Wyck Brooks who was the most committed to undoing Cooper's critical reputation. Brooks's foundational critique of Cooper appears in his 1915 *America's Coming of Age*—the book F. O. Matthiessen describes in *American Renaissance* as Brooks's most rigorous, most intellectually engaged, and most critically discriminating volume of criticism (Matthiessen, xvii).

In his analysis of American culture, Brooks recapitulates Santayana's emphasis on a divided American mind using two of the historical figures that are central to Santayana's analysis. For Brooks, American national culture is composed of an original puritanism that split into a "highbrow" "current of Transcendentalism" that reached its nadir in the philosophies of Jonathan Edwards and Ralph Waldo Emerson before becoming feminized, passive, and intellectually lazy, and a "lowbrow" "current of catchpenny opportunism" that coalesced in the figure of Benjamin Franklin before ultimately producing "the atmosphere of contemporary business life" (10). Brooks argues that this bifurcated culture, this slightly redefined "genteel tradition," has stifled cultural and literary development in the United States, that even in the second decade of the twentieth century the nation is still "like a vast Sargasso Sea—a prodigious welter of unconscious life, swept by ground-swells of half-conscious emotion" from which very few authors of merit have been able to emerge (164).

Following Santayana, Brooks regards Emerson, Hawthorne, and Poe as qualified successes whose writings can do no better than present a "fastidiously intellectual" "shadow world . . . in which only two colors exist, white and black," while hailing Walt Whitman as the only American literary figure who has been able to transcend the strictures of his native culture (113). Whitman, Brooks argues, was "a great vegetable of a man, all of a piece in roots, flavor, substantiality, and succulence, well-ripened in the common sunshine" who offered America, "for the first time . . . something organic in American life" (112). Within his organic self, "the hitherto incompatible extremes of the American temperament were fused"; he "cast into a crucible" "all those things which had been separate, self-sufficient, incoördinate" in American culture, and "they emerged, harmonious and molten, in a fresh democratic ideal, which is based upon the whole personality" (112, 118).

As critical as they were to establishing the centrality of Emerson, Poe, Hawthorne, and Whitman within an emerging American national literature, these arguments of Santayana and Brooks alternately exclude and dismiss Cooper. Never a subject of discussion in Santayana's work, where he looms as a silent and unacknowledged specter of the genteel tradition that disgusts him, Brooks describes Cooper as a participant in a womanish and domestic "literature of necessity" (47). Entirely secondary to a higher "absolute literature," Cooper's variety of literature, Brooks argues, was "simply a cog in the machinery of life" whose practitioners, "*like prudent women* who, having moved into a new house, energetically set to work laying down carpets, papering walls, cutting and hanging the most appropriate window-curtains, and pruning the garden—making it, in short, a place of reasonable charm and contentment" (47; emphasis added). Authors who participated in this "literature of necessity," Brooks argues, "were moralists . . . shot through with all manner of baccalaureate ideals" who produced texts that were rendered "barren" by "ulterior" objectives of "success or salvation" that were as ruinous to literary production as "the ulterior object of *making money*" (50, 53; emphasis added).

Brooks's patronizing claim that Cooper's art performs the "woman's work" of a more masculine and "absolute" American literature is clearly meant to demean, as is his quick but stabbing suggestion that any awareness of market forces produces a debased literature. The more lasting violence that Santayana and Brooks exact against Cooper, however, is their almost entire erasure of the literary and political situations that surround his work. As two of his early-twentieth-century defenders, Robert Spiller and Vernon Louis Parrington, argue, Cooper emerged from a federalist political tradition and he grappled with the federalist/democratic binary throughout his career. Cooper's father was a federalist, he attended Yale College during the reign of the arch-federalist Timothy Dwight, and, as a landowner who wished to maintain his holdings against the wishes of an increasingly democratic populace, he had deep federalist sympathies himself.[5]

The political system that the Santayana/Brooks strain of Americanist criticism endorses, however, is clearly democratic. Brooks glorifies Whitman because he embodies "a fresh democratic ideal" and subsequent criticism has followed his lead. In a move that is representative of the much larger trend, D. H. Lawrence opens his 1933 *Studies in Classic American Literature* with a discussion of Benjamin Franklin and continues on to Crèvecoeur, whose yeoman agrarianism anticipates Jeffersonian democracy, and arrives at Cooper with no more historical or political context than this. Similarly, the first sentence of the prologue to Henry Nash Smith's 1950 *Virgin Land* is Crèvecoeur's question, "What is an American?" From there, Smith opens his book with a discussion of Jefferson and follows the familiar democratic trajectory that culminates in a chapter on democracy's bard, Walt Whitman, before ever engaging Cooper. Even Leo Marx's 1964 *Machine in the Garden*, which one might reasonably expect to engage Cooper, opens with a discussion of Hawthorne, proceeds into a discussion of Shakespeare, and then entirely overshoots Cooper and his historical moment as it moves from discussions of Robert Beverly and Jefferson to Emerson, Thoreau, Melville, Twain, Henry James, and F. Scott Fitzgerald.

Cooper's status has improved substantially since the canon debates of the 1980s and the 1990s, but it is still difficult to determine how to interpret his environmental politics. In *The Lay of the Land* (1975), Kolodny argued without hesitation that "the gutting of forests and the increase of the population" in and around Cooperstown were events that Cooper had watched "with dismay;" that Cooper's subsequent creation of Templeton in *The Pioneers* marked a deliberate attempt "to correct" the environmental "abuses" that he had witnessed in his own lifetime; and that Marmaduke Temple, the landowning aristocrat of *The Pioneers*, was a "well-intentioned conservationist" for attempting to regulate fishing and hunting seasons and for his interest in similar means of protecting forests (72, 91).

As I have already mentioned, however, Kolodny's argument was subject to quick rebuke. For Cecilia Tichi in *New World, New Earth*, the situation was simple: "early Americans" did not lament environmental change as Kolodny claims Cooper does; they welcomed it. "Far from heedlessly vandalizing the environment," she argues, "early Americans saw its modification—in fact, its reform—as an ideological imperative that must proceed together with America's moral regeneration" (viii). Within this frame, Tichi explains that the true center of Cooper's novel should be Marmaduke Temple, not Natty Bumppo, because it is he, the "national paragon," who must "mandate environmental reform in the name of civilization" (169). Because Cooper was skeptical about the national project of transforming the New World into a "New Earth," Tichi interprets Cooper's entire artistic project as a failure that ends in "moral allegory" and "diatribe unleavened by satiric skill," a "fecal commemoration of a rotten New Earth" (187).[6]

While no other critics use such language to deconstruct Cooper's environmental concerns, the deconstruction of Kolodny's interpretation has continued apace. In Tichi's wake, critics have suggested even more explicitly that ecology plays no role in *The Pioneers* and that the presence of game laws in *The Pioneers* says more about class than it does about any interest in conservation. Richard Godden has written, for instance, that "Temple's game laws" are "too often taken ecologically. Temple as conservationist arises exclusively from twentieth-century misreading; his interest in deer, maple and bass, like his interest in coal and canals, expresses a preoccupation with development" (125). And while Charles Swann has not leveled accusations of misreading, he has suggested that class, not conservationism, is the best context for reading Temple's game laws because "the history of game laws *is* a history of class laws" (97). From such a perspective, Temple's game laws do not indicate a legitimate concern for environmental exhaustion, as Kolodny suggests they may, but "a democratic rhetoric referring to the rule of law which conceals the way in which a would-be American aristocracy is in danger of replicating an aristocratic Europe" (Swann 100).

Recontextualizing Cooper and Restoring His Environmental Politics

Tichi, Godden, and Swann submit Kolodny's initial claims about Cooper's environmental concerns to valuable scrutiny, but they perform two misreadings, neither of which are surprising: they tacitly interpret environmental politics as an exclusively late-twentieth-century phenomenon, and they never consider reading Cooper in any political context other than the democratic trajectory that has been standard to American literary criticism since the work of Santayana and Brooks.[7] When Cooper is read in the context of the federalism that he was surrounded by in his youth, the environmental concerns in his texts, which can otherwise seem extremely problematic, become quite apparent and wholly legitimate.

Crèvecoeur's *Letters from an American Farmer* is frequently called upon as a familiar touchstone for studies of early-nineteenth-century American literature, but less familiar federalist histories by William Cooper and Timothy Dwight provide better approximations of the political views that Cooper was exposed to and (to some degree) sympathized with, and they provide much better points of entry into James Fenimore Cooper's view of the relationship between American culture and the North American environment.[8] Following the methods and concerns of Jeremy Belknap's *History of New Hampshire* (published in three volumes between 1784 and 1792), William Cooper's 1810 *A Guide in the Wilderness* and Timothy Dwight's *Travels in New England and New York* (published in four volumes during 1821 and 1822) record the history of the United States in environmental, social, and religious terms, and they devote significant space to describing United States expansionism as a wholly benevolent process that nonetheless needs strict guidance to prevent it from becoming wasteful and environmentally unsustainable.[9]

When Fenimore Cooper discusses processes of European settlement and the North American environment in the Leatherstocking series, he writes in conversation with these texts—sometimes extending their arguments and sometimes rejecting them. The most obvious difference between the federalist histories and Cooper's historical romances are Cooper's deep misgivings about the environmental consequences and sustainability of American expansionism. The federalist histories envision United States expansionism as the extension of individual enterprise into a virgin void, and they identify environmental exhaustion as a real but remediable threat to the progress of national expansion. In the Leatherstocking series, on the other hand, Cooper presents American expansionism as a much more complex and insidious national project involving the military, linguistic, and scientific subjugation of a sociopolitically embedded un-virgin space, and he rejects the managerial optimism of his father and Timothy Dwight to present resource exhaustion as an unsolvable impediment to the expansion of American "civilization."

Throughout the four volumes of his *Travels in New England and New York*, Dwight explains that settlement involves unattractive phases characterized by tree stumps and burnt tree trunks like the ones that snow obscures from Elizabeth Temple's view at the beginning of *The Pioneers*. None of the ugliness involved in the process, however, prevents Dwight from declaring that newly settled valleys in the bloom of cultivation present the "richest prospect in New England," if not "in the United States," that North America is filled with inexhaustible resources, and that the transformation of wilderness into civilization can be accomplished using methods that are alternately good and bad (1: 257). In one of his most ecstatic moments, for instance, he views the Connecticut River valley from the summit of Mount Holyoke and finds that

> [a] perfect neatness and brilliancy is everywhere diffused, without a neglected spot to tarnish the luster or excite a wish in the mind for a higher finish. All these objects united present here a collection of beauties to which I know no parallel. When the eye traces this majestic stream, meandering with a singular course through these delightful fields . . . it will be difficult not to say that with these exquisite varieties of beauty and grandeur the relish for landscape is filled. (1: 259)

This vision, one of the most enraptured of Dwight's entire four-volume travel narrative, is surely a legitimate response to a remarkable place, but its effect is aided by the elevated, panoramic, and godlike perspective of Dwight's gaze.[10] At ground level, however, Dwight, like Belknap and William Cooper, cannot avoid the fact that such idyllic scenes depend on the perpetuity of the immanently exhaustible natural resources that make them possible. Of these three authors, only Belknap, in the earliest of the texts I am discussing here, entirely avoids issues of resource scarcity. Belknap never admits any real limits to nature's resources, but he does suggest that human impact—deforestation in particular—may result in permanent climate change, and he offers detailed advice on "rural economy," or how to make the best use of whatever natural resources may be available at any particular location (Belknap 3: 248).[11]

William Cooper and Dwight, writing slightly later than Belknap, are deeply anxious about the durability of environmental resources. Cooper's text is written in direct response to a letter from William Sampson that is torn between bragging and worrying about deforestation. Sampson suggests Cooper should boast "of having cut down two millions of trees" only before asking Cooper, several pages later, if "too great zeal for clearing may render [timber] in some time as scarce as it is now abundant" (2, 4). The best Cooper can do is confirm that forest exhaustion is a real threat, but Dwight, who is reluctant even to make this concession, demonstrates more clearly that the only response to environmental depletion within a federalist vision of American society is a faith in the regenerative capacity of the natural world that he weds to a laissez-faire faith in the ultimate triumph of the type of "good" federalism that Cooper spells out in his *Guide*.

This passage, which I have mentioned briefly before, offers Dwight's most vehement critique of deforestation:

> The people of Newbury appear to have cut down their forest with an improvident hand: an evil but too common in most parts of this country. Unhappily it is an increasing evil, and may hereafter put a final stop to the progress of population long before it will have reached to the natural acme. Almost every person complains of this imprudence; and yet not a single efficacious nor hopeful measure is adopted to lessen or even check it. . . . Forecast is certainly no predominant trait in the character of man, else an evil of this magnitude would create very serious apprehensions. (2: 238)

The particular vigor of this statement is worth emphasizing. Dwight considers this "improvident" destruction of forest "evil," and he recognizes that the situation in Newbury is merely representative of a much larger problem. The consequences, for Dwight, are clear and drastic: the misuse of resources may hinder population growth, and, to read what I think runs just beneath the surface of Dwight's statement, may prevent the nation from reaching its "natural acme," which Dwight clearly believes to be total transcontinental domination.

Dwight is troubled by the fact that in Newbury's representative situation "not a single efficacious nor hopeful measure is adopted to lessen or check" the course of environmental destruction, but he does nothing to suggest any regulatory measures. His most common response, to the contrary, is to emphasize that forests "renew themselves" (1: 75). In the first volume of his *Travels*, for instance, Dwight writes to his imagined British reader that "it may seem strange to you, accustomed as you are to see forest trees planted in great numbers and preserved with great care, that the inhabitants of this country should so soon after its colonization have cut down their forests in this extensive manner . . . this wanton manner without any apparent reason" (1: 74–75). To explain this strange phenomenon—and to diffuse the environmental anxiety that I believe neither William Cooper nor James Fenimore Cooper can entirely ignore—Dwight explains that "the wood of this country is its fuel" and that the trees of New England "renew themselves" in a "manner and by a process totally superior to any contrived by the human mind"; they are "furnished by the Author of Nature with the means of perpetual self-restoration" (1: 75). "Good grounds," he continues "yield a growth [of wood] amply sufficient for fuel once in fourteen years," and, with proper husbandry, "the forests of New England become in a sense ever living and supply plentifully the wants of the inhabitants" (1: 75).

The only solution to environmental depletion for Dwight is nature's regenerative capacity, which he believes to be greater in North America than anywhere else. William Cooper, however, mounts an argument in his *Guide* that Dwight would absolutely affirm: the only way to ensure a prosperous and sustainable settlement (in social, economic, and environmental terms) is to institute a benevolent federalist social and political plan. Where Cooper sees failed settlements (among which I believe Dwight's Newbury would qualify), he sees the failure of "plans" in which large landlords "have reserved favorite tracts, retained mill sites in their own hands; . . . opened expensive roads, and built costly bridges at their own charge . . . too early insisted with rigor upon payment, and forced the purchaser to surrender a part or the whole of his possession" (37). Cooper's plan, which he promotes throughout the *Guide*, involves large landowners granting land to both rich and poor settlers, actually selling rather than leasing tracts of land, and cultivating goodwill and a sense of community among settlers by practicing extreme patience with lien holders and accomplishing large-scale improvements through communal effort.

William Cooper and Timothy Dwight feel that an ill-managed federalist settlement governed by greedy and speculative patricians can produce results just as devastating to the raw materials of national prosperity as the type of thoroughly self-serving democratic mob that Fenimore Cooper represents in the pioneering Ishmael Bush clan of *The Prairie*. Despite the fact that he always harbored deep misgivings about democracy, Fenimore Cooper breaks from the federalist faith of his father and Timothy

Dwight. In structuring the central conflicts of *The Pioneers* around the looming specter of environmental exhaustion that his forefathers ignored or downplayed, Fenimore Cooper suggests that he has no faith that any social or governmental system can control the environmental rapacity that he recognizes to be a fundamental component of an essentially violent and imperialistic Euro-American culture.

Scholars such as Godden and Swann have certainly identified the self-interest involved in Marmaduke Temple's creation of game laws, but such arguments fail to recognize that the federalist vision promoted by William Cooper and Timothy Dwight relies upon a benevolent aristocratic self-interest and that in several key places Fenimore Cooper extends the problem of resource exhaustion beyond any sense of personal interest as he implies that it impinges on regional and national prosperity. In his *A Guide in the Wilderness*, William Cooper is quite clear that the best interests of landowners should also serve the best interests of their tenants, and Judge Temple's laws represent an attempt at fulfilling the type of managerial perfection that William Cooper envisions. Judge Temple's laws are flawed, though. They solidify the class system, and they are ecologically counterproductive.[12]

To put it bluntly, Temple's laws are failures, and they indicate Cooper's loss of faith in the federalist system. This loss of faith is particularly grim for Cooper because it leaves him politically isolated; he goes into an intense confrontation with environmental problems in *The Pioneers* without any faith in any political force that could possibly alleviate them. Cooper opens his novel with an introduction that tells his readers that "the Otsego is beginning to be a niggard of its treasures," and he creates the dramatic pigeon-shooting and fishing scenes that present careless environmental destruction that Judge Temple cannot control. His loss of faith in the federalist view of nature comes through most clearly, however, when Temple remarks that settlers are " 'already felling the forests as if no end could be found to their treasures, nor any limits to their extent . . . twenty years hence we shall want fuel' " (9, 105).

Temple may not be able to enforce his own game laws, but he makes this point stick in an argument with Richard Jones, who constantly preaches nature's illimitability, and he makes his point in terms that are vague enough to suggest that the problem extends well beyond the bounds of Templeton. More than two hundred pages later, when the novel again turns to a discussion of the state of forests, Cooper absolutely rejects Dwight's faith in forests' regenerative capacity when he has Temple remind Billy Kirby that the maples he is damaging " 'are the growth of centuries, and when once gone, none living will ever see their loss remedied' " (228).

By the time Natty Bumppo flees Templeton for the uninhabited wilds where he reappears in *The Prairie*, he and Cooper have both abandoned any faith in federalism's ability to ameliorate environmental destruction. When Natty turns westward, he concedes that not even a federalist patrician such as Oliver Edwards, who has been trained by Natty himself in the bosom of the nation's nature and who has married a woman in Elizabeth Temple who appreciates nature's beauty, can quell either his own rapacious impulses or those of such reckless individuals as Richard Jones and Billy Kirby.

Ultimately, Cooper cannot see a way out of the patterns of environmental destruction he confronts in *The Pioneers*, but as the Leatherstocking series continues his rejection of established federalist modes of viewing the environment and avoiding environmental crisis develops into a thorough critique of the United States' orientation toward the natural space it occupies. Although his engagement with the problem is often less explicit than it is in *The Pioneers*, throughout the rest of the Leatherstocking tales Cooper sustains a critical counternarrative against any triumphalist notion of North American environmental virginity or illimitability. From *The Last of the Mohicans* to *The Deerslayer* (the second and final novels of the series), Cooper situates American expansionism as the product of military, linguistic, and scientific violence taking place in a wholly unromantic space that does not constitute virgin ground so much as an already bloody field that Europeans and white Americans have recently come to occupy simply as the most violent, insidious, and numerous forces in play.

In *The Spy*, Cooper presents the North American environment as contested space, or "neutral ground," but beginning with *The Last of the Mohicans* he begins to mount a more radical rejection of the "virgin land" myth. Rather than empty or virgin space, in each of the Leatherstocking tales after *The Pioneers* (*The Last of the Mohicans*, *The Prairie*, *The Pathfinder*, and *The Deerslayer*) Cooper consistently describes the North American environment as a space of bloody conflict. As the first novel of the Leatherstocking series to descend into the prehistory of *The Pioneers*, *The Last of the Mohicans* describes the North American continent as a space that has been shaped by violence since European settlement. Cooper insists that "there was no recess of the woods so dark, nor any secret place so lovely, that it might claim exemption from the inroads of those who had pledged their blood to satiate their vengeance, or to uphold the cold and selfish policy of the distant monarchs of Europe" (11). He recognizes that "European arms" represent a clear "threat to nature, powerful though the presence of the forest is," and that the European "imperial adventure" "has at its end the defilement of nature" (Rans, 109, 108, 107). The village of Templeton, Cooper suggests at the outset of *The Last of the Mohicans*, is not simply the product of what Timothy

Dwight would describe as "equivocal," or mysterious, "generation"; it is built in a region that was first "a bloody arena," a "scene of strife and bloodshed" (*Mohicans* 13).

The Last of the Mohicans suggests that North American space has been a zone of contest since the European incursion, but Cooper makes more radical claims in *The Prairie* and *The Deerslayer*. In both of these novels, he denies any sense that the North American continent had *ever*, at least within human history, constituted a virgin or empty space. As Ishmael Bush and Thomas Hutter push their predictable ideas of property ownership into various frontier zones, Cooper emphasizes that their claims of ownership are not the first but merely the newest—that every North American space *has always* existed under military and political mediation. Through the voice of Natty Bumppo in *The Prairie*, for instance, Cooper insists that " 'The Teton and the Pawnee and the Konza, and men of a dozen other tribes claim to own these naked fields,' " which Ishmael Bush is attempting to possess, and in his own undisguised narratorial voice Cooper adds that Bush's attempt at legitimizing his land grabbing is a "wild conceit" (78).

Cooper's rejection of the virgin land myth is more radical in *The Deerslayer* by virtue of its deconstruction of the myth in an even more remote historical moment. Here, in a novel set in 1745 and well beyond the geographical boundaries of regular European settlement, Cooper punctures the myth of virgin land by planting a fortified house, "Muskrat Castle," in the middle of the most unspoiled natural space that he ever describes (39). The very fact that Tom Hutter's "castle," which contains numerous symbols of European power and violence, has come to be stationed in the middle of the lake in the first place is a constant reminder that this seemingly primitive location is already overwritten with conflicts of ownership—Hutter has built the castle in the lake because Native Americans, who do not recognize his claim of ownership, have repeatedly burned him out of the homes he built on dry land. As Natty and Hurry Harry discuss the implications of this fortified house that seems to float in the middle of the lake, they enumerate the claims of ownership that hang over the place: they mention that the only " 'lawful owner' " of the place is " 'the King,' " but that "Tom Hutter . . . has got possession and is like to keep it as long as his life lasts," while at the same time Native Americans " 'come and go' " but leave the impression that " 'the country seems to belong to no native tribe in particular' "—all of this despite the fact that " 'Mohawks' " are in a position to cede the land should a " 'heavy enough' " buyer emerge (37–38).

From particular points of view—particularly those that read Cooper's engagement with issues of property and class in the context of his own loss of property and status—it is certainly possible to interpret Cooper's rejection of the virgin land idea as little more than a legitimization of Europe's bloody involvement in what was always a violently negotiated space. Within the frame of federalist historiography and Cooper's engagement with it, however, his rejection of the virgin land myth forces violent European (and later, American) imperialism to appear as the violent acts that they are without being distorted by a screen of cultural myth that transforms the acts into sanitized and ambivalent expansions into empty space. This argument is further supported, I believe, by evidence that Cooper understood European and American imperialism to be vast and complex mechanisms composed of seemingly innocuous forces—namely, language and science.

Cooper invests language with significant spatial agency in *The Last of the Mohicans* and *The Deerslayer*, but the vehicle of spatial politics in *The Prairie* is natural history, a science that Cooper places in the vanguard of American expansionism. In *The Last of the Mohicans* and *The Deerslayer*, Cooper does something in his place descriptions that Timothy Dwight and William Cooper never do in their historical works: he peels away the layers of language that have been superimposed over particular places over spans of time, and he identifies the most recent layers of language as racially and environmentally destructive.

Cooper performs this archaeology of place names at the outset of *The Last of the Mohicans*. In a passage that would seem horribly and unnecessarily circumlocutious to D. H. Lawrence, Leslie Fiedler, or Richard Chase, Cooper refuses to simply state that the action of the story occurs around Lake George, a place Dwight visited and described in his *Travels,* without any sort of equivocation whatsoever. Cooper explains, instead, that the central action of the story will occur around a lake that the French had named " 'du Saint Sacrement,' " that the English had named Lake George, and that the Native Americans had named " 'Horican' " (12).

The process of naming, Cooper recognizes, erases not only a Native American name but also the violent act of *renaming*—the names "Lake George" and "du Saint Sacrement" were only established, Cooper writes, because European nations had "united to *rob* the untutored possessors of the wooded scenery of their native right" (12; emphasis added). Cooper finds this history of naming significant enough to expand it into a footnote where he suggests an even deeper linguistic history of the place. In this footnote, he admits that since the Indians have multiple languages and dialects the lake may have even more names; he translates the Indian name "Horican" into "The Tail of the Lake," which is significantly devoid of the religious and nationalist connotations of the French (du Saint Sacrement) and English (Lake George) names; and he cheapens the enduring and legal "Lake George" appellation by describing it as "vulgar" (12).

This same attention to place names (which loosens the coherence of Cooper's plots and adds a layer of complexity that would never improve his standing in the main line of Americanist criticism) also appears in *The Deerslayer*, with the added caveat that here the arrival of an English name is clearly understood to herald a place's destruction. One of Natty's reactions to seeing Glimmerglass lake is to ask Hurry Harry, " 'Have the governor's, or the King's people given this lake a name' " (44). Natty feels that to give a place an English name is to " 'disturb natur,' " and he is relieved to find that the place has " 'no pale face name, for their christenings always foretel waste and destruction" (45). Despite finding pleasure in the absence of an official English name, Natty understands that the place still exists in a historical and social matrix involving "red skins," who would "have their own modes of knowing it" and who would be " 'likely to call the place by something reasonable and resembling,' " even if he does not know the names himself (45).

Cooper clearly understands that language is an agent of imperial violence and erasure, and he describes language as one of the first mechanisms of imperialism to affect a place after European incursion. In *The Prairie*, however, Cooper draws science into the vanguard of American expansionism through his treatment of Obed Battius, whom Richard Chase dismisses as "a scientist-pedant who has stepped out of the pages of Smollett or Fielding to investigate the flora and fauna of the plains" who is "tiresome" and who appears in "comic passages" that "are incredibly bad" (59).[13] Regardless of the literary history that may have influenced Cooper's development of the character, Battius is also a significant representative in *The Prairie* of natural science, the science that has been complicit with imperialist expansion since the two phenomena developed concurrently in seventeenth century Europe, the science that so intrigued Emerson in the early 1830s.

The politics of natural science have been laid bare since Michel Foucault's groundbreaking critique of European rationalism in *The Order of Things*. By now, however, it is fairly commonplace to recognize, as Lee Rust Brown does in the context of Ralph Waldo Emerson's interest in natural history, that natural science emerged "in the early sixteenth century" and "grew along a course parallel to that of European exploration and colonial expansion" (97). Mary Louise Pratt, who deals with natural science more directly than Brown, goes farther. For her, natural science is deeply complicit with European imperialism and pursues complementary goals. Natural science's drive toward the total "systematization of nature," she recognizes, "coincides with the height of the slave trade, the plantation system, colonial genocide in North America and South Africa, slave rebellions in the Andes, the Caribbean, North America, elsewhere" (36).

In the Leatherstocking series, Battius, as a natural scientist, amounts to what Pratt has described as the "image of a European bourgeois subject simultaneously innocent and imperial," and the science that he brings into the American West asserts a seemingly "harmless hegemonic vision that instills no apparatus of domination" (Pratt 34). The scientific "apparatus of domination" that Battius represents is certainly less bloody than the military means of domination that appear in *The Last of the Mohicans*, *The Pathfinder*, and *The Deerslayer*, but it is far more insidious.

In *The Prairie*, this imperial natural science has penetrated the continental interior far beyond the reach of any significant military power, and even if Battius is a failure of a naturalist, his presence points to the fact that natural science has already reached and moved beyond the ground he occupies with the Bush clan. As soon as Battius enters the novel, Cooper uses him to explain that even though Ishmael Bush and his family have penetrated the continent far beyond the bounds of "civilization," they have not moved—and perhaps cannot move—into territory unknown to science. Battius, after all, has just completed a two-day walk in the wilderness "without seeing even a blade of grass that is not already enumerated and classed" (69). The place has already been penetrated, and every organism in it classified, by a quick-moving science that is already pushing into the West's outer reaches, even as Battius speaks, with explorers such as Lewis and Clark (whose expedition is, after all, the reason that Duncan Uncas Middleton enters the novel in the first place). Battius brings to *The Prairie* the natural scientist's ability to read a place—and to read the scientific knowledge that has already been cast over it. Battius never finds any organisms that are unknown to science, but everywhere he looks he finds evidence of science's presence, and by constantly articulating the otherwise invisible presence of science Battius offers a reminder that the entire continental span has already been penetrated, classified, and brought to order by a scientific force that we would never notice without him.

In the American canon that was crafted by critics from Brooks and Santayana to Fiedler, which privileged Emerson and tacitly endorsed his abstract and imperialist vision of nature, Cooper's work became virtually invisible. Within the ahistorical, apolitical aesthetic that these critics crafted, his texts and the environmental anxieties they contain became unreadable. He came to exist only as a failure who possessed, in Fiedler's words, "all the qualifications for a great American writer except the simple ability to write," whose works are "monumental in their cumulative dullness," nearly "unreadable" because of their "hysteria" and "piety," appropriately "read . . . in large print and embellished with pictures," and remembered "if at all, as children's books, exciting and incredibly boring by turns" (191, 180). In the context of the abandoned federalist tradition, however, James

Fenimore Cooper is an author who abandons the typical federalist faith in environmental inexhaustibility, who deconstructs the American mythology of virgin land, and who recognizes American culture as a destructive and imperial force. He is an author whose environmental politics clearly ran counter to those of both mainstream American culture and the emerging American literary institution, and his canonical erasure is an expression of American Literature's evasive environmental politics.

Chapter 3

Henry Wadsworth Longfellow, United States National Literature, and the American Canon's Erasure of Material Nature

In his Leatherstocking series, James Fenimore Cooper deconstructs the myth of virgin land and the rhetoric of manifest destiny by insisting that North America has a history prior to the arrival of Europeans and by suggesting that European expansion is and always has been a bloody imperial project even when clothed in the unassuming garb of natural science. Cooper deconstructs dominant myths and ideologies while pointing out the problems that cannot be resolved: how to balance the rights of the individual and society, how to govern effectively when the democratic mass is as dangerous as imperfect federalist leadership, how to build a new nation without ruining the resources that are the basis for both its cultural exceptionality and its material power. And Cooper performs this deconstruction while writing for popular audiences, while refusing to abandon female readers, while allowing nature to remain immanently feminine rather than the transforming it into the type of masculine abstraction that it becomes in Emerson's *Nature*.

Like Cooper, Henry Wadsworth Longfellow was tremendously successful in popular, commercial terms throughout the nineteenth century but fell into a slow critical decline that began rather innocuously in mid-nineteenth-century debates with Edgar Allen Poe and Margaret Fuller and then accelerated in the early twentieth century as he became an even more consistent target of Santayana and Brooks than Cooper. As the most successful, most widely read poet of the nineteenth century who also happened to be a very domestic man, Longfellow, more any of the other figures who bore similar characteristics (Cooper, Washington Irving, William Cullen Bryant, John Greenleaf Whittier) embodied Santayana's "genteel tradition." When Santayana and Brooks set out to demolish this tradition they effectively broke Longfellow, whose reputation, despite a mild revival over the last twenty years, has not yet recovered.

As Longfellow has faded from public consciousness and critical acclaim, so too has a unique environmental politics that motivates much of his poetry. From the beginning of his career, Longfellow worked tirelessly to build a transnational American literature upon the body of a unique North American natural world that he always casts in physical, terrestrial terms, and this goal motivates—even animates—much of his enduring poetry (such as *Evangeline* and *The Song of Hiawatha*). Cooper deconstructs the dominant environmental rhetoric of the nineteenth century; Longfellow creates a transnationalist and environmentally determined theory of American literature. Together, Cooper and Longfellow demonstrate a diversity of environmental thought within nineteenth-century American literature that has been rendered invisible by the processes of canonization that gradually bestowed cultural capital upon Emerson's environmental philosophy to the detriment of all others.

Longfellow's Literary Manifestoes

Henry Wadsworth Longfellow's environmental politics are woven intricately into a vision for American literature that he defined repeatedly throughout his career. Three times during his career, Longfellow argued that any legitimate national literature of the United States should spring from European literary roots but depend upon the influence of North American nature for its uniqueness. He presents this argument in his 1824 "The Literary Spirit of Our Country," in his 1832 "Defence of Poetry," and in his 1849 *Kavanagh*.[1] After the first of these manifestoes, which establishes the fundamental position that persists throughout subsequent arguments, each restatement of Longfellow's position participates in a debate about the status and the future of American literature that drew the support of figures such as James Russell Lowell and C. C. Felton and the ire of hypernationalistic and nativist Young Americans such as Evert Augustus Duyckinck and Cornelius Mathews.[2]

When it is mentioned at all, Longfellow's theorization of an American literature is regularly reduced to a single essay—usually the 1832 "Defence of Poesy"—or dismissed as a voice in the crowd.[3] Admittedly, Longfellow published his first literary manifesto, "The Literary Spirit of Our Country," when he was very young—he published it in the *United States Literary Gazette* in 1825. Regardless of its early date, however, this manifesto is critical to understanding the endurance of Longfellow's commitment to an environmentally determined and transatlantic American literature. It offers a backstory to the more fully developed 1832 "Defence of Poetry," which *has* attracted some critical attention, just as Longfellow's discussion of United States national literature in his 1849 *Kavanagh* carries his plan for American literature into mid-century.

Over the course of these three pieces, Longfellow remains committed to a middle course between American literary nativism and the imitation of European models, he laments the impediments to literary culture that exist in the United States, and he always argues that the North American environment must be the source of any emergent American national literature. While Longfellow's theoretical commitments remain consistent, however, each subsequent argument presents a more vehement engagement with general and critical American cultures. As Longfellow moves from "The Literary Sprit of Our Country" to "The Defence of Poetry" and eventually to *Kavanagh*, he sharpens his critique of print culture in the United States, and he takes issue with the New Americans, such as Cornelius Mathews, who were arguing at the time for the creation of a nationalistic American Literature that would sever itself entirely from British and European culture.

From the very beginning of his career, Longfellow believed that any U.S. national literature would have to base its claims of vitality and originality on the qualities of its natural environment because the new nation could match neither the educational superstructure nor the deep cultural legacies that had produced enduring literary traditions in Europe. In "The Literary Spirit of Our Country," for instance, Longfellow resigns himself to the enduring influence of "English taste" in literature, but he claims that the exceptionally sensitive "poetic mind" would be deeply affected by a North American nature that is "more exquisite than elsewhere" (793). On this continent, in the United States, Longfellow believes that "nature has exhibited her works upon the most beautiful and magnificent scale" and that this "vast theatre" can be "the school in which the genius of our country is to be trained" (793). Here, the environment bears such "an influence upon the mind . . . that the features of the intellect are moulded after those of nature" (793).

Longfellow's second literary manifesto, "The Defense of Poetry," seems more representative of what we regard today as mainstream nineteenth-century literary criticism, which is to say it seems more Emersonian. After summarizing the national zeitgeist—he finds the nation gripped in a pervasive sense of utility, proud of its territorial size, and enraptured with "the magnificence and beauty of our natural scenery"—he remarks that "the true glory of a nation consists not in the extent of its territory, the pomp of its forests, the majesty of its rivers, the height of its mountains, and the beauty of its sky; but in the extent of its mental power"(60).

From this point, Longfellow launches into a long rant about a nation's power being manifest in "the majesty of its intellect,—the height and depth and purity of its moral nature . . . in what nature and education have given to the mind . . . in the world within us . . . in the attributes of the soul . . . in the incorruptible, the permanent, the imperishable mind. True greatness is the greatness of the mind;—the true glory of a nation is moral and intellectual pre-eminence" (60).

It can be argued, based on passages such as these, that Longfellow envisioned American national literature to be purely a poetry of the mind that had become terribly stunted by a national spirit preoccupied with materialistic utility.[4] Such interpretations, however, overlook Longfellow's continued obsession with the destining power of the North American environment. Regardless of how concerned Longfellow is about the state of American culture or how much he wants to locate national power in the intellect, his belief in environmental determinism is just as strong in "The Defence of Poetry" as it is in "The Literary Spirit of Our Country."

Here, as in the previous essay, the natural world offers the best avenue toward a viable and original American literature. Longfellow still believes, in 1832, that nature shapes "the character of the mind, the peculiar habits of thought and feeling, and, consequently, the general complexion of literary performances," and he extends this sentiment into a claim that the effects of "natural scenery and climate" on the mind are "the most obvious . . . in their influence upon the prevailing tenor of poetic composition" (70). He supports his argument with claims that the particular environments of England, Italy, Spain, and Portugal have shaped each nation's literature, and he ultimately recommends that American authors submit the formation of a new national literature to nature's deterministic power. Openly desiring that "our native poets would give a more national character to their writings," Longfellow simply suggests that "they have only to write more naturally, to write from their own feelings and impressions, from the influence of what they see around them, and not from any pre-conceived notions of what poetry ought to be, caught by reading many books, and imitating many models" (74, 75).

Longfellow and the Nineteenth-Century American Literature Debates

Longfellow's suggestion in "The Defence of Poetry" that an American literature would develop on its own due to the influence of the natural world differs drastically from other early- to mid-nineteenth-century manifestoes of American national literature. No manifesto presents a more different vision, for instance, than Cornelius Mathews's hyper-nationalistic 1847 "Nationality in Literature"—the essay, it seems, that caused Longfellow to restate his theory of environmentally determined poetry for a third time in his 1849 prose tale, *Kavanagh*. In "Nationality in Literature," Mathews (who is remembered today as an overzealous member of the Young Americans who often irritated his more conventional associates such as Evert Duyckinck) is frustrated to distraction by the fact that "this great country . . . has no native literature, but is, in letters, in a state of colonial and provincial dependency upon the old world" (60).[5] The United States, he finds, exists in an "old literary domination"; it is "overmastered by the literature of England" and mired "in a state of pupilage" that can be best overcome through the cultivation of "a clear development of the idea and the necessity of nationality" (61).

American national literature, as far as Cornelius Mathews is concerned, should involve "home writers . . . home themes, affording opportunity for descriptions of our scenery . . . events . . . [and] the manners of the people" all "*penetrated and vivified by an intense and enlightened patriotism*" (62; emphasis added). Nationalism, Mathews argues, "guard[s] the soil and preserve[s] the sacred independence of nations," but it also inspires great literature (65). Using Greece, Rome, and England as examples because their "writers have been most penetrated by the sense of nationality," Mathews argues that nationalism, "instead of narrowing the domain of . . . great writers, has made their chief works the peerless gifts and priceless treasures of the whole intellectual world" (63). Mathews feels that American authors "slavishly adhere to old and foreign models," and he demands that they abandon their "unnational spirit" to finally create a new American literature (65). It should be thoroughly independent of Europe, Mathews argues; it should be (quoting a speech he had earlier presented in New York City) " 'instinct with the life of the country, full of a hearty, spontaneous, genuine home feeling; relishing of the soil of the spirit of the people,' " and it should " 'sound of the great voices of nature, of which she is full' " (65–66).

Mathews's "Nationality in Literature" shares one idea with Longfellow's manifestoes—it believes that any emergent American literature would require the particularly powerful influence of the North American environment. However, it attacks the internationalism of Longfellow and other like-minded intellectuals such as C. C. Felton (the classicist who was Longfellow's colleague at Harvard before eventually becoming the college's president) until it finally arrives at a plan that would have American literature actually look like the literature of a "Nature's Nation"—a nation *sui-* or *ex natura*, composed only from nature without any inheritance from European culture.

Beyond simply being angry that the United States has not produced a spectacular nativist literature, in "Nationality in Literature" Mathews is irritated by the fact that patriotism "has been denied in a quarter of respectability" by elites such as Felton, who had just written an article in *The North American Review* disclaiming patriotism as tawdry and counterproductive in the march toward an American national literature. Mathews's entire argument in "Nationality in Literature" is written in explicit response to the critique of literary patriotism that Felton incorporated into his October 1846 review of "Simms's *Stories and Reviews*." In this review, which strays significantly from its primary subject—two works by William Gilmore Simms—Felton argues that "national literature cannot be forced like a hothouse plant" while he accuses (through suggestion rather than name-calling) the New Americans of producing merely "a good deal of unmeaning talk about American literature" without doing anything substantial to bring such a national literature into being (377).

Felton's discussion of the New Americans manifests itself in a critique of "certain coteries of would-be men of letters, noisy authorlings" who "waste their time and vex the spirits of long-suffering readers, by prating about our want of an independent national American literature" (377). As if this condemnation of Mathews is not sufficiently direct, Felton goes on to level a damning dismissal of Mathews's ill-fated novel, *The Career of Puffer Hopkins*, before articulating his own theory of American literature. Just as Mathews recognizes in "Nationality in Literature," Felton's opinion is that "an intense national self-consciousness, though the shallow may misname it patriotism, is the worst foe to the true and generous unfolding of national genius"(377). Any viable national literature must speak to the universal rather than the national or provincial, Felton believes, and the New American dismissal of "the English language and its glorious treasures" amounts to a calamitous rejection of the nation's "birthright" (377). This dismissal, moreover, requires American authors to "limit themselves to American subjects . . . as if, forsooth, the genius of America must never wander beyond the mountains, forests, and waterfalls of the western continent" (377).

When Mathews turns Felton's position on its head in "Nationality in Literature," he is not merely rejecting the theory of national literature held by a Harvard classicist. He is rejecting the internationalist and environmentally determined theory of American literature that Longfellow had already once restated since his 1824 "The Literary Spirit of Our Country." And it was Mathews's 1847 reaction against Felton in "Nationality in Literature," it seems, that inspired Longfellow to once again redefine his position in his 1849 *Kavanagh*, a tale that he began writing in 1847 shortly upon the heels of Mathews's essay.

Longfellow's *Kavanagh* tells a conventional tale of country romance, but in the center of the tale a new character named Mr. Hathaway—modeled after Cornelius Mathews—enters the scene with no purpose beyond sparking an extended debate about national literature with Longfellow's persona in the text—a school teacher and aspiring author, Mr. Churchill.[6] *Kavanagh* cannot be properly classified as either a romance or a novel (historical or otherwise), but it is a self-conscious work of fiction, and as such it is not surprising that Longfellow never actually speaks the name of Cornelius Mathews. Hathaway appears, however, attempting to enlist Churchill in "a new magazine he was about to establish, in order to raise the character of American literature, which, in his opinion, the existing reviews and magazines had entirely failed to accomplish" (754). The journal, which Hathaway plans to call "The Niagara," is similar in its plan to *The Arcturus*, which Mathews edited with Evert Duyckinck from 1841 to 1842, and both Hathaway's nativist literary vision and his overzealous rhetoric point unequivocally toward the brash Cornelius Mathews whose unchecked passion embarrassed his friends.

Over the course of the discussion that springs up between these two characters, Hathaway offers a number of claims that allow Longfellow to methodically refine the theories of national literature that he offered in 1825 and 1832. As he lays out the plan for his new nativist literary magazine, Hathaway explains he wants an American national literature that is as grandiose as the North American environment and as wild, uncultivated, and free:

> We want a national literature commensurate with our mountains and rivers,—commensurate with Niagara, and the Alleghanies, and the Great Lakes! . . . We want a national epic that shall correspond to the size of the country; that shall be to all other epics what Banvard's Panorama of the Mississippi is to all other paintings,—the largest in the world! . . . In a word, we want a national literature altogether shaggy and unshorn, that shall shake the earth, like a herd of buffaloes thundering over the prairies! (754–55)

Such a literature, for Hathaway, must be absolutely " 'original' " (or unrelated to any existing literary tradition) and absolutely national (" 'If it is not national,' " he argues, " 'it is nothing' ") (756, 755).

Longfellow uses this series of claims to explain his own faith in the American environment's ability to eventually cultivate a national literature and to reassert the value of European literary models in the face of nativist literary isolationism. While Longfellow essentially agrees with what Hathaway calls " 'the influence of scenery on the mind,' " he qualifies his earlier manifestoes' broad claims of environmental determinism by having Churchill—again, his own persona in the text—explain that " 'scenery' " cannot " 'create genius' " but " 'only develop it' " (755). It is not so much a concession on Longfellow's part so much as a careful qualification made necessary by what he regarded as Mathews's cockeyed and overly emotional hyper-nationalism, which threatened what Longfellow and Churchill believed would be the "natural" development of an American literature (756). As Longfellow explains through the mouth of Churchill, " 'national literature is not the growth of a day' " but of " 'centuries;' " " 'our own is growing slowly but surely, striking its roots downward, and its branches upward, as is natural; and I do not wish, for the sake of what some people call originality, to invert it, and try to make it grow with its roots in the air' " (756).

Longfellow expects the particular qualities of the North American environment to shape whatever genius arises in the United States, but he wants to allow nature the time it takes to create a national literature that is " 'universal' " and internationally engaged rather than narrowly nationalistic and mired in a patriotism that " 'is often ridiculous' " (756). Regardless of nature's power to shape the literary mind, in *Kavanagh* as in each of his previous literary manifestoes, Longfellow neither believes nor desires that American literature will ever be able to exact the clean break from British literature that Hathaway—and Cornelius Mathews—want. Churchill, constantly speaking for Longfellow, simply cannot "see how our literature can be very different from theirs. Westward from hand to hand we pass the lighted torch, but it was lighted at the old domestic fireside of England" (756). Moreover, he does not recognize this extension of the British tradition as " 'an imitation' " so much as " 'a continuation' " that " 'we may well be proud of' " (756). There is nothing in *Kavanagh* to dilute, in other words, the staunch sense of transatlantic unity that inspires Longfellow to write near the end of his "Defence of Poetry" that any aspiring American poet "should make . . . the whole body of English classical literature, his study" (77).

Longfellow's Un-Emersonian Nature

In the scattered fits and bursts that he devotes to Longfellow in *American Renaissance*, F. O. Matthiessen argues that *Evangeline* (1847) and *The Song of Hiawatha* (1855) demonstrate the chief problem with Longfellow's poetry: his poetic forms "were not brought into fusion with his native themes" (174). Longfellow's manifestoes were all but forgotten by the time Matthiessen published *American Renaissance* and their approach was thoroughly out of step with the modernist program that Matthiessen promoted. These manifestos, however, suggest that Longfellow's fusion of European forms and "native themes" was entirely intentional.

In "The Literary Spirit of Our Country," "Defence of Poetry,"and *Kavanagh*, Longfellow asks that poets turn to American nature for inspiration and for literary subject matter while maintaining ties to European literary traditions, and he argues repeatedly that any American exceptionality in culture or literature would have to be environmentally determined. In *Evangeline* and *Hiawatha* Longfellow attempts to carry this poetic project forward, and while he fuses the forms of Scandinavian sagas with North American subjects he presents the natural world in a way that is wholly different from Emerson's system of environmental abstraction. Longfellow, rather, consistently represents the natural world as a terrestrial and material, grounded and tactile phenomenon, and in these two long poems he spends tremendous amounts of space describing it because it bears such incredible cultural significance.

Nearly half of *Evangeline* constitutes a ranging tour of the North American continent, and throughout the poem Longfellow depends upon an environmental gaze that despite its frequent panoramic sweep remains fixed on a physical, terrestrial American environment.[7] After the village of Grand-Pré is burned and its inhabitants are dispersed by the British navy, the poem follows Evangeline Bellefontaine's search for her fiancé, Gabriel Lajeunesse, as she travels down the Mississippi to Louisiana and from there to the American West. The entire second section of "Part the Second," in fact, catalogs what Evangeline sees as she travels "through a wilderness sombre with forests":

> cotton-trees . . . broad lagoons, where silvery sandbars / Lay in the stream . . . china-trees . . . groves of orange and citron . . . a maze of sluggish and devious waters . . . towering and tenebrous boughs of the cypress . . . trailing mosses . . . herons . . . columns of cypress and cedar . . . the whoop of the crane and the roar of the grim alligator . . . water-lilies in myriads . . . (43–45)[8]

After Evangeline reaches the Louisiana home of Basil the Blacksmith and finds that Gabriel has "sought in the Western wilds oblivion of self and of sorrow," her continued search for Gabriel takes the poem into the West, where Longfellow again presents a sweeping, panoramic representation of the North American continent (47). The poem's movement into the West allows Longfellow to cartographically enclose the expansive natural space that he expects to nourish a national literature, and he does this in a language of scale, wonder, beauty, and luxuriance that constantly emphasizes the exceptionality of the North American environment.

The same claim of environmental exceptionality motivates Longfellow's *The Song of Hiawatha*, which makes an explicit claim of its own environmental determination. The "stories," "legends and traditions" the poem relates, Longfellow explains, come "From the great forests and the prairies, / From the great lakes of the Northland, / From the land of the Ojibways, / From the land of the Dacotahs, / From the mountains, moors, and fen-lands / Where the heron, the Shuh-shuh-gah, / Feeds among the rushes"(141). They do not come from any person in particular, but explicitly from *places*—"great forests and prairie," "great lakes," ancestral "lands," and "mountains, moors, and fen-lands."

After his opening claim of nature's literary agency, Longfellow claims that Native American oral literature (which he did take seriously) is itself evidence of the natural world's artistic agency.[9] The "legends and traditions" that *Hiawatha* relates, Longfellow's narrator explains, have come to him "from the lips of Nawadaha," an Indian "singer," who, in turn, heard them directly from the natural world (141). Nawadaha, Longfellow writes, found the stories "In the bird's nests of the forest, / In the lodges of the beaver, In the hoof-prints of the bison, / In the eyry of the eagle" (141). "In the moorlands and the fen-lands, / In the melancholy marshes" "All the wild-fowl said them to him;" "Chetowaik, the plover sang them, / Mahng, the loon, the wild goose, Wawa, / the blue heron, the Shuh-Shuh-gah, / And the grouse, the Mushodosa" all sang the stories of *Hiawatha* to Nawadaha, the Indian singer who pulled a native literature out of the natural world (141).

The Nation's Shifting Sense of Nature and Longfellow's Hedge Against the Future

While Longfellow was arguing for an environmentally determined American literature and working to create it, the nation's perception of its own environment was gradually but perceptibly changing—as the nineteenth century wore on, it became harder to believe in the limitlessness and the immortal virginity of the North American continent.[10] In 1823, one year before Longfellow penned his first theory of environmentally determined American literature, James Fenimore Cooper had already announced his departure from optimistic federalist environmental rhetoric in *The Pioneers*. In 1832, the same year that Longfellow reiterated his initial position on American Literature in "Defense of Poesy," the *New York Daily Commercial Advertiser* published a letter from George Catlin that proposed a national park in the American West as the only possible way to intervene in a broad pattern of environmental destruction. This letter, which Catlin also published as "Letter No. 31: Mouth of Teton River, Upper Missouri" in his *North American Indians* considers the "extinction" of the American bison to be "near at hand" and claims that "the rudenesses and wilds of Nature's works . . . are destined to fall before the deadly axe and desolating hands of cultivating man" (*North American Indians* 292–93).[11]

Fifteen years later, in 1847, the same year that Longfellow achieved tremendous success with the release of *Evangeline* (it went through six printings in three months), George Perkins Marsh articulated his first critique of American land use, deploring the "injudicious destruction of the woods" and similar "tokens of improvident waste" ("Address to the Agricultural Society"). Eventually, with *Man and Nature* in 1864, Marsh would offer the nineteenth century's most stringent critique of American environmental destruction. Writing in a rhetorical register that anticipates the environmentalist rhetoric of the late twentieth century, Marsh argues that

> [m]an has too long forgotten that the earth was given to him for usufruct alone, not for consumption, still less for profligate waste. Nature has provided against the absolute destruction of any of her elementary matter, the raw material of her works. . . . But she has left it within the power of man irreparably to derange the combinations of inorganic and organic life. . . . Man is everywhere a disturbing agent. Wherever he plants his foot, the harmonies of nature are turned to discords. The proportions and accommodations which insured the stability of existing arrangements are overthrown. . . . Man pursues his victims with reckless destructiveness; and, while the sacrifice of life by the lower animals is limited by the cravings of appetite, he unsparingly persecutes, even to extirpation, thousands of organic forms which he cannot consume. (36–37)

From Marsh's perspective, modern humanity is destructive to the point of derangement. It is hopelessly reckless—so reckless, in fact, that it is impossible to repair the destruction that it leaves in its wake.

James Fenimore Cooper reacted to this shifting conception of North American nature with frustration and resignation while subtly deconstructing the myths of virgin land and innocent exploration. Emerson's response was to formulate a way to continue believing in the health, virginity, and limitlessness of the continent's natural environment even when all of these things were beginning to seem problematic. Longfellow also recognized—or at least sensed—the nineteenth century's shifting sense of environmental awareness, and his writings show him reacting to it in ways that are different from either Cooper or Emerson. This awareness of environmental destruction punctures Longfellow's narratives of nature's grandeur in surprising moments, and it causes him to prepare a series of countermeasures that would preserve his environmentally determined American literature against the possibility of nature's ultimate end. All of this—Longfellow's sense of an environmental shift and his reaction against it—appears in *Evangeline*. This poem begins and ends with descriptions of the timeless, pristine, and explicitly un-threatened forest that surrounds the Acadian village of Grand-Pré, and it spends incredible space on a panoramic tour of the North American continent; it is punctured, however, almost at its center, by a stark admission of North American nature's destructibility. In lines that simultaneously praise American progress and throw the endurance of Longfellow's literary program into doubt, Longfellow writes that "lands may be had for the asking, and forests of timber / With a few blows of the axe are hewn and framed into houses" (60–61).

The replacement of forests with houses was something that Longfellow could not—and would not have wanted to—denounce, but it still presented him with a tremendous problem. For all of their positive implications, it was not "houses," but nature, forests, that he believed could shape the cultural development of the United States, and as much as he recognized the threatened status of North American nature, Longfellow still *needed* to believe that the Acadian environment could continue to endure as it does in his poem. The literary program that he had theorized and refined since his youth depended upon it.

Structurally, *Evangline* keeps the Acadian environment alive. It is as pure, inexorable, and immutable at the end of the poem when Longfellow returns to it as it is at the poem's beginning. But the problem within the bounds of the United States is different. Here, especially in the final half of the poem, Longfellow adopts an apocalyptic, even postapocalyptic, view of the natural world and imagines a way to preserve its cultural force even beyond its actual end.

Almost immediately after the iconic pioneering axe punctures Longfellow's poem, he narrates a voyage down the Mississippi River and begins interpreting the natural world as a glorious ruin—in much the same way that Walter Benjamin relies upon the image of the ruin in *The Origins of German Tragic Drama*—that can retain its cultural value even after its destruction as a viable physical entity.

As he narrates this voyage down the Mississippi, Longfellow slips into the same discourse of architecture that Benjamin uses to formulate his idea of the ruin. On the Mississippi, for instance, the "tenebrous boughs of the cypress / Met in a dusky arch, and the trailing mosses in mid-air / Waved like banners that hang on the walls of ancient cathedrals" (43). Rows of trees are "columns," "colonnades," and "corridors," and when beams of moonlight penetrate the forest canopy, the light shines into "broken vaults . . . as through chinks in a ruin" (44–45).

In describing nature with architectural metaphors—even metaphors of ruined architecture, Longfellow is preparing North American nature to become the same type of culturally significant ruin that Walter Benjamin understood to operate in the *Trauerspiel*, a form of baroque sixteenth-century German drama. In the *Trauerspiel*, Benjamin explains, ruins and fragments of antiquity—"the highly significant fragment, the remnant"—were the ideal materials for the creation of new art (178). The ruin embodies history, and, as an artistic medium, fragments of ruined greatness allow for the creation of new "structure[s]" that would, even "in destruction, still be superior to the harmonies of antiquity" in their original states (177–78).

In each of his manifestoes, Longfellow argues that Native American cultures grant North America a cultural history that rivals Europe, but he also clearly suggests that Native American culture is most powerful to white culture when the Natives themselves have disappeared. By the same token, if North American nature were to collapse as the viable physical entity that allows him to make claims of American exceptionality and to argue for an American national literature, it could still serve the purposes of U.S. national culture. Even in a ruined state, it could grant the United States a sense of deep history that it lacked. Even in decay North American nature would suggest greatness, perhaps still determine the nation's character, and possibly fulfill Longfellow's environmentally determinist literary program. After all, as Benjamin recognizes, "in the ruins of great buildings, the idea of the plan speaks more impressively than in lesser buildings, however well preserved they are" (235).

Erasing Longfellow and Naturalizing American Literary Personality in the Early Twentieth Century

Longfellow believed that American literature's distinctiveness would come from a distinctly American nature, and he composed poems in *Evangeline* and *The Song of Hiawatha* that attempt to offer examples of just such an environmentally determined American literature. These poems map a geographical space that they explicitly define as exceptional; they claim this space as both an artistic subject and art's destining force; they argue that a new national literature can emerge out of the North American continent; they cultivate an environmental gaze that consistently focuses on a natural world that is terrestrial and material rather than abstract in the mode of Emerson; and they prepare American literature for an existence beyond the death of North American nature.

Like Cooper, Longfellow had his share of critics during his lifetime. Poe famously accused him of plagiarism. Margaret Fuller, while dismissing Poe's claims on the grounds that Longfellow's very poetic project *depends* upon poetic borrowing and imitation, argued in "American Literature: Its Position in the Present Time, and Prospects for the Future" that Longfellow "had no style of his own" and that the derivative style he did have simply sucked the life out of his poems (154).[12] In her own words, "This want of the free breath of nature" in his poetry, "this perpetual borrowing of imagery, this excessive, because superficial, culture which he has derived from an acquaintance with the elegant literature of many nations and men out of proportion to the experience of life himself, prevent Mr. Longfellow's verses from ever being a true refreshment to ourselves" (154).

It was not Poe and Fuller, however, who excised Longfellow from the American canon. He was firmly entrenched in the American cultural memory—still recognized, in fact, as one of the United States' representative authors—when Santayana and Brooks began their work of canon construction at the turn of the twentieth century. To Santayana and Brooks, Longfellow's literary manifestoes were simply unimportant—unworthy of discussion, in fact—his vision of transatlantic literary unity seemed weak-minded and unimaginative, his poetry seemed childish and fit for no higher purpose than children's reading, and he mattered most as the representative figure of an American culture that by the turn of the twentieth century had become soft, feminized, and "genteel."[13]

When Santayana confronted Longfellow, he bridged the gap between nineteenth-century critical discussions that concerned themselves primarily with the development of a national literature and the twentieth-century conversations that finally accomplished an American canon at Longfellow's expense. In "The Moral Background," for instance, Santayana described "Rip Van Winkle," "Hiawatha," and "Evangeline" as the best literary productions of New England's mid-nineteenth-century "Indian summer of the mind," but—continuing the sentiments of Mathews and Fuller—he condemned the writings of Irving and Longfellow as unorginal or un-American: they "lacked native roots and fresh sap because the American intellect itself lacked them. Their culture was half a pious survival, half an intentional acquirement; it was not the inevitable flowering of a fresh experience" (78).

It is precisely this insistence upon new, uniquely American experience that shaped the nineteenth-century response to Longfellow's work, but Santayana inaugurated a new line of critique—the line that was pursued with particular vigor by Van Wyck Brooks—when he condemned Longfellow for his gentility, which was always an attack upon his masculinity. As I have already mentioned, Santayana first identified gentility as a national problem for the United States in "The Genteel Tradition in American Philosophy," but in two subsequent essays, "Genteel American Poetry (1915) and "The Moral Background" (1920), he made it quite clear that he found Longfellow the best illustration of gentility.

In "Genteel American Poetry," for example, Santayana deploys the usual critique of antebellum American poetry as "a boundless field of convention, prosperity and mediocrity," but for the first time he also describes Longfellow's poetry as the expression of an aged and atrophied femininity: "[I]t was a simple, sweet, humane, Protestant literature, grandmotherly in that sedate spectacled wonder with which it gazed at the terrible world and said how beautiful and how interesting it all was" (73). For Santayana, Longfellow's poetry does not merely represent a feminine literature. It represents the most negative form of femininity that Santayana can muster—a naive and visually impaired femininity that lacks even sexual or generative vitality.

Whenever Santayana discusses the "genteel tradition," Longfellow looms as an omniscient example. For Van Wyck Brooks, however, Longfellow is a subject of direct, persistent, and consistently gendered attack. Much like Cooper, Brooks considers him a member of the "first generation of American writers" who wrote "like prudent women" preparing a home for habitation (47). The work of both Cooper and Longfellow constitutes a "literature of necessity," in Brooks's formulation, that "like the first warm blaze in a newly constructed hearth . . . takes away the sense of chill" and makes "the room . . . at once cozy and cheerful" (47). By no means do either Cooper or Longfellow accomplish what Brooks regards as the primary purpose of a poet: "to revivify a people" (51).

In the introduction to his 1934 *Three Essays on America*, which reprints some of *America's Coming-of-Age*, Brooks offers an apology to Longfellow and the other authors he feels he may have treated unfairly in the earlier book. He explains that he and his generation "were tired of hearing Longfellow called 'the Just,' and we inscribed our shards against him," ultimately confessing that "in Longfellow's case, and that of most of the others . . . I attempted no rounded estimates. I meant merely to brush them lightly, with reference to a point of view that seems to me now sufficiently incomplete. But the tone of my remarks was sometimes rash, even to the point of impudence" (11).

Despite his attempt to apologize for his early treatment of Longfellow, Brooks's opinion never really changes. Much to the contrary, just two years after this apology, Brooks would offer the twentieth century's most sustained critical dismissal of Longfellow in his 1936 *Flowering of New England*. In this text, which attempts to mask its disdain for Longfellow by acknowledging that he "had an original mind. He was an innovator in metres and rhythms; he introduced new modes of feeling; he touched his world with a magic that was mild but unmistakable," Brooks pins Longfellow down as, once again, a womanish poet, a poet for children and, (in a new twist) an impotent poet (317 or 318).

When it comes to Longfellow, *The Flowering of New England* is Brooks's book of insincere concessions. Its conciliatory tone marks a significant departure from earlier work, but with each begrudging compliment comes a swipe at the "burden of youthful nostalgia" in Longfellow's poems or a condescending remark about the fact that Longfellow "seemed to write for the joy of sharing his treasures, as if he were glad to be thought a mere translator, a simple storyteller, a nursery minstrel" (168, 317 or 318).[14]

Of these pejorative titles that Brooks bestows upon Longfellow, "nursery minstrel" may be the most telling. It moves Brooks, in ways that "translator" and "storyteller" do not, directly toward his primary problem with Longfellow and his poetry: simply that they are engaged with a wholly feminine and domestic sphere of human life that Brooks regards as emasculating. Before Brooks drops the subject, he suggests that Longfellow's poetic process involved "walking in his garden," certainly a feminine place, "among the birds, to the trilling of the frogs in his pond" composing "the stories he was telling his children" and "passing them on to a larger world that was an extension of his household" (510). His compositional process, for Brooks, essentially amounted to "woman's work" (although it may not have been physical labor in the way that domestic "woman's work" is often imagined, the very fact that it happened in a feminine domestic space would have carried strong enough implications for Brooks) that stripped him of his masculinity so that he himself became childlike and told these poetic stories "with a childlike air of trust" (510). In the end, this male but domestic poet suffered from a "flaccidity" that "debarred him from the front rank" of American litterateurs (512).

Domestic, and by implication rendered impotent *by* his domesticity, the Longfellow of Brooks's account was essentially little more than a child himself, and "child," it is important to remember, bears no positive implication in the scope of Brook's argument where real poets are first and foremost expected to be men—firm, potent, vigorous men, like Whitman. For all this emasculating domesticity, Longfellow only remains important, for Brooks, as one of "the popular New England authors," like Whittier and Holmes (whom he includes in this group earlier in the paragraph), "whom every child could understand" and whose works "remained as classics indeed, but mainly for children" (530).

Thus, Santayana and Brooks effectively buried Longfellow beneath an attack on domestic literature that stood essentially unchallenged until Jane Tompkins's *Sensational Designs* defended domesticity and questioned the critical institution's modernist aesthetics. And since David Leverenz's *Manhood and the American Renaissance* furthered Tompkins's line of inquiry by illuminating nineteenth-century "dramas of beset manhood," critics have controlled a critical apparatus capable of redeeming Longfellow's domesticity—and a considerable number of scholars have used it. Despite its critical redemption, however, Longfellow's domesticity is just one element of a poetic project that underwent as near a complete erasure as is possible for an author who enjoyed Longfellow's nineteenth-century status.

Longfellow's vision of an environmentally determined American literature may have ultimately proven untenable, but in at least one way it was remarkable: it yoked American literature to the North American environment and forced the two to be invested in each other. It marked a high point in American literature's awareness of and dependence upon the natural world. When Santayana and Brooks performed their erasure of Longfellow, however, they could not entirely discard nature from the literary sphere. They wrote in a moment when nature bore particularly high cultural capital and when the new sense of environmental scarcity had sparked a sustained and very public conservation movement. In the thirty-year period preceding the 1911 publication of Santayana's "The Genteel Tradition in American Philosophy," the nation had witnessed the appearance of John Muir's preservationist essays in journals such as *Scribner's*, the *Atlantic*, the *Outlook*, and the *Overland*; the creation of the Yosemite, General Grant, and Sequoia national parks; the formation of the Sierra Club with the help of Muir and Robert Underwood Johnson; the appointment of Gifford Pinchot as the director of the national Division of Forestry; the formation of the Audubon Society; and the beginning of John Muir's very public battle to save the Hetch Hetchy Valley from being turned into a reservoir for the city of Los Angeles. By the time Brooks published his *America's Coming-of-Age* in 1915, the battle for the Hetch Hetchy had ended, Muir had died, the natural world had been revealed, for a moment, as the field of political conflict that it always is, and the conservation of nature had become a subject of both household and national debate.[15]

Santayana's "The Genteel Tradition in American Philosophy" even participates in the nature-oriented spirit of the early twentieth century by suggesting Americans turn to nature as a remedy for their own gentility. In this essay, which directly addresses an American audience, Santayana argues that "the mountains and the woods should make you at last ashamed to assert" the central claim of American gentility, that "the conceited notion that man, or human reason, or the human distinction between good and evil, is the center and pivot of the universe" (63). Before the essay ends, Santayana goes so far as to claim that "the society of nature," can remove "the yoke of this genteel tradition itself . . . from your shoulders"; the mountains and woods of North America, which Santayana describes as "virgin and prodigious . . . allow you, in one happy moment, at once to play and to worship, to take yourselves simply, humbly, for what you are, and to salute the wild, indifferent, noncensorious infinity of nature" (62–64).

With the natural world still so immanently important to American culture, Santayana and Brooks promote a literary program that strips the American environment of any power to shape or create a national literature (thus severing Longfellow's intimate link between American literature and American nature) while subsuming the culturally important rhetoric of nature into a new vision of American literary personality. When Santayana and Brooks proclaim Whitman the true beginning of any real American literature, Whitman essentially *becomes* American nature, effectively removing the physical environment from the American literary equation and replacing it with a new, "*natural*," American self.[16] Brooks accomplishes this in *America's Coming-of-Age* at the same moment that he explains Whitman's greatness in terms that approximate the language of environmental determinism that Longfellow uses in his manifestoes. For Brooks, Whitman reveals "something organic" in American life and is himself organic (112). As I have already mentioned in my discussion of Cooper, Brooks finds Whitman "a great vegetable of a man, all of a piece in roots, flavor, substantiality, and succulence, well-ripened in the common sunshine" (112). By transforming Whitman into something organic—specifically, a succulent, raw, undressed, and certainly phallic vegetable—Brooks manages to maintain the convincing language of the earlier environmental determinist models of American national literature while allowing the influential force of a physical nature to fade behind walls of naturalistic language and personality.

As Brooks appropriates the language of environmental determinist models of national literature, he also manipulates the national relationship to the vast category of "the organic" by recasting the nation itself as a sort of organic protoplasm. In Brooks's formulation, the nation is envisioned as a pre-human figure suspended in a process of Darwinian evolution:

> America is like a vast Sargasso Sea—a prodigious welter of unconscious life, swept by ground-swells of half-conscious emotion. All manner of living things are drifting in it, phosphorescent, gayly colored, gathered into knots and clotted masses, gelatinous, unformed, flimsy, tangled, rising and falling, floating and merging, here an immense distended belly, there a tiny rudimentary brain (the gross devouring the fine)—everywhere an unchecked, uncharted, unorganized vitality like that of the first chaos. It is a welter of life which has not been worked into an organism, into which fruitful values and standards of humane economy have not been introduced, innocent of those laws of social gravitation which, rightly understood and pursued with a keen faith, produce a fine temper in the human animal. (164–65)

Despite the fact that it makes an unmistakable appeal to "the natural" through its Sargasso Sea metaphor, this passage performs a semiotic reversal that first of all sublimates the natural world into the world of the sign, thereby removing all agency from the realm of the environmental component of the passage, and then transfers whatever value the organic possessed away from the natural world to the exclusively human sphere. The United States, its literature, and its culture are not *determined by* an organic sphere—they *are* the organic, they *are* nature.

Ultimately, Brooks's replacement of literary environmental determinism with a cult of a naturalistic Whitmanian personality eroded nature's literary agency and its literary/cultural capital at one of the most dramatic moments in the history of U.S. environmental politics, and it gave to the American critical tradition that developed in Brooks's wake a method of discussing literature that had almost no connection at all to any sense of a material nature. It preserved, as these passages from *America's Coming-of-Age* demonstrate, a naturalistic rhetoric that possessed considerable cultural power in the historical moment but only by relegating the environmental language of earlier manifestoes of U.S. national literature to a realm of signification that is entirely removed from any actual environmental signifier. Rather than an environment that shapes a national literature, Brooks offers an American culture that *is* nature, a primordial and evolutionary "Sargasso Sea," and one poet, Walt Whitman, who had emerged out of this "welter of life" as a true "organism" who contained a self from whence all of the environment's qualities could be mined.

The critical decisions of George Santayana and Van Wyck Brooks were not inevitable events so much as deliberate actions of an implicit environmental politics that overwrote and silenced the vastly different literary plans of nineteenth-century literary figures such as Henry Wadsworth Longfellow. Santayana and Brooks were repelled by Longfellow's social conservatism and poetic restraint, but when they rejected his poetry on these grounds and in favor of new modernist literary projects they also discarded elements of his thinking—his focus on a material nature and his terrestrial environmental gaze—that could have contributed to a much more environmentally engaged course for American literature in the twentieth century. Even Santayana himself, had he given Longfellow a fairer reading, would have appreciated the poet's frequently non-anthropocentric environmental vision of a natural world that Santayana believed to be the great hope for a culture that was mired in gentility.[17]

As the twentieth century progressed, however, the environmental politics of American literature would become the politics of evasion and displacement that Santayana and Brooks theorized and legitimized in their canonical decisions. American authors who wrote about the environment in the early twentieth century—and who wanted to be received as serious writers of "literature"—faced several clearly defined options: they could chafe against this literary culture of environmental disengagement, as Willa Cather and John Steinbeck would; they could follow its natural trajectory, as Hemingway would, to a thoroughly imperialist orientation toward the natural world; or they could simply disregard American literature's conventional environmental philosophy, as Zora Neale Hurston and Jean Toomer would, to create a wholly different relationship with nature based on a liberatory absorption into the environment rather than an exploitation of it. Whatever course of action these authors chose, they indelibly worked within a critical climate and a literary tradition that Santayana and Brooks helped construct against the material nature and terrestrial environmental vision of Henry Wadsworth Longfellow.

Chapter 4

Willa Cather and John Steinbeck, Environmental Schizophrenia, and Monstrous Ecology

As the twentieth century dawned on the United States, the nation was seriously confronting the fact that its nature was neither unlimited, nor virginal, nor indestructible, and the Progressive Era's focus on conservation, preservation, and pollution remediation served as hedges against the material, cultural, and spiritual threats posed by the possibility of environmental exhaustion. American literature, though, was entering a period of fragmentation that would deeply impact its relationship with the natural world. The ahistorical, apolitical aesthetic system championed by Santayana and Brooks was being put into practice by the new wave of modernist authors while the historical and political modes were not dying but being marginalized by critics as "lowbrow," to call upon the term that Brooks uses in *America's Coming-of-Age*.[1]

From the 1890s until sometime in the 1920s, authors could write about the natural world and advocate for its conservation or preservation and still find substantial and eager audiences.[2] This worked marvelously for John Muir and John Burroughs, and, to a lesser extent, for Mary Austin, but the modernist shift widened the disconnect between audience size and critical success. It became difficult to write about nature and simultaneously produce "literature." As more time passed, as the early decades of the twentieth century, with all their lurking radicalism and revolutionary foment, became the recidivist 1930s and 1940s with their anticommunist paranoia, it became difficult to argue for environmental reform even in the "lower" register where Muir and Burroughs had operated with such popularity in earlier decades.

In the early twentieth century writing about nature carried a series of consequences. It could meet with commercial success, or it could meet with charges of radicalism, but, whatever the case, it was effectively barred from the realm of "high literature." This situation posed a fundamental problem for authors, such as Willa Cather and John Steinbeck, who understood the guiding principles of the emerging ecological sciences, who recognized ongoing environmental destruction as a problem, and who viewed themselves as participants in the American literary tradition. They could not speak plainly about the environmental realities that concerned them. As a result, both Cather and Steinbeck produced bodies of work that walk the line between the expectations of "literature," which they wanted to meet, and the environmental realities that they could not help but express even if they had to express them with great care and subtlety.

These negotiations of art and politics produced two bodies of work that contain what I believe is best described as a tenuously managed environmental schizophrenia carefully held in check by forces that are both internal and external to the individual texts themselves. Cather and Steinbeck, and the characters they create, avoid venturing into radicalism by tactically retreating into the tried and true Emersonian approach to nature with its tendency toward abstraction, with its skyward environmental gazes, and with its metonyms of environmental health, and they do it because they know the world outside their books is intricately tuned to detect and destroy any trace of radicalism, whether such attacks might appear in reviews that discredit environmental sentiment as empty sentimentalism or as evidence of communist sympathies.

The Unavoidability of Environmental Politics in Willa Cather's World

Since the mid-1990s, critics have understood that Cather was deeply interested in ecological science and that environmental concerns became a part of mainstream politics during the Progressive Era. We now know, for instance, that Cather went to the University of Nebraska planning to become " 'a great anatomist or a brilliant naturalist' " at a time when the university was dominated by the presence of the ecologist Charles Besey, and we know she cultivated friendships with classmates F. E. Clements and Edith Schwartz who would go on to become influential ecologists in their own rights (Rosowski, 37). Similarly, we know that between the time Cather was nine years old in 1882 and forty-nine years old in 1922 more land was protected by the federal government—in the form of national parks, national monuments, national forests, and wildlife preserves—than at any other time before or since.[3]

For all we know about Cather's scientific interests, and for all we know about how much land was put into preservation and conservation programs during this period, it is still too easy to imagine environmental politics as a silent or invisible issue during the early twentieth century, as something that played itself out in bureaucratic offices hidden from public view. When Cather moved to New York City to work for *McClure's* magazine in 1906, however, she entered social and professional communities that would soon become so fixated on conservation that Cather would not have been able to avoid the issue.

Conservation had been a topic of public discussion from the beginning of Theodore Roosevelt's administration. In his first address to Congress, which the *New York Times* published on December 4, 1901, Roosevelt identified "forest and water problems" as one of the most pressing concerns facing the nation at the turn of the twentieth century, and conservation issues became newsworthy from time to time throughout his first term. In the fall of 1907, though, conservation became an issue that the press would cover consistently through the two remaining years of Roosevelt's administration, through the single-term presidency of William Taft (1909–1913), and throughout the two-term presidency of Woodrow Wilson (1913–1921). As Roosevelt brought his presidency to a close between 1907 and 1909, the *Times* published roughly 270 articles that touched on conservation issues in one way or another. During Taft's administration, the *Times* published nearly 1,400 articles on conservation-related issues, and during Woodrow Wilson's administration the newspaper issued approximately 2,700 more articles on the same subject, which amounts to nearly one article per day between 1913 and 1921 even as the nation's attention was firmly fixed on World War I from 1914 to 1918.[4]

The media's steady coverage of conservation issues began in November 1907 when Roosevelt announced plans for a governors' conservation conference that he would host at the White House in May 1908. On November 18, 1907, the *Times* printed the invitation Roosevelt sent to the nation's governors; it laid out Roosevelt's basic idea that national prosperity relies directly upon the sustainability of the nation's natural resources, it identified resource conservation as the most pressing issue facing the nation, and it expressed the president's opinion that "the abundant national resources on which the welfare of this nation rests are becoming depleted, and in not a few cases are already exhausted" ("Roosevelt Invites Governors to Meet").

Nearly six months later, on May 10, 1908, the *Times* began what would become a week of extensive coverage of the Governors' Conference on Conservation with an article that forecast the event as stunningly portentous. It would be the first time a president had called all the nation's governors to the White House, it would be the first time the White House had "sheltered a large convention of a great public issue," it would be the first time "the question of the conservation called for the consideration of the Nation's natural resources had been made the subject of a great deliberative body." For these reasons, the *Times* found the conditions "favorable for many interesting phases of historymaking possibilities" and approached the event as a wholly new way of enacting political change—it would mark "a new and distinct step forward in the political methods of the country" ("Governors to Meet at the White House").

From May 10 until May 17, the *Times* reported on pre-and post-conference parties, the conference's agenda, and the conferences's results. By all accounts, it was a spectacularly successful affair. The attendees generally agreed with Roosevelt's concerns (one headline from the May 14 *Times* reads, "Governors Cheer Roosevelt's Talk"), they agreed to work together to unify state and federal conservation efforts, they agreed to continue meeting on a formal and regular basis both with and without the president, and they passed a resolution, which the *Times* printed on May 16, that spelled out their wholesale support of the president's conservation agenda.[5]

The resolution that was passed at the end of the Governors' Conference and the decision to plan similar meetings in the future were both important events, but the Governors' Conference might be more important for the fact that it spawned several subsequent developments that kept the press, and the nation, focused on conservation. On June 8, 1908, Roosevelt acted on an idea that was well received during the Governors' Conference and announced the creation of a new National Conservation Commission charged with undertaking a complete inventory of the nation's natural resources ("To Guard Our Resources"). This commission would present its conclusions six months later, on December 10, in Washington, D. C., and on December 27, with just three months remaining in his presidency and with William Howard Taft waiting in the wings as president-elect, Roosevelt announced one last conservation conference—this time it would be the North American Conference on Conservation of Resources, which would take place over five days beginning on February 18, 1909 (just weeks before Taft's inauguration on March 4) and include delegations from Canada and Mexico ("Roosevelt Invites Canada and Mexico").[6]

Intentionally or not, the pace of Roosevelt's conservation agenda—with major announcements, conferences, and commission reports appearing at regular intervals over the last two years of his presidency—was perfect for news outlets such as the *New York Times*. It allowed newspapers to announce coming events, report on the buildup to the events as they approached, and report on their results. All of this took place in measured succession so that a new conservation story sprang up virtually every time an old one finished running its course.

In this manner, conservation remained a current issue for the better part of two years, and the steady presence of conservation in public discourse had the unanticipated consequence of shaping Taft's platform as he campaigned for the presidency in 1908. At nearly every opportunity, Taft asserted that his presidency would continue Roosevelt's policies, and whenever he made such claims he usually referred specifically to Roosevelt's conservation initiatives. He did this in the official, detailed platform he delivered when the Republican Party nominated him as its presidential candidate on June 15, 1908, he repeated his position in speeches he delivered later in June and in August, and he tacitly reaffirmed it by appearing with Roosevelt at the conservation conventions and commission meetings.[7] In this manner, even news stories on "pure" politics—reports on political conventions and stump speeches—became stories that kept the extended discussion of conservation alive.

This world of intense environmental debate was Cather's world even to the extent that her professional life intersected with environmental politics. Cather published articles in the same magazines—*The Century*, *The Overland Monthly*, *Collier's*, and *Scribner's*—that published the writings of John Muir before and during his campaign to save the Hetch Hetchy Valley, and she would eventually publish her first four novels—*Alexander's Bridge* (1912), *O Pioneers!* (1913), *The Song of the Lark* (1915), and *My Ántonia* (1918)—with Houghton, Mifflin, the same company that published four of Muir's long prose works between 1901 and the year of his death, 1914, in addition to four travel narratives, a collection of his letters, and a biography that it printed posthumously.[8]

When Muir committed himself to resisting the Hetch Hetchy project in 1907, Cather had already been working as an editor at *McClure's* for a year, and in 1908 she became the magazine's managing editor—a position she would hold until 1912, one year before Congress and Woodrow Wilson passed legislation to permit the flooding of the valley. While Cather was managing *McClure's*, the nation's magazines and newspapers granted overwhelming support to Muir's cause. Editors of two other New York–based magazines, Lyman Abbott of the *Overlook* and Robert Underwood Johnson of the more influential *Century*, devoted themselves and their publications to Muir's campaign, and by the end of the prolonged debate most of the nation's magazines and newspapers had joined the effort along with a long list of prominent citizens.[9]

McClure's did not directly engage the Hetch Hetchy controversy, but it could not entirely avoid the era's environmentally attuned zeitgeist. In July 1908, just a month before Cather became managing editor of the magazine, *McClure's* published a short but glowing biography of Gifford Pinchot by Will C. Barnes, and in April 1909—now under Cather's direction—it printed Rudolph Cronau's "A Continent Despoiled," which presents a vitriolic condemnation of the nation's misuse of natural resources. One month later, *McClure's* would publish Judson C. Welliver's "The National Water Power Trust," which defends Theodore Roosevelt's conservation policies by exposing another example of corporate greed overriding the public good: private power companies attempting to consolidate the rights to all of the valuable hydroelectric sites in North America.

Environmental Desire and Environmental Schizophrenia

When Longfellow registered a fissure in the idea of an immutable and permanent North American nature, he wrote well before the furor of early-twentieth-century environmental politics, and the loss of nature mattered most to him for the implications that it held for his particular vision of American literature. By the time Cather began her writing career, however, environmental loss had accelerated and become a national issue that would have been difficult to ignore for anyone who held Cather's ecological sensibilities, her central position in a New York magazine industry that had become involved in the environmental politics of the period, and her interest in writing novels that she imagined to have grown out of the long grasses of the prairies.

To put it simply, Cather seemed to have all the makings of an environmental activist, but she was not one, and would never become one. She was suspicious of the types of social activism, or muckraking, that she had been a part of at *McClure's*, and she did not believe that there was any place for politics in art.[10] In several essays, Cather clearly states that the novel *should not* become the vehicle for social agendas and that she had lost her zeal for muckraking. In her 1936 essay "Escapism," for instance, she mocks the current sentiment that the novelist's "first concern should be to cry out against social injustice" and confesses that "when I first lived in New York and was working on the editorial staff of a magazine, I became disillusioned about social workers and reformers" (970). It was not just the social workers that lost their luster for Cather but the entire mission of social activism. If she ever had any real interest in reform movements (and Woodress is adamant in *Willa Cather: Her Life and Art* that she did not), it clearly had no place in her vision of literature. In her literary credo, "The Novel Démeublé," which also appeared in 1936 (as an essay in *Not Under Forty*), Cather postulates that "[i]f the novel is a form of imaginative art, it cannot be at the same time a vivid and brilliant form of journalism" (836).[11]

When Cather abandoned social activism in favor of literature that avoided overt politics, she simultaneously abandoned the sphere of women's writing (which had been associated with social activism throughout the nineteenth century's abolition, temperance, women's suffrage, and urban reform movements) and committed herself to the masculine tradition that had been steadily moving away from politics since at least the middle of the nineteenth century. Her disavowal of social activism carried with it an a priori rejection of any overtly political confrontation with the processes of environmental destruction that were rapidly changing the very places that she was using to ground her novels.

Both *O Pioneers!* and *My Ántonia* admit widespread environmental change, but, with activism out of the question, they defuse the potentially revolutionary force of such change in ways that have traditionally been received—in a highly oversimplified fashion—as simple, mindless nostalgia. It takes no grand feat of literary analysis to recognize that there is nostalgia in Cather's writings, but Cather's use of nostalgia is always controlled and purposeful; as critics have begun to realize in recent years, it is usually used to highlight problems that Cather recognized in the national culture of her own era.[12]

In *O Pioneers!*, two manifestations of nostalgia battle against each other. Carl Linstrum's backward gaze recalls the prairie as it was before it was developed into an agricultural grid; his gaze forgets all of the privation that drove his family to move back to the city, but it recalls the original glory of the prairie and illuminates the history of a place that has become an agricultural grid. Against Carl's nostalgia, which maintains a memory of the original prairie even while it forgets his family's pain and failure, Alexandra Bergson poses what might best be described as a nostalgia for the present. Especially during the first two major sections of the novel—which record her big dream of large-scale agricultural success and the fulfillment of this dream—Alexandra views the current moment as the fulfillment of a historical process, imagines the present itself as a pivotal moment in history, and erases the ugly imperialism that contributed to it.[13] The nostalgia that runs throughout *My Ántonia* is not polyvocal as it is in *O Pioneers!*, but it is no less complex. Every time Jim Burden looks backward to his boyhood and youth on the glorious prairie, his gaze is forced through the filter of Cather's introduction to the novel, which casts him as a speculator with a deep romantic streak. It is a brief but cutting description of Jim, and it should expose everything else he does and says to very careful scrutiny.

The environmental nostalgia that runs through both *O Pioneers!* and *My Ántonia* produces a subtle environmental schizophrenia that operates on at least two distinct levels. In the simpler sense, "environmental schizophrenia" is a way to describe the innocent and unreconciled double-mindedness of the novels and the characters that populate them. Cather never drives any of the characters or novels to a resolution of their contradictions. The novels and characters express tremendous love for the land yet document and participate in the destruction of what they love about it.

In the other sense, though, the environmental schizophrenia of Cather's novels contains a type of political power that I do not believe we can recognize without thinking about the philosophical discussion of the schizophrenic figure that Gilles Deleuze and Felix Guattari carry out to such great effect in *Anti-Oedipus*. For Deleuze and Guattari, the schizophrenic figure is both a product of and a threat to capitalism. S/he is deaf, mute, and catatonic, withdrawn into a fractured self through which desire flows freely and unchecked, and s/he is capable of sliding through space and time to "everywhere something real has been and will be produced" (*Anti-Oedipus* 87). While capitalism commodifies the self through the repression of individual and social desire, the schizophrenic unleashes all repressed desire—becomes a welter of uncontrolled desire—until it removes both the mind and the body from processes of capitalist production. By giving itself over to the unchecked flow of desire, which is inherently "revolutionary in its own right," schizophrenia holds the power even to unhinge the capitalist order. It is because of this, Deleuze and Guattari argue, that capitalism controls, confines, and imprisons schizophrenia—capitalism preserves itself by checking its coursing flows of unchecked desire (*Anti-Oedipus* 116).

O Pioneers! and *My Ántonia* are crisscrossed with currents of environmental yearning and lamentation. Like the schizophrenic of Deleuze and Guattari's formulation, Cather's characters move through space and time to locate real, authentic, or original environments, and in the process they undercut the narratives of unapologetic progress that are promoted by Alexandra Bergson and Jim Burden. Always, though, the environmental desire that flows through Cather's work is arrested before it becomes radical, and it is often arrested by a return to an Emersonian relationship to the environment that maintains its faith in nature's permanence and purity through metonyms of environmental health and a tightly controlled environmental gaze.

Cather's Canonically Modulated Environmental Schizophrenia

In *O Pioneers!* and *My Ántonia*, the Nebraska prairie is both stultifying and magnificent. It breaks Carl Linstrum in *O Pioneers!* and essentially kills John Bergson; it is "bewildering . . . depressing and disheartening . . . an enigma" unlike any other land (13–14). It is a site of extreme privation for European immigrants, and it blots out Jim Burden's sense of himself in *My Ántonia* just as it had blotted out Cather's own identity as a child.[14] At the same time, however, the prairie in *O Pioneers!* is "the great fact," a powerful place that wishes to "preserve its own fierce strength, its peculiar savage kind of beauty, its uninterrupted mournfulness"; in *My Ántonia* Jim Burden's "first glorious autumn" is glorious because the prairie is wild, free, fenceless, and full of motion (*O Pioneers!* 10, *My Ántonia* 27).[15] In each of the novels the original uniqueness and power of the prairie—its essence—is bound up in its most distinct single feature—its native grasses.

O Pioneers! and *My Ántonia* are both driven steadily away from this dually interpreted original environment by characters who play critical roles in converting it into a highly ordered agricultural space. Alexandra Bergson and Jim Burden both privilege optimistic environmental narratives that emphasize the glory of the prairie's transformation, but Cather punctures each of their grand narratives to reveal an undercurrent of environmental longing that privileges a benevolent vision of the prairie during an earlier moment. These ruptures, which are provided in large part by Carl Linstrum in *O Pioneers!* and Cather's narratorial interventions in *My Ántonia*, insert unwieldy flows of environmental desire into Jim and Alexandra's master narratives that are ultimately controlled through various forms of Emersonian environmental misdirection.

From the beginning of *O Pioneers!*, Cather establishes that Alexandra Bergson is a visionary. When she first appears, she is a girl "who seemed to be looking with . . . anguished perplexity into the future" (9). As Alexandra matures, she accomplishes her father's mission of forging a highly ordered space out of the wide expanse of the indomitable prairie, and she manages "the big chance" of land speculation when other settlers fail (41). All in all, watching her big dreams act themselves out on the prairie is an exhilarating experience for Alexandra. The prairie—especially when she sees it within the scope of the plan she has for it—seems "beautiful to her, rich and strong and glorious" (41–42). It is so glorious, in fact, that it brings her to tears.[16]

Carl Linstrum exists in the first part of *O Pioneers!* as a "bitter" and sullen boy whose family is failing at frontier life, and he ultimately exits the narrative when his family abandons its homestead and returns to St. Louis (10). He reappears at the beginning of Part II, however, sixteen years after John Bergson's death, and he returns to a place that is radically different: now, Cather writes, "The shaggy coat of the prairie . . . has vanished forever. From the Norwegian graveyard one looks out over a vast checkerboard, marked off in squares of wheat and corn; light and dark, dark and light. Telephone wires hum along the white roads, which always run at right angles" (49).

As soon as Carl finds himself alone with Alexandra, he punctures her sense of triumph by stating that he prefers the original, untamed prairie to the new prairie of Alexandra's own creation. In what could be construed as an expression of a very simplistic nostalgia, Carl says,

> "I think I liked the old Lou and Oscar better, and they probably feel the same about me. I even, if you can keep a secret,"—Carl leaned forward and touched her arm, smiling,—"I even think I liked the old country better. This is all very splendid in its way, but there was something about this country when it was a wild old beast that has haunted me all these years. Now, when I come back to all this milk and honey, I feel like the old German song, 'Wo bist du, wo bist du, mein geliebtest Land?'—Do you ever feel like that, I wonder?" (75)

Carl's question is nostalgic insofar as it looks back to an idealized past—its retrospective view of the prairie erases the distinctly negative view of the place that he himself held early in the novel—but it also gives expression to an environmental anxiety that Alexandra seems to sense but evade throughout the novel.

When she wants to see the inexorable perpetuity of the natural world that used to be written all over the face of the prairie, Alexandra casts her gaze skyward; when she wants to reexperience the former glory of the place, she looks toward the bits of native prairie grass that endure within the fences of cemeteries; and when she is consolidating her power as a landowner she incorporates "Crazy Ivar," the only figure in the novel who lives in total ecological harmony with the prairie, into her own family as if his assimilation grants her operation a sense of ecological benevolence. When Carl asks his pivotal question, Alexandra immediately shifts the discussion from the terrestrial nature that Carl recognizes as fundamentally—and unfortunately—changed to a nature that is construed as abstract and astronomical. Alexandra turns her attention to the unchanging heavens and directs Carl's gaze to the place where a fragment of original prairie remains: Alexandra, Cather writes, "paused and looked thoughtfully at the stars" before immediately diverting Carl's attention to the old Norwegian graveyard that reappears throughout the novel as a final preserve of native prairie grass (75).

By the time Carl asked Alexandra if she missed the old prairie, she had already learned to depend on an averted and restricted environmental gaze to repress any potentially subversive environmental desire from undercutting the narrative of success that she was constructing for herself. Relatively early in *O Pioneers!*, after the mildly traumatic moment in which Alexandra tells her brothers that she plans to expand the family's landholdings, Alexandra re-centers herself against the vision of unchanging nature that she finds in the night sky. After her talk with her brothers, she stands against a windmill "looking at the stars which glittered so keenly through the frosty autumn air" and thinking "of their vastness and distance, and of their ordered march" (45). With Alexandra's eyes focused above the space that is capable of being entirely transformed and with her mind on vastness, distance, and cosmic order, Cather writes that "it fortified her to reflect upon the great operations of nature, and when she thought of the law that lay behind them, she felt a sense of personal security" (45). Similarly, the graveyard that Cather recalls after Carl's question had always existed within the scope of the novel as a veritable museum of native prairie biota. From the opening chapter of the novel it is a place where the native endures, "where the grass had, indeed, grown back over everything, shaggy and red, hiding even the wire fence" (10).

Jim Burden is at least as involved as Alexandra Bergson in drastic environmental change, and he deals with such change just as she does—by looking away from it and fixing his gaze on what are essentially taxidermied remains of a formerly wild, free, glorious, and clearly exceptional place. Cather, however, treats Jim Burden differently. While both Alexandra and Jim contain multiple orientations toward the environment and mechanisms to control them, in *My Ántonia* Cather works to expose everything Jim does as dubious—including the relationship to the environment that he creates for himself.

Cather quickly undermines Jim's narrative before she ever turns the novel over to him. In the novel's introduction, as it appears in the original version of 1918, the female narrator (presumably Cather herself), who will ultimately present Jim's narrative "substantially as he brought it to me," presents Jim as a conniving social climber with a stilted worldview and an explicitly contradictory relationship with the natural world (6).[17] This narrator states quite frankly that Jim's "career was suddenly advanced by a brilliant marriage," that she rarely spends time with Jim because "I do not like his wife," and that Jim possess a "naturally romantic and ardent disposition" (3). On the heels of these serious blows to Jim's reliability, Cather's female narrator specifically identifies Jim's relationship with the environment as a point of conflict. Jim "loves with a personal passion the great country" of his youth, but "he is legal counsel for one of the great Western railways" that "runs and branches" through the very place he loves (4, 3). Jim has a great "faith in" and "knowledge of" this land,

and he has "played an important part in its development," but his "part" has moved in particularly exploitative directions:

> He is always able to raise capital for new enterprises in Wyoming or Montana, and has helped young men out there to do remarkable things in *mines* and *timber* and *oil*. If a young man with an idea can once get Jim Burden's attention, can manage to accompany him when he goes off into the wilds hunting for lost parks or exploring new canyons, then the money which means action is usually forthcoming. (4; emphasis added)

Joseph Urgo, who claims that Jim Burden is a preservationist, grounds his argument on this passage. In Urgo's words, "Jim Burden is emblematic of the conservation debate. He is both a legal counsel for the railroads (and so he profits from development), and he is a preservationist, someone you can count on for funding 'big Western dreams' of uncovering secret canyons and lost parks" (50). Urgo makes his central claim, however, without acknowledging that Jim's grand plans involve "mines, timber, and oil" and that Jim funds young men who want to take "action" in the "lost parks . . . [and] new canyons." Although the word is vague, this "action" seems much more likely to involve the extraction of natural resources rather than any sort of preservation (or conservation, for that matter), especially considering Jim's lines of work.

All things considered, Jim's relationship to the natural world is much less preservationist (or conservationist or environmentalist) than Urgo admits. The more compelling facet of Jim's relationship with the natural world concerns how he maintains his own multiplicities—how he can continue to love the land of his childhood and continue to be involved in its erasure.

The burden of environmental guilt Jim Burden faces in his narrative is more intense than the one Cather creates in *O Pioneers!*. In the earlier novel, the prairie may have been glorious but in the early years it was also a bitter place that killed or broke vigorous men. In *My Ántonia*, however, the prairie lacks the menacing half of this binary. Mr. Shimerda dies and the prairie has collected a wide variety of broken individuals (Pavel and Peter, for instance, and all of the "Working Girls" whose lives have been made difficult by conditions on the prairie), but very little blame falls on the prairie itself. To Jim Burden, the prairie of his boyhood is a wholly magnificent—even magical—place even though he remembers his first encounter with the prairie as an encounter with a profound black nothingness against which he "felt erased, blotted out"; from the beginning he paints the prairie as the mother of a nation (13).

As he moves away from his initial definition of the prairie as a generative nothingness, Jim sings a song of its glories until he elevates it to the sublime. He revels in its openness and lack of fencing: "all the years that have passed have not dimmed my memory of that first *glorious* autumn . . . there were *no fences* in those days, and I could choose my own way over the grass uplands, trusting my pony to get me home again" (27). He fixes his environmental gaze upon the prairie's native grasses, which he argues are the locus of the prairie's incredible motion and vivacity: "[A]s I looked about me I felt that the grass was the country, as the water is the sea. The red of the grass made all the great prairie the color of wine-stains, or of certain seaweeds when they are first washed up. And there was so much motion in it; the whole country seemed, somehow, to be running" (18). And in Jim's most enraptured moment, the wild fenceless prairie of his boyhood, with all of its native grasses, becomes a sublime, transfigurative space of heroic and biblical scale:

> All those fall afternoons were the same, but I never got used to them. As far as we could see, the miles of copper-red grass were drenched in sunlight that was stronger and fiercer than at any other time of the day . . . the whole prairie was like the bush that burned with the fire and was not consumed. That hour always had the exultation of victory, of triumphant ending, like a hero's death—heroes who died young and gloriously. It was a sudden transfiguration, a lifting-up of day.
>
> How many an afternoon Ántonia and I have trailed along the prairie under that magnificence! And always two long black shadows flitted before us or followed after, dark spots on the ruddy grass. (35)

For Jim, the death of the prairie as he found it in his boyhood would amount to the loss of the pure and original, the loss of the exceptional, and the loss of a source of the sublime. His reaction to this incredible source of loss, which he has helped precipitate, is like Alexandra's. He simply looks away. Having already established that the prairie's grasses metonymically represent a pure and vibrant prairie, Jim fixes his environmental gaze on the scant patches of prairie grass that remain, and when he comes face to face with the colossal changes that have taken place on the prairie he manipulates visual perspective to further mediate the environmental losses that he witnesses.

As time passes and the native prairie recedes before the plow, Jim and Ántonia repeatedly and "instinctively" retreat to the one place where the native grasses remain—the grave of Ántonia's father, Mr. Shimerda

(239). Although the place is clearly significant because it is tied to Mr. Shimerda and his terribly traumatic death, it is also magnetic because it contains some of the last remaining prairie grass that Jim represents as the soul of the original prairie. The gravesite is a persistent "little island" "with a sagging wire fence around it" that contains the "tall red grass that was never mowed" (94).[18] This place and its metonymic grass, Jim explicitly points out, continued unchanged "when the open-grazing days were over, and the red grass had been ploughed under until it had almost disappeared from the prairie; when all the fields were under fence, and the roads no longer ran about like wild things, but followed the surveyed section-lines" (94). This gravesite is a monument to Mr. Shimerda and to the prairie itself, but Jim does not recognize it *as* a monument. For him, it is the original prairie still alive, and its perpetual existence allows him to extend the life of the highly significant original prairie even beyond its effectual end.

While Jim usually enforces a constricted environmental gaze that focuses strictly on Mr. Shimerda's metonymic grass, he is equally capable of widening the lens and recasting the prairie as a panorama of expansionist triumph that obliterates environmental loss from a different direction. Near the end of *O Pioneers!*, Jim adopts this panoramic gaze to praise the new, thoroughly controlled, thoroughly agricultural prairie. During a trip to "the high country, to visit Widow Steavens," he reports that

> [t]he wheat harvest was over, and here and there along the horizon I could see black puffs of smoke from the steam thrashing-machines. The old pasture land was now being broken up into wheatfields and cornfields, the red grass was disappearing, and the whole face of the country was changing. (229)

For Jim, the pastures, the harvest, and the new wooden homes he also witnesses all mean "happy children, contented women, and men who saw their lives coming to a fortunate issue" (229). In aggregate, he finds "the changes . . . beautiful and harmonious . . . it was like watching the growth of a great man or of a great idea" (229).

This statement, Jim's only unequivocal praise of prairie development in the entire novel, is remarkable for the circumstances it involves and for what it does not say. Jim only experiences this moment of enthusiasm when he is in a "high country" that grants him a particular perspective. From this vantage point, the entire place loses its particularity and becomes more like an Albert Bierstadt panorama than the actual place Jim loves. It becomes more like the *idea* of American "progress," which of course is an idea that rarely admits the costs it entails, and it is only from this perspective that the life of the prairie cannot be measured in the motion of its rapidly disappearing grasses.

On that particular highland, with the prairie spread out across his horizon, the situation was right for Jim to find the new prairie "beautiful and harmonious," or for his own personal interests (his love for the place as it was) to become secondary to a grand, panoramic idea of progress. It is not insignificant, though, that after his triumphalist vision he repeatedly moves in the opposite direction—away from the heights, where change is visible on an overwhelming scale and back to ground level where draws, gullies, and fences limit the line of sight to remaining bits of native prairie. Between the mountaintop scene and the end of the novel, Jim encloses himself in Ántonia's homestead, with its concentric rings of trees and hedges, where he experiences the type of domesticity he imagined in his highland vision, and immediately before his final departure from Black Hawk he wanders away from the train station into the pastures, draws, and hillocks "where the land was so rough that it had never been ploughed up, and the long red grass of early times still grew shaggy" (272). Even after helping create a new prairie, seeing it, and registering the loss of the original environment, Jim finds a way—somewhere behind the train station—to find a bit of the "old road, which used to run like a wild thing across the open prairie," the same prairie that he says used to run like a wild thing itself (273). As long as this patch of old road exists, just as patches of native prairie grass continue to exist, Jim will be able to believe that the prairie of his boyhood still exists, and he will be able to maintain his contradictory stance toward the environment; he will be able to maintain a fragile but absolutely necessary equilibrium in his schizophrenic relationship with the natural world.

Steinbeck, Ecology, and American Culture

More than any other factor, the male literary tradition and its established modes of mediating environmental loss shaped Willa Cather's evasion of environmental crisis, but she still understood, as John Steinbeck would demonstrate later in the century, that environmental activism also faced tremendous opposition from a hostile American culture. This, after all, is the moral of Crazy Ivar's story in *O Pioneers!*. Ivar knows that he is different because he practices a strange (ecocentric) Norwegian religion, but it is not his religion so much as it is his unusual symbiotic relationship with nature that earns him his "Crazy" moniker. Alexandra treats Ivar's unorthodox relationship with the natural world as a commodity worth exploiting, but for her brothers, Lou and Oscar (who often speak for the larger community), Ivar is a pariah, largely because he can live "without defiling the face of nature any more than the coyote that had lived there before him had done" (24). Because of his unique relationship with nature, Ivar is faced on every side with incarceration. He fears being sent to an asylum that "they have built . . . for people who are different" (and it is significant that the word is "different" rather than something like "insane" or "crazy"), but even when he is ultimately incorporated into Alexandra's household he simply experiences a more pleasant variety of institutionalization (60). As a part of Alexandra's farm, he functions semiotically as an emblem of environmental benevolence and understanding—in his mere existence he keeps his old ecologically symbiotic mode of life alive and stands as a constant resource of unorthodox agricultural advice for Alexandra.

John Steinbeck was born in 1901, practically in the middle of the progressive conservation movement that would erupt around Cather in New York City several years later, and his connection with ecology—while still largely informal—would be composed of at least as many strands as Cather's. Despite his background, however, Steinbeck would be no more successful than Cather in articulating anything like an unequivocal environmentalist position. While Cather's work demonstrates how the American literary tradition could control the flow of environmental desire, Steinbeck's writing focuses more intensely upon Crazy Ivar's problem: the precarious position of the environmental radical in the United States.

In the Summer of 1923, with his sister, Steinbeck took a course in marine biology at the Hopkins Marine Station in Pacific Grove, California. His instructor was Charles Vincent Taylor, who was deeply influenced by William Emerson Ritter, the renowned zoologist, marine biologist, and founder of the Scripps Institute of Oceanography who promoted an idea of ecological interconnection, or "superorganicism," that captured Steinbeck's imagination. In 1930, he befriended the marine biologist Ed Ricketts, who in turn exposed him to another important early ecologist—W. C. Allee, the specialist in animal group behavior, whose influence Ricketts had felt as a zoology student at the University of Chicago.[19]

Thus, Steinbeck was an intellectual heir, twice-removed on each side, of two incredibly important twentieth-century ecologists. His exposure to these strains of ecological thought allowed him to imagine humans as members of a larger biological community, and it allowed him to register environmental loss in scientific terms. It enabled him to create a series of characters, including Joseph Wayne in *To a God Unknown* (1933), Muley Graves in *The Grapes of Wrath* (1939), and Doc in both *Cannery Row* (1945) and its sequel, *Sweet Thursday* (1954), who feel a powerful transcendental connection to the natural world, and it even allowed him to participate in the ecological expedition that he records in *Sea of Cortez* (1941).[20]

Steinbeck is unique among U.S. authors because he may have recognized the scope, scale, and implications of twentieth-century environmental destruction better than any other "major" American author before Edward Abbey, who published his environmentalist polemic, *Desert Solitaire*, in 1968, the year of Steinbeck's death. This awareness of environmental crisis is most explicit in Steinbeck's late nonfiction works, *Travels with Charley* (1962) and *America and Americans* (1966). In *Travels with Charley*, he is frustrated by "chemical wastes in the rivers, metal wastes everywhere, and atomic wastes buried deep in the earth or sunk in the sea," he argues that the pervasive and felicitous waste that he sees in the United States is a particularly American phenomenon, and he emphasizes its extreme foolishness (26). As insightful as they are, Steinbeck's comments about the state of the environment in *Travels with Charley* are fleeting. In *America and Americans*, though, he rereads the whole of United States history in terms of environmental catastrophe and recognizes that the Untied States operates on an outmoded and unsustainable system of environmental ethics:

> I have often wondered at the savagery and thoughtlessness with which our early settlers approached this rich continent. They came at it as though it were an enemy, which of course it was. They burned the forests and changed the rainfall, they swept the buffalo from the plains, blasted the streams, set fire to the grass, and ran a reckless scythe through the virgin and noble timber. . . . This tendency toward irresponsibility persists in very many of us today; our rivers are poisoned by reckless dumping of sewage and toxic industrial wastes, the air of our cities is filthy and dangerous to breathe from the belching of uncontrolled products from combustion of coal, coke, oil, and gasoline. Our towns are girdled with wreckage and the debris of our toys—our automobiles and our packaged pleasures. Through uninhibited spraying against one enemy we have destroyed the natural balances our survival requires. All these evils can and must be overcome if America and Americans are to survive; but many of us still conduct ourselves as our ancestors did, stealing from the future for our clear and present profit. (377)

This polemic extends through five additional pages. It follows the westward wake of environmental destruction that accompanied U.S. expansion, describes the nineteenth century as environmentally "merciless," and concludes that the "atom bomb" is the culmination of the American tradition of environmental recklessness (379).

If Steinbeck had offered these observations and cultural critiques in isolation, no one would claim that he fell short of an unequivocal environmentalist position. As numerous scholars have pointed out, however, he constantly represses his pessimism with proclamations of faith in an American culture that he portrays as bumbling and mistake-prone but still essentially good-hearted.[21] In the words of Joel Hedgpeth, "Steinbeck is always apologizing for saying bad things and reassuring us that he still loves us all" (Hedgpeth 306).

The ultimate flaw in Steinbeck's environmentalism, according to John Timmerman, is that he offers no "specific program to rectify" the United States' flawed environmental ethic, but the body of Steinbeck's work suggests that there is a very distinct reason his environmentalism went no farther than it did (312). His environmentalist sympathies were held in check by an American culture that he regarded as hegemonic and particularly hostile to any type of radicalism—including both ecological science and environmentalist activism. Anyone who stepped forward and delivered a strident environmental message, Steinbeck believed, would be assaulted with charges of monstrosity and threatened with a ceremonial murder that would reaffirm the nation's environmentally exploitative status quo.

Steinbeck and Monstrosity

Monstrosity was central to Steinbeck's understanding of American culture from the beginning of his career, and two of his early works of fiction, *To a God Unknown* (1933) and *Of Mice and Men* (1937), demonstrate that he understood the cultural history of monstrosity and its role as a regulatory device for American culture. A significant portion of *To a God Unknown*, for instance, focuses on the Renaissance belief that monstrous birth defects are caused by the wayward imaginations of expectant mothers. Throughout the novel, Rama, a mystical matriarch and duenna to a young, expectant mother named Elizabeth, speaks of "children born with tails, with extra limbs, with mouths in the middle of their backs," and Elizabeth, accordingly, lives in fear of having experiences that will transform her unborn child into a monster (99).

As much as he recognized it has a history, though, it is clear that Steinbeck also understood that monstrosity is a cultural weapon. His writings suggest as several scholars have recently argued, that, "monsters are . . . political beings" who are "chosen with deliberation to do quite specific narrative and social work" (Ingebretsen 26). Monsters are used to map social edges and centers, they "delineate and buttress the norms of behavior and belief understood to be matters of 'common sense,' " and when they are ceremonially murdered their deaths are always intended to strengthen a "communal body" (Ingebretsen 26).[22]

Well before Steinbeck associated ecology and environmental activism with it, monstrosity functioned as a device for social regulation in *Of Mice and Men*. Lenny, the story's protagonist, bears physical marks of monstrosity—he possesses superhuman strength, works like a machine, and lacks normal human capacities for judgment and restraint—but he is most menacing to the ranch community as a threat to women and (along with his partner, George) to the community's almost overdetermined heteronormativity. Lenny never intentionally harms anyone, but he does physically assault—even kill—the wife of the ranch's foreman. The incident enters the script of monstrosity, though, when the crime is immediately registered as an assault upon the purity and virtue of womanhood that requires immediate and fatal vengeance to restore the community's expectations of normal human behavior and the sanctity of femininity. Beyond the incident with Curley's wife, which ultimately precipitates his death, Lenny is monstrous because he shares an exclusive homosocial relationship with George. Lenny and George are constantly called to answer for their unusual relationship throughout Steinbeck's narrative, and the particular way that Lenny is ultimately killed is shaped by George's love for his friend and his desire to remove from himself the mark of monstrosity that the relationship placed upon him. In an act that denies the larger community the curative public killing that would have reaffirmed its concepts of normalcy, deviance, and the consequences of deviance, George kills Lenny privately and thus proves to the public community that his bond with Lenny did not overstep the bounds of its unspoken codes of normal heterosexual male behavior.

To a God Unknown and *Of Mice and Men* demonstrate just how well Steinbeck understood monstrosity as a historical phenomenon and a culturally regulative device, but as his career progressed monstrosity became a much larger problem. Beginning with *The Grapes of Wrath*, Steinbeck was no longer exclusively concerned with the insular communities that he engaged in *To A God Unknown*, *Tortilla Flat*, and *Of Mice and Men*; his focus became national, and, accordingly, the community that wielded the deadly brand of monstrosity against all forms of radicalism became national as well.

The Grapes of Wrath is a pivotal novel for Steinbeck because it marks the shift of his focus to the national scene, but it also announces the fundamental assessment of American culture that would endure throughout the rest of his career. Although it is a position that he often undercuts, this novel cringes at the scope and scale of American technocapitalism. The culture of "progress" that displaces the Joad family and their values of agrarianism, independence, and toughness is advanced by faceless conglomerates and by cyborg men who seem melded to their tank-like tractors. Everyone (including Tom Joad and Jim Casy) who exists outside this new and menacing mainstream culture, moreover, is forced to live a precarious life on a cultural border that is vigilantly patrolled and violently defended—often by very real political figures—against subversives and radicals.

Outside of *The Grapes of Wrath*, Steinbeck's nonfiction writings of the 1950s and 1960s contain his most pointed condemnations of American culture. In these pieces, Steinbeck offers his most strident arguments that American culture is a hegemonic construct that is tightly regulated by a group of "leaders" who "are surely screwballs" and resist "any reform movement" by deploying familiar charges of political monstrosity against any emergent source of radicalism (*America and Americans* 364). "The stalking horror" of the moment, Steinbeck writes, is " 'Communism,' with its thread of confiscation of private wealth, and 'Socialism,' which implies that they might be forced to share their wealth with less fortunate citizens" (*A and A* 364). In 1954, Steinbeck was so frustrated with the cultural situation of the United States that he declared, in an essay entitled "I Am a Revolutionary," that

> [t]he so-called masses are more lumpen now than ever. Any semblance of the emergence of the individual is instantly crushed and the doctrine of party and state above everything has taken the place of the theory of liberated men.
>
> The victim of this savagely applied system is the individual. Individuality must be destroyed because it is dangerous to all reactionary plans because the individual is creative and creativeness outside the narrow pattern of the status quo cannot be tolerated. (90)

Steinbeck's Monstrous Ecology

Steinbeck may have issued his most compact critique of American land ethics in *Travels with Charley* and *America and Americans*, but a much earlier text, *The Log from the Sea of Cortez*, offers the clearest vision of how his environmentalist impulses were controlled by his vision of a threatening American culture. The *Log* is the record of an ecological expedition that Steinbeck undertook with Ed Ricketts in 1940. It records the events of the expedition, but record keeping is not is primary function. More than anything, it is an extended attempt to justify ecology to an American culture that is more of a "lumpen mass" and more likely to deploy monstrosity against a radical science than it is in any of Steinbeck's writings outside of "I Am a Revolutionary."

In the *Log*, Steinbeck establishes a fundamental critique of American culture that he transfers onto Mexicans and Native Americans throughout much of his narrative; he refuses to articulate the ecological and preservationist purpose of the expedition; and he ultimately illustrates exactly how he understood American culture to control ecological radicalism through the threat of monstrosity. Before he ever reaches Mexican waters—in incidents that occur in Monterey as he tries to charter a boat and in San Diego as the expedition makes its final stop in a U.S. port—Steinbeck mounts an implicit argument that American culture is deeply opposed to ecology and capable of extreme violence. In Monterey, he has tremendous trouble chartering a vessel because all of the port's charter boat captains considered him and his shipmates "suspicious," "crazy," and "ridiculous" because any expedition that did not involve sardine fishing, much less an ecological exploration, was "nonsense" (7–8). Later, in San Diego, Steinbeck encounters a place that is stockpiled with military equipment, overrun with robotic soldiers, and managed by "military mind[s]" who think neither about the massive power of their weapons nor the people who will be destroyed by them (35).

Steinbeck writes that after the *Western Flyer* left San Diego, "the great world dropped away very quickly. We lost the fear and fierceness and contagion of war and economic uncertainty" (173). The narrative he offers, however, tells quite another story. The rest of the text is haunted by Steinbeck's experience in Monterey, by the images of war and violence that he took away from San Diego, and by the more general antipathy toward ecology that he sensed from mainstream U.S. culture.

Long before Steinbeck reaches Mexico, in fact, he begins projecting his anxieties about the United States onto Mexico. He fears that he will encounter a repressive military regime that will consider "the work we intended to do" as "suspicious" because "it would seem ridiculous to the military mind to travel fifteen hundred miles for the purpose of turning over rocks on the seashore and picking up small animals, very few of which were edible; and doing all this without shooting at anyone" (23). Steinbeck had already been called "ridiculous" in Monterey, and he had already experienced a "military mind" in San Diego that, upon his return, would assess the value of the "thousands of pickled animals" that his crew had collected over the course of six weeks and four thousand miles at "five dollars" (84).

As soon as Steinbeck enters a Mexican port, he stops projecting the U.S. military mind onto Mexico, but in his first port-of-call, Cape San Lucas, he turns an interaction between "Mexicans" and cormorants into a drama about the relationship between ecology, radical politics, and the regulatory practices of a hegemonic culture—clearly, issues that he brought with him from the United States. Steinbeck describes fishermen on the coast shooting cormorants that are dispersing baitfish that have been drawn conveniently close to the shore (for the fishermen) by a tuna cannery's discarded "entrails and cuttings" (48). In Steinbeck's dramatization of this situation, the birds are disrupting an established situation: they are "considered interlopers, radicals, subversive forces against the perfect and God-set balance on Cape San Lucas, and they are rightly slaughtered, as all radicals should be" (48). At the same time, the fishermen become more than what they are: they are men who do not understand ecological principles, who cannot see beyond their economic self-interests to the larger, interconnected whole of the situation, and who become cultural Brahmins preserving the order of their world by murdering the deviant. It is a scene that takes place in Mexico and involves Mexicans, but it deploys the same rhetoric that Steinbeck uses in his nonfiction to excoriate political "screwballs" and in his fiction to describe the precarious positions of his numerous outcasts that live on the fringes of society.

As much as Steinbeck feared encountering a militaristic regime in Mexico, he dreaded the task of explaining his expedition to an underclass of "Indians" that he knew would be primarily concerned with issues of subsistence. Before any biological collecting ever takes place, Steinbeck writes that "we had known that sooner or later we must develop an explanation for what we were doing which would be short and convincing. It couldn't be the truth because that wouldn't be convincing at all . . . [so] we developed our story and stuck to it thereafter. We were collecting curios, we said" (83–84). When the men finally begin their collecting, they do indeed hear the "embarrassing question" that they anticipated: " 'What do you search for?' " (92). Steinbeck considers a range of answers but eventually settles on the prepared lie:

> We search for something that will seem like truth to us; we search for understanding. We search for that principle which keys us deeply into the pattern of all life; we search for the relations of things, one to another, as this young man searches for a warm light in his wife's eyes and that one for the hot

> warmth of fighting. These little boys and young men on the tide flat do not even know that they search for such things too. We say to them, "we are looking for curios, for certain small animals." (92)

While he is genuinely sensitive to their situations, even these "Indians" gradually point Steinbeck back to problems in the United States. Instead of thinking about how he could explain himself to the people in front of him, Steinbeck quickly asks a question that returns him to problems in the United States: "How can you say to a people who are preoccupied with getting enough food and enough children that you have come to pick up useless little animals so that perhaps your world picture will be enlarged?" (84). This passage appears to speak directly to the Mexicans involved in the biological collecting, but two elements of this comment—its nebulous appeal to "a people" and its emphasis on food and subsistence—link it to comments about conditions in the United States that Steinbeck offers ten pages earlier when he writes that "[s]ome time ago a Congress of honest men refused an appropriation of several hundreds of millions of dollars to feed our people," meaning by "our people," of course, U.S. citizens (74). Subsistence, in Steinbeck's mind, is a problem that is not exclusive to Mexico. He knows that the United States struggles to feed its own people and obliquely suggests that the problem of presenting ecology and environmentalism to audiences in the United States is at least as problematic as presenting these concepts to audiences in Mexico.

Steinbeck never achieves any satisfactory answer to the purpose of the Gulf expedition and at the end of the *Log* ultimately abandons any attempt to explain its real value when he writes, in a tone of resignation, "Here was no service to science, no naming of unknown animals, but rather—we simply liked it. We liked it very much. The brown Indians and the gardens of the sea, and the beer and the work, they were all one thing and we were that one thing too" (224). Despite Steinbeck's inability to describe it, the voyage of the *Western Flyer* does seem to have a very distinct purpose, even if it is unspeakable. In the Log's introduction, Steinbeck writes that the intent of the voyage was to "collect and preserve" the animals "of the littoral"—a very succinct statement of intent—but he also reveals that simultaneous to their acts of preservation, "Fifty miles away the Japanese shrimpboats [were] dredging with overlapping scoops, bringing up tons of shrimp, rapidly destroying the species so that it may never come back, and with the species destroying the ecological balance of the whole region" (2, 3). The destructiveness of this shrimping fleet looms over the whole of the *Log*. It is important enough in Steinbeck's recollection of the expedition to appear in his introduction but then it disappears only to resurface two hundred pages later as a "large destructive machine . . . committing a true crime against nature and against the immediate welfare of Mexico and the eventual welfare of the whole human species" (206–207). The positioning of the destructive Japanese fishing fleet at the beginning of the work and near its end casts its net over the whole text and suggests that the purpose of Steinbeck's expedition, though he cannot say it, is to see and preserve the Gulf of California before it is thoroughly destroyed through this type of exploitation.

The voyage of the *Western Flyer* is a type of environmentalist intervention in the wrecking of the natural world that does not expose its participants to the charge of monstrosity because it refuses to explain what it is doing or why it is doing it. Steinbeck seems to have known that this type of environmentalist intervention would not fundamentally change the American culture that he knew to be the root of the problem, but he contemplated it at length—and remained committed to it—in a number of texts that he wrote between the 1940s and 1960s. In *Cannery Row* and *Sweet Thursday*, the two novels that convert Ed Ricketts into a character named Doc who owns a biological supply company in Monterey, Steinbeck tries to believe that science can solve the ecological crises of the twentieth century. Although he hardly discusses it at all in either of these novels, Cannery Row is a tremendous industrial machine that exploited and exhausted the California sardine population in the mid-1940s (Shillinglaw vii). Essentially under the eaves of Cannery Row, Doc plods among tidal pools searching for starfish and other marine animals that he can preserve and sell to Eastern universities.

Steinbeck does not articulate it as such, but Doc's preservative work is a hedge against the very process of environmental exploitation that the title of *Cannery Row* implies. When he kills his specimens, inserts dye into their veins, and ships them to students who will study them, Doc nominates species for induction into a transcendental scientific mind where they will have eternal life regardless of the mortal fate of the species. It is the same notion of preservation that was practiced in natural science museums beginning in the sixteenth century, the same notion of preservation that was fueling the development of the African Hall exhibit in the American Museum of Natural History in New York City in the first half of the twentieth century.[23]

Bottling specimens of animal life so they could be preserved for science offered Steinbeck some interesting possibilities, but he ultimately recognizes its deficiencies. In *Cannery Row*, this mode of preservation allows Steinbeck to imaginatively sever the barrier that divides the sphere of the human from the nonhuman. This binary dissolves in the storeroom of Doc's laboratory, where "little unborn humans, . . . whole and . . . sliced thin and mounted on slides" are situated among "rattlesnakes, and rats, and honey bees and gila monsters," and it disintegrates when Doc happens upon the body of a dead girl, suspended lifeless but immaculate in a tide pool, during a collecting mission (27).

When Doc encounters this body in the tide pool, the entire episode bears the marks of sublime experience. Doc breaks out in goose bumps, he begins shivering, his eyes fill with tears, and he feels that the image of the girl's face has been "burned" on his mind (105). It is not the moment of abject horror or disgust that it could have been, however. He hears music, he recognizes that the girl is "pretty," even "beautiful," and that she is an image of "comfort and rest" (105). For all of the shock involved, the most interesting aspect of this scene is the way that Steinbeck constructs the sublime. Here, the sublime does not signal the sudden presence of God, nor is it necessarily triggered by the presence of death—that the girl is dead is less important to the sublime effect of the scene than the fact that she is an image of humanity fully and beautifully incorporated into nature. She is entirely enclosed—as if in one of Doc's specimen bottles—within a crevice of rock and a bed of algae (which seems like kelp in Steinbeck's description), and the transcendent beauty and peace of her face is the result of her submerged state: "Just under water it was and the clear water made it very beautiful" (105).

Within the whole scope of his work, the collection of specimens for scientific preservation is the only hedge against environmental destruction that does not carry the threat of monstrosity (this fact alone may account for Steinbeck's sustained commitment to this form of preservation), and it is the only way Steinbeck can imagine a total integration of the human and the natural. In the end, it is an attenuated type of preservation—its goals depend upon an idealized scientific mind that might be able to grant a sense of immortality to a biological species, but only by remaining necessarily isolated from the problematic American culture Steinbeck blames for the environmental crises of the twentieth century. Even beyond its lack of cultural agency, this scientific mode of preservation cannot accomplish any of its goals—whether the preservation of species or the creation of a new human orientation toward the environment—outside of death.

Steinbeck remained committed to nonradical forms of environmentalist intervention until the very end of his career. Just two years before his death, he submitted an open letter to *Popular Science* asking the public to continue funding ocean research. He wrote the letter as the official historian of a deep ocean drilling program that lasted from 1961 to 1966, but his financial plea is based upon a very broad claim that oceanic exploration might be able to alleviate the problem of global overpopulation.[24] In this letter, which is entitled "Let's Go After the Neglected Treasures Beneath the Seas: A plea for equal effort on 'inner space' exploration," Steinbeck suggests that humanity should pursue "improving" fish species so that they will be more useful to humans, cultivating "the huge agriculture of the seas," and, in what is really his magic bullet, finding a way to make plankton, "this boundless bank of protein," "available for our bellies" (86).

The whole body of Steinbeck's work—even "Let's Go After the Neglected Treasures Beneath the Seas," when it speaks of modern, North American *homo sapiens* as a wasteful species that unnaturally "raids" the earth of its resources and kills more than it needs to consume—reveals that Steinbeck recognized multiple forms of environmental abuse, understood its human and ecological ramifications, and recognized the problem as a cultural predilection toward irresponsible and wasteful overconsumption fueled by twentieth-century corporate capitalism. Despite what his writings reveal, Steinbeck never says anything to suggest that waste should be reduced, that ecological damage should be stopped, or that patterns of consumption should be changed. As his *Popular Science* article illustrates, his primary inclination is to look for solutions to environmental problems in science rather than social activism.

If Steinbeck had ever pursued an environmentalist social agenda, he would have had to adopt a type of public voice that he associates with monstrosity in *To a God Unknown* and *Sweet Thursday*. In these novels Steinbeck clearly suggests that radicalism only becomes monstrosity when it finds public expression. Joseph Wayne, the protagonist of *To a God Unknown*, senses a spiritual connection to the earth, considers himself a part of the land, and ultimately comes to regard the health of the land as more important than his own. When the parish priest learns of all this, he articulates the relationship between voice, radicalism, and monstrosity that guides Steinbeck's politics: " 'Thank God this man has no message. Thank God he has no will to be remembered, to be believed in.' And, in sudden heresy, 'Else there might be a new Christ here in the West' " (177). Joseph Wayne would only become dangerous if his radicalism became a "message," which is also the case with "the Seer" in *Sweet Thursday*. This character refuses to participate in what he recognizes as the mainstream and materialistic culture of the United States and accordingly lives on the beach as a hermit. In a conversation with the seer, Doc comments that he is "surprised they don't lock you up" because it is "a crime to be happy without . . . a whole hell of a lot of stuff," and reaffirms the connection between voice and monstrosity that Steinbeck initially defined in *Sweet Thursday* when he tells the seer that "You may not be preaching it, but you're living treason" (61). For each of these figures, becoming a "new Christ" would bear the same old price. As it always is with Steinbeck, to live treasonously is one thing, but to articulate a radical position is to risk monstrosity.

Willa Cather and John Steinbeck are important, and they are important together, because they illustrate a number of facts that commonly go unacknowledged: environmental politics was a vital field during the early twentieth century, American authors were deeply engaged with this environmental politics, and there was no comfortable place for environmental politics in the literary field during this period. When Cather was writing about the Nebraska prairies, the aesthetic she prescribed to—the aesthetic that drew a boundary between political literature and "real" or "high" literature, the aesthetic that allowed her to claim a place in the respected American literary tradition—prevented her from lamenting environmental loss more directly than she did, and by the time Steinbeck's career reached its end environmental politics were doubly impossible within the literary field. The canon, which was well defined by the 1960s, held no place for it, and it was prohibited within the field of American culture.

Cather and Steinbeck show us the limits of the literary field, but they are also interesting because of what they do within the zone of impossibility. With overt environmentalist politics out of the question because of what it would mean to them as serious authors and citizens in a nation vehemently opposed to such politics, the environmentalist desires within their writings are funneled into second options. Cather's characters look to the abstract and astronomical, as was Emerson's wont, to fortify themselves against the possibility of environmental ruin, and they focus on metonyms of environmental endurance even when Cather herself seems to stand aloof from these characters, undermining their credibility, puncturing their triumphant narratives, and, it seems, doubting their faith in nature's indestructibility. As Steinbeck and his characters study the ecology of the western littoral, they too seem to place faith in the metonym. They preserve organisms as though their scientific preservation can serve as a hedge against forms of environmental destruction that are too large and too powerful to be stopped in a national culture that would attack and destroy any movement that tried to intervene against it. In every instance, the environmental politics in the work of Cather and Steinbeck is restrained, and both authors seem to already mourn for environmental losses that they anticipate but feel they cannot stop.

In the life of the nation, the resurgence of environmental activism initiated by Rachel Carson and *Silent Spring* would challenge this pervasive tone of environmental resignation, but not before Carson was assaulted from multiple directions (which is the very fate Steinbeck predicted for any figure who articulated a clear environmentalist position) and her book was tacitly shuffled into a quickly developing subfield of nature or environmental writing that would keep her out of the main line of "Literature," American or otherwise.[25] Throughout most of the twentieth century, alternative orientations toward the environment were only available to those like Carson who were willing to take the risks involved with public activism, and to those, such as Zora Neale Hurston and Jean Toomer, who wrote outside of the dominant U.S. literary traditions and cultures.

Chapter 5

Zora Neale Hurston, the Power of Harlem, and the Promise of Florida

Willa Cather and John Steinbeck were hardly the only authors to register environmental loss in the early twentieth century, but their canonically modulated methods of repressing environmental anxiety are largely representative. William Faulkner, for instance, was equally aware of widespread environmental destruction, and a range of scholars have recently shown that much of his work reflects a keen understanding of Mississippi's environmental history. While Cather and Steinbeck tended to grant the natural world intrinsic or ecological value, Faulkner found nature important as a place where boys could become men and where the threatened masculinities of grown men could be rejuvenated. When he and his fictional characters confronted nature's ultimate end, however, they depended on the same metonyms of environmental health we have tracked from Emerson to Cather and Steinbeck. As Ike McCaslin does in *Go Down, Moses*, Faulkner silences any potential environmental lamentation he could have offered and insists that the immortal essence of his privileged wilderness, Mississippi's "Big Bottom," will always remain virgin and indomitable even when reduced by sawmills and expanding cotton operations to a final, pubic, and metonymic "∇-shaped section of earth between hills and River" (*GDM* 327).[1]

As Faulkner watched the deterioration of Mississippi's natural world and began adopting ways to remain disconnected from the increasingly unavoidable problem, Zora Neale Hurston was becoming frustrated with the politics and patronage of Harlem and preparing to carve out a new liberatory, regenerative, and utopian blackspace in the Southern United States. Hurston had arrived in Harlem in 1925 and experienced a short period of incredible success—her short stories were published in Charles S. Johnson's *Opportunity* and won prizes in the magazine's literary contest, she founded and co-edited *Fire!!* with Langston Hughes and Wallace Thurman, and she fashioned herself, for a short while, into the central spectacle of the Harlem Renaissance.[2] As time passed, though, she found herself caught between a manipulative white community that supported her financially and a group of powerful African American leaders that conspired to control her. Hurston's ultimate response to this situation—which has been criticized since the early twentieth century as an escape into nostalgia and an abandonment of liberatory racial politics—was to create an alternate zone of black autonomy in the South, the very region that many African Americans had fled during the Great Migration.

For Hurston, the South—and Florida in particular—was a space that could accommodate a vibrant black community outside of Harlem's system of patronage and control. Although she had lived through some of the South's most frightening racial violence, Hurston still believed the place to be a haven for African Americans in general and African American artists in particular, and her writings work to reclaim the hostile space for the use of African Americans.

The white tradition of environmental thinking, which I have discussed throughout this book, is preoccupied with environmental purity, the perpetual availability of environmental resources, and fears of environmental destruction; it treats nature as a pure Other—as something that should be revered and protected but is still Other. But Hurston's approach is fundamentally different. Instead of focusing on the issues of purity, availability, and durability, she offers a vision of enmeshment within an immanently physical natural world that is imbued with racial and cultural significance.

Hurston, Harlem, and Power

When Hurston arrived in Harlem in 1925, she found "a place where being black was not a burden but an act of beauty, not a liability but a state of grace" that "fully restored" the sense of community and the sense of "*me*-ness that Zora had felt so profoundly as a child in Eatonville" (Boyd 94). For all the joy that Hurston found in Harlem, however, the place came with its own set of peculiar difficulties. It was a place with high rents and low salaries where success as an artist was not necessarily enough to avoid being entangled in an economy of patronage and power. For Hurston, success and patronage were inextricably bound together from the beginning of her experience in Harlem. When she won a host of awards in the *Opportunity*'s literary contest shortly after coming to New York (she won more awards than anyone including second place awards in fiction and drama and two honorable mention awards in the same categories), the awards ceremony she attended was both her coming-out party as an emerging force in Harlem literary community and her induction into the system of patronage that would fund her but humiliate her for most of the next seven years.[3]

Between 1925 and 1932, Hurston enjoyed the support of three patronesses: Annie Nathan Meyer, Fanny Hurst, and Charlotte Osgood Mason. Two of them, Meyer and Hurst, attended *Opportunity*'s awards banquet. Hurst had presented Hurston with the second place prize that she won for "Spunk" (Boyd 104–105). Meyer, the founder and longtime trustee of Barnard College, approached Hurston after the banquet and soon granted her enrollment at Barnard, which would ultimately offer Huston her first experience with the mixed blessings of the Harlem Renaissance patronage system. Although Meyer was successful in getting her into Barnard, she had to struggle to fund Hurston's education. The college would not grant Hurston a scholarship on the basis of the academic record she brought from Howard, and Meyer cast about soliciting money from those whom Virginia Gildersleeve, the dean of Barnard College, called " 'outside persons interested in the Negro race' " (Boyd 101).

Meyer's efforts were mostly successful, but they left Hurston in financial straits nonetheless. She could still not pay all of her fees, and she was burdened by the seemingly endless small expenses that attended the Barnard experience. In an October 12, 1925 letter to Meyer, for instance, Hurston concedes that her first semester at Barnard will have to be her last because she has had to spend "so much money for necessities—books, gym outfit, shoes, stockings, maps, tennis raquet [*sic*], . . . a bathing suit, gloves and if I am here in the Spring, I will need a golf outfit" (Kaplan 66). Five days later, in another letter to Meyer, Hurston writes, "Today I have 11 cents—all that is left of my savings, so you can see there is some justification for my doubts as to whether I can remain there [at Barnard]. I must somehow pay my room-rent and I must have food" (Kaplan 67).

Hurston remained nearly penniless until Meyer brought her situation to the attention of Fannie Hurst. Hurst was already becoming involved with Hurston when Meyer approached her about the money problem (well after the *Opportunity* banquet Hurst had procured Hurston's address from Carl Van Vetchen and invited her to her home), and she immediately interceded by making Hurston her personal secretary. Hurston lived with Fanny Hurst for a month, and her secretarial stint was short, but her relationship with the famous novelist endured. They shared a sense of style, they made public outings together, and Hurston's attachment to Hurst improved her standing at Barnard among both her classmates and the college's administration, which found a scholarship for her in 1926.

By all accounts, Annie Nathan Meyer and Fannie Hurst genuinely *liked* Hurston and they wanted to help her; and Hurston, for her part, liked them and appreciated their support. Even in the best circumstances, though, the relationships were uneven and sometimes—deliberately or not—humiliating. Of all the support Hurston gained, Meyer's came with the fewest strings attached. Having helped found Barnard in the late 1880s, she served on its board of trustees until her death in 1951 and constantly worked to recruit students to the college. When Meyer managed to have Hurston admitted, Hurston became the only black student enrolled at Barnard at the time, but recruiting students for the college was essentially what Meyer did. The language that Hurston uses in her letters to Meyer, however, reflects a sense of abjection—even if it is feigned abjection.[4] In the first letters she sends to Meyer, Hurston emphasizes her indebtedness when she writes, "I must not let you be disappointed in me," and she accentuates the stark racial and class differences between herself and Meyer by frequently referring to herself as "your little pickaninny" and "your most humble and obedient servant" (Kaplan 62–69).

Even though Hurston developed a closer bond to Hurst than Meyer, this relationship was also fraught with inequality. For all their common interests, the two authors never played on an even field. As much as Hurst promoted Hurston's writings, she clearly treated her differently than her other friends, and by announcing her as " 'Princess Zora' " in social situations she clearly used Hurston as a social novelty in ways that Hurston would certainly have understood (Patterson, 166). Beyond the uneven terms of their friendship, Hurston never achieved her patron's financial success or publishing advances despite the fact that they enjoyed similar levels of acclaim as writers.

By the time Hurston met her third major patron, Charlotte Osgood Mason, she had largely succeeded at Barnard. She had discovered anthropology and become comfortable in the company of Melville Herskovits, Ruth Benedict, and Gladys Reichard; she had forged a lasting bond with Franz Boas, and she had already conducted her first anthropological fieldwork in Florida—a six-month project that was funded, at Boas's urging, by the Association for the Study of Negro Life and History and the American Folklore Society (Boyd 142).[5] When Hurston finally did meet Mason in September 1927, the elderly white woman was already supporting Langston Hughes, Alain Locke, and numerous other Renaissance figures.

As with Meyer and Hurst, Hurston's relationship with Mason was mixed. Hurston felt—or at least reported feeling—that she was destined to meet Mason. She reported having had dreams of the moment from her childhood, and she professed feeling a psychic and even telepathic connection to the elderly white woman whom she called "Godmother."[6] Mason supported Hurston financially from 1927 to 1937; with no other avenues of support available to her and lacking the advanced degrees that would have allowed her to solicit support from major organizations, Hurston had few options but to accept Mason's offer under the terms that were extended to her.[7]

The deal that Hurston struck with Mason was, in the words of Cheryll Wall, "a Faustian compact" (*Women* 155). It required that Mason retain the rights to all of the anthropological materials Hurston collected in her field work, and it subjected Hurston to much more severe forms of humiliation than she experienced in her relationships with any of her other patrons. Tiffany Ruby Patterson writes, for instance, that " 'Godmother' liked to hold court from a throne-like chair while the godchildren occupied low stools at her feet. Part of this ritual called for lush cascades of flattery and self-deprecation from her Negroes" (171). Even when Hurston was not in New York to perform in Mason's court, she still worked under the long shadow of her patron. Hurston reports in *Dust Tracks on a Road* that Mason could read her mind even "at a distance" and that she would receive letters from Godmother out of the blue while she was working in "Alabama, Florida, or in the Bahama Islands" that chastised her "for what I was thinking" (128). Whether this psychic connection was "real" or not is secondary to the fact that before her ultimate break from her Hurston could not escape Mason's grip regardless of where she went or what she did. She depended upon her patron for all of her material needs, and while she was working in the field she had to itemize everything she bought, including—a detail that appears in every description of the Hurston-Mason relationship—"everything from dues to professional organizations to Kotex" (Wall *Women* 154).

With her financial patrons, Hurston was forced to negotiate the tenuous boundary between friendship and servitude—for the most part, she liked her patrons and she certainly needed them, but she rarely trusted them and knew that their relationships were often mutually exploitative. Her relationship with the period's race leaders, particularly with Alain Locke, was equally strained. Huston knew all of the black leaders of the early twentieth century, and she strained against the influence of them all. She knew W. E. B. Du Bois, for instance—she participated in his Krigwa Players, she helped establish the group's Little Negro Theatre, and she provided several of the plays that the Theatre performed in 1925—but she, Langston Hughes, and Wallace Thurman all rebelled against Du Bois's aesthetic system (and the power with which he promoted it) when they compiled the first and only edition of their deliberately scandalous journal, *Fire!!* (Boyd 117–18).[8]

Although she knew Du Bois and although she had an extended and sometimes fiery relationship with Walter White, Alain Locke was Hurston's most intimate link to the power brokers of the Harlem Renaissance.[9]

Without Locke, in fact, Hurston may have never gone to Harlem at all. She had attracted Locke's attention while she was a student at Howard University (she was a member of Stylus, the Howard literary club that Locke himself helped found in 1915), and in1924 he had told Charles S. Johnson to solicit a story from her for his magazine. She gave Johnson "Drenched in Light," he published it in *Opportunity*, and then he urged her to move to Harlem. When she made the move, she made it already having personal relationships with two of the most powerful men in the Renaissance. Hurston knew that Locke was a key catalyst to her success, she was comfortable with the role he had played, and she thanked him repeatedly for everything he had done for her.

At the same time, though, Locke was a burden. As early as 1929, Hurston was imagining him as a wheedling, scheming fraud. In a letter to Langston Hughes, she writes that "the trouble with Locke is that he is intellectually dishonest. He is too eager to be with the winner, if you get what I mean. He wants to autograph all success, but is afraid to risk an opinion first hand" (Kaplan, 144). Whatever Hurston thought of Locke, he was not a person she could dismiss. He was Harlem's gatekeeper, and he was Charlotte Osgood Mason's most trusted confidant. When Hurston's play *From Sun to Sun* turned into a financial disaster in 1932, Mason discussed Hurston with Locke. According to both Hemenway and Boyd, Mason confessed her misgivings about Hurston to Locke, and he added fuel to the fire. Mason "felt that Zora lacked leadership skills—and that other people . . . were actually exploiting her to get ideas for their own work" while Locke, joining in the spirit of the moment, "wondered aloud how Zora could afford the rent on her New York apartment and questioned why Godmother was continuing to give her a monthly allowance 'with nothing to show for it' " (Boyd 233).

Locke has been described as "Godmother's chief advisor on all things Negro," and he often acted as Mason's agent; in this role he had even kept an eye on the development of *From Sun to Sun* for Mason from the beginning—a fact that prompts Boyd to call him "a theatrical spy of sorts" (Boyd 228, 229). It is, therefore, wholly unsurprising that Locke was called upon to inform Hurston of Godmother's state of mind. He told her, according to Hemenway, "that she could no longer expect money from Godmother. He pointed out, like a professor to a student, that her apartment was far too expensive for her reduced income, and that she should be writing to black colleges about employment" (183). Both Hemenway and Boyd recognize that the end of the relationship between Hurston and Mason was partially determined by economics—the United States was mired in the Great Depression in 1932—but only Boyd admits that Locke's behavior amounted to an act of base "meddling" and self-preservation (234). He was working to "protect Godmother's [financial] interests (and his own); if Hurston went off the books, there was a greater chance that he would remain on them" (Boyd 233).

Despite the boldness of Locke's confrontation, Hurston essentially acquiesced to the news he delivered. She understood she was a financial burden to Mason and that she was being judged all along on her monetary success. In the years following that fateful meeting, Hurston remained in contact and on fairly congenial terms with Locke. In 1938, though, he issued such a biting review of *Their Eyes Were Watching God* that Hurston attempted to make public the fundamental criticism of Locke that she expressed to Langston Hughes in 1929. Those original sentiments run throughout a document that she sent in February 1938 to James Weldon Johnson as a personal letter and to *Opportunity* as "The Chick with One Hen" (which the magazine never printed):

> I get tired of the envious picking on me. And if you will admit the truth you know that Alain Leroy Locke is a malicious, spiteful litt[l]e snot that thinks he ought to be the leading Negro because of his degrees. Foiled in that, he spends his time trying to cut the ground from under everybody else. So far as the young writers are concerned, he runs a mental pawnshop. He lends out his patronage and takes in ideas which he soon passes off as his own. And God help you if you get on without letting him "represent" you! (Kaplan 413)

Creating a Floridian Blackspace

At the critical moment in 1932 when *From Sun to Sun* failed to turn a profit and Alain Locke told her that she was dead weight Godmother could not continue to bear, Hurston viewed Harlem itself—particularly its economies of patronage and power—as part of her problem. Harlem simply would not allow her to conduct her artistic and anthropological work. Her immediate response to this situation was to return to Florida. From 1932 on, Hurston made Florida her home (she traveled frequently to New York, other parts of the South, and the Caribbean Islands, but she was rooted in Florida), and she worked to re-envision the South as a viable space for the practice of African American life and art.

Coming to grips with who Hurston became and the writings she produced after this pivotal moment in 1932 has been difficult for Hurston's critics. They have frequently reacted negatively to her work, and much of their frustration seems rooted in how Hurston related to and represented the South. Shortly after the publication of *Their Eyes Were Watching God*, Alain Locke and Richard Wright issued reviews of the book that articulated what they felt to be basic flaws in Hurston's work, and these criticisms have never entirely gone away. Locke suggested that Hurston needed to "get over oversimplification" and "come to grips with motive fiction and social document fiction" while Wright, in a separate review, accused Hurston of minstrelsy and pandering to "a white audience whose chauvinistic tastes she knows how to satisfy" (18, 17). Although the language is somewhat different, these same concerns motivate Hazel Carby's much more recent suggestions that Hurston ignored the northward and urban movement of black Americans during the early twentieth century; that her "representation of African-American culture as primarily rural and oral" is a "particular [and flawed] response to the dramatic transformations within black culture;" and that each of these tendencies (to ignore both the spatial and cultural changes that African Americans were experiencing in the early twentieth century) amount to an overarching "discursive displacement of contemporary social crises in her writing" (121).

Hurston's explanations of her return to the South seem to support Carby's claims. When she first informed Charlotte Osgood Mason of her desire to return to the South in an April 1832 letter, Hurston laid out "several good reasons": "1. atmosphere to work. 2. Escape New York. 3. Health 4. Chance of self-support" (Kaplan 250). And, several years later, when she explained the same relocation to Thomas E. Jones (the president of Fisk University), she wrote that "I returned to my native village for quiet, atmosphere and economical existence in addition to my love of the place" (Kaplan 316). In each instance—in more or less overt ways—Hurston portrays her return to the South as an *escape* and, with references to "my native village," quietude, and a "love for a place," as a retreat into what may be viewed as a socially disengaged and nostalgic fantasyland.

Despite what these letters may suggest about a nostalgic outlook and an abandonment of politics, though, Hurston knew the situation she was re-entering in the South and she knew her return—and what she planned to do there—was a political intervention in its own right. When Hurston moved from Jacksonville, Florida, to Memphis, Tennessee, in 1915 (eventually to land in Baltimore, Maryland, in 1917), she was participating—albeit with different motivations than many—in the Great Migration that carried scores of African Americans northward in the early twentieth century and abandoning the South in the middle of the fifty-year period that witnessed the lynching of nearly 2,500 African Americans (Tolnay and Beck ix).[10]

Of the Southern states, Hurston's Florida had been an even more dangerous place for African Americans than any other state in the region—more dangerous, in fact, than the "Deep South" states of Mississippi, Georgia, Louisiana, Alabama, and South Carolina—from 1882 to 1930. The most recent definitive data show that during this period Florida experienced nearly eighty black victims of lynching per one hundred thousand African Americans, which is nearly thirty more victims per hundred thousand than the next state, Mississippi, which had approximately fifty-three (Tolnay and Beck 38).

When Hurston returned to the South in the late 1920s to carry out anthropological field research and in the 1930s to settle more or less permanently in Florida, she was returning to a region that was still witnessing prolific mob violence despite the fact that lynching (in the form of vigilante kidnapping, torture, and murder rather than the "legal lynchings" that were becoming more common) was on the decline throughout the South.[11] When she returned for her first anthropological expedition in 1927, two of the state's most notorious lynchings had taken place in regions of the state that she had known in her childhood and adolescence.

In 1920, while Hurston was earning her associate's degree from Howard University in Washington, D. C., a mob of whites, incensed by blacks who were attempting to vote, traveled three miles from Winter Park, Florida, to Ocoee (just thirteen miles from Eatonville) and killed seven people including the prosperous black landowner, July Perry. In the aftermath of the incident, which included continued white violence toward the all-black town, Ocoee was entirely abandoned.[12] Three years later, while Hurston was still at Howard, one of the nation's most dramatic lynchings occurred in Rosewood, Florida. In this instance, which has been described as "one incident in an era of extraordinary racial anxiety and conflict," at least eight African Americans were killed and the all-black community of Rosewood was burned to the ground by a mob acting on a white woman's unfounded accusation of rape (Colburn 176). Even in the 1930s—when the worst of the South's lynching was over and when Hurston was back in Florida—thirteen more people were lynched in the state, including Claude Neale and Joseph Shoemaker, whose lynchings attracted national attention.[13]

Although Eatonville was peaceful and relatively isolated during Hurston's early life, Florida was riddled with racial violence throughout her childhood and adolescence, it was violent while she was largely out of the state in the first half of the 1920s, and it was still violent when she returned to conduct research later in the decade and to essentially settle in the state in 1932. None of this was lost on Hurston. While on an anthropological expedition in Florida in March 1927, she wrote to

Lawrence Jordan that "crackers" were not bothering her and that she hoped "they don't begin [to] as I go farther down state" (Kaplan 94). On the same expedition she began carrying a gun. In Hemenway's opinion, she did this for the purpose of defending herself in the rough-and-tumble African American labor communities that she was trying to mine for folktales, but such a measure of self-defense would have been prudent in the context of the state's pervasive racial violence (Hemenway 111).[14] In 1938, while she was working for the Federal Writer's Project in Florida, Hurston wrote an essay entitled "The Ocoee Riot" that she planned to include in a collection of essays entitled "The Florida Negro." The project was never completed and "The Ocoee Riot" was never published in Hurston's lifetime, but the essay, a gritty journalistic description of the Ocoee incident that would have satisfied Locke's and Wright's demands for overtly political writing, stands as powerful evidence that Hurston was deeply affected by the state's tradition of racial violence.

For all of its violence, Florida was still the only state in the South to experience positive migration in the early twentieth century. While scores of African Americans were fleeing the South between 1900 and 1930, Florida's black population grew by nearly one hundred thousand with an increase of more than fifty-four thousand African Americans in the 1920s (Tolnay and Beck 214). Hurston, of course, was one of those fifty-four thousand, and she returned, in part, because she knew that a unique situation was brewing in Florida. In her introduction to *Mules and Men*, Hurston recalls telling Frans Boas that " 'Florida is a place that draws people—white people from all over the world, and Negroes from every Southern state surely and from some of the North and West' " (1). In Florida, she "knew that it was possible . . . to get a cross section of the Negro South in the one state;" the state was still a haven of blackness and Hurston's immersion in it amounted to a bold and defiant attempt to create a better environment for the practice of everyday black life and art than the one she found in Harlem (*Mules and Men* 1).

As early as 1929, Hurston had envisioned a community of black artists in Florida that would match Harlem's solidarity and celebration of black life without its strictures and humiliations. In May 1929, she wrote Langston Hughes telling him, "I have a chance to buy a beautiful tract of land slap on the Indian River, which as you probably know, passes for the most beautiful river in the world" (Kaplan, 145). She imagines a "dandy club house right on the water" and the entire parcel of land turned into "A Negro art colony. You, and Wallie [Wallace Thurman], and Aaron Douglas and Bruce [Nugent] and me and all our crowd . . . a little town of our own . . . we could have lots of fun and a lovely place to retire and write on occasion . . . a neat little colony of kindred souls"

(145–46). She tells Hughes that no one had ever sold land on the Indian River to an African American but that the city council had already held a meeting and not only granted Hurston the right buy but also the right to "sell to any of my friends so long as they belong to my social caste" (145).

Hurston's plan did not materialize, at least in part because she, Hughes, and her other friends were just as "dead broke" as she perceived the people in Florida to be, but she was quite serious about the possibility of developing a black art community in the state (Kaplan, 145). Beyond pushing the Indian River land issue to the point of city council meetings, she repeatedly discussed the possibility of developing a black art community in Florida with her friends over the better part of the next ten years.

Despite the fact that her plans never came to fruition, after she left Harlem in 1932 Florida became the place where Hurston would conduct all of her serious artistic work throughout the rest of her career; it was her psychic and (usually) her literal home, where she would go when she needed to "polish off" a book without distractions or economic strictures (Kaplan 404).[15] At the same time, though, Hurston never envisioned her return to Florida as a retreat from the black art community or even necessarily as an abandonment of racial politics. Even more than a personal artistic haven, Hurston always thought of Florida as a site that was perfect for the development of an artistic community like the one she tried to develop on the Indian River.

As soon as Hurston arrived in Florida in 1932, fresh off the heels of the pivotal talk with Alain Locke that apprised her of her standing with Charlotte Osgood Mason, she began trying to enact the vision of a black art community that had inspired the Indian River idea in 1929. This time, rather than trying to form what may best be called a personal refuge or commune, Hurston focused on founding a viable black theatre, which she attempted to accomplish in association with Rollins College and Bethune-Cookman College, and on founding schools of African American art.

In all of these endeavors, Hurston exuded optimism and felt she was fulfilling dreams she had shared for years with Mason and Locke. As she presented it to Edwin Osgood Grover, her attempt to found a theatre in the Eatonville area with the backing of Rollins College was an attempt to establish a "*real* Negro theatre," which she believed had still not developed in Harlem or anywhere else in the United States (Kaplan 259; emphasis added). It would be an opportunity, she wrote to Locke in 1933, to build "not just the [theatre's] building but the heart, the reason for the building to be;" and all of this meant that she would be "<u>doing</u> some of the things that we used to dream of" (Kaplan 281).

As ambitious as Hurston's plans for a new theater were, they are all the more interesting because they are founded on a desire to create a type of counter-Harlem in Florida. In a 1933 letter to Mason, which insists, just as her letter to Locke does, that she is doing what "you and I have dreamed of doing for so long," Hurston suggests that this particular project is more likely to succeed because she is no longer battling what she calls "the handicap of Harlem" (Kaplan 276). Thus unfettered, she believes that "if we can give real creative urge a push forward here, the world will see a New Negro and justify our efforts" (Kaplan 276).

Karla Kaplan points out that although the phrase " 'New Negro' was much in use among Harlem literati," Hurston used the phrase very rarely (276). In the context of the plans she is outlining in this letter to Mason, it is an intentional replication of the naming project that Alain Locke initiated with *The New Negro*—just as Locke's book called the Harlem Renaissance into being, Hurston co-opts his phrase to call into existence her own spatialized black renaissance in the heart of Florida. She believes that her theater at Rollins College will "surpass by far . . . what has been done by Paul Green et al [in African American drama] at the University of North Carolina"; she writes that in addition to its "special stress on music and drama" this particular place encourages "painting carving, sculpture—all forms of art" (Kaplan 276). Further developing her sense of central Florida as a new center of black art, she insists in a letter to Locke that "we can build here a theatre that will be talked of *around the world*," and she asks Locke to imagine what could happen if the type of community she wants were to ever develop: "if we had Bruce Nugent and one or two others. Lawd, Lawd!" (Kaplan 282).

Hurston had some success with drama at Rollins College and in and around Eatonville, but it ultimately proved grueling, unsustainable, and irregular work. Hurston made another concerted effort at establishing a genuine black theater in 1934 after being invited to Bethune-Cookman College in Daytona Beach. As she wrote to Carl Van Vetchen in January 1934, the president of the college, Mary McCleod Bethune had recruited Hurston "to establish a school of dramatic arts based on pure Negro expression at her school in Daytona Beach" (288). Although Hurston wrote in that letter that "she is after my own heart," her relationship with Bethune quickly soured and, as she explained to Thomas E. Jones when she was pursing a job at Fisk University, she shortly "decided to abandon the farce of Bethune-Cookman's Drama Department" (Kaplan 288, 318).[16]

Despite being consistently disappointed by the institutions that supported her, Hurston continued to imagine the development of a black art community outside of Harlem. In 1937, when the Guggenheim

Foundation's Henry Allen Moe asked Hurston to identify causes that his organization could support, she gave him the names of two black artists ("Iven Tate, painter and elevator boy at Orange General Hospital, Orlando, Florida," and Ollie Stewart, a Baltimore-based writer) and suggested that that the foundation fund "a school of music and dancing for all the Negroes" (Kaplan 405). Although she does not specify where such a place should be built, the school that she envisions is still faithful to her original vision of black art communes on the Indian River and at Rollins College: it would

> formalize and make respectable Negro musical methods . . . [its] professors would be the people who make the songs and dances. It could be something more dynamic than most people would realize at first glance. It could support itself by concerts and tuition fees. [written in margin:] Imagine, Duke Ellington, Fats Waller, Louis Armstrong as guest professors! Ethel Waters, Bill Robinson, etc." (405, "[written in margin]" is Kaplan's editorial note.)

To some degree frustrated with her adventures in drama, Hurston turned to writing fiction. And in returning to this medium (she had not written fiction in years) Hurston launched a spatial project that was related to all of her plans for a black art community in Florida. Rather than calling other black artists to a new place that she found more liberating than Harlem, Hurston began taking possession of the place in her writing. Her narratives, with all of the cultural agency that Michel De Certeau grants to stories, reclaim what was a racially violent and volatile space for the practice of a vibrant African American everyday life that is deeply rooted in the space it occupies.

As Melvin Dixon explains in *Ride Out the Wilderness: Geography and Identity in Afro-American Literature,* "nature" and "wilderness" have held central places in African American expression from the very beginning. In the earliest slave stories and songs, nature and wilderness were both spiritual and physical locations of tribulation and salvation—spaces, whether real or imaginary, outside of slavery that often had to be traversed at great peril in the process of gaining freedom. By the early twentieth century, though, African American thinkers such as Booker T. Washington, W. E. B. Du Bois, and Jean Toomer were all rethinking "nature" in different ways. Hurston departed from them all.

Washington, Du Bois, and Toomer, though they encounter nature in significantly different ways, all take for granted that Southern space—including both its "natural" and "built" environments—is essentially white space, or space under the absolute control of an oppressive white regime. Beginning with *Jonah's Gourd Vine*, however, Hurston begins to challenge this assumption of white control. In this novel, she follows a cast of central characters as they travel from Southern Alabama to the Florida panhandle and then into Eatonville and Central Florida. *Their Eyes Were Watching God* pursues a program of spatial politics that is much more deliberate: she maps out a particular space for the practice of a vibrant black life and depicts an absolute physical, psychic, and spiritual immersion into the place that constitutes an entirely different method of discussing the environment than the white, Emersonian tradition that had come to dominate the field by the early twentieth century.

Before Hurston began her writing career, several ideas of "nature" and even a particularly Southern "nature," were circulating among African American intellectuals. Not surprisingly, perhaps, Booker T. Washington was perfectly capable of slipping into a highly Emersonian rhetoric of nature as a recuperative retreat. In the middle of *Up From Slavery* (1901), for instance, he writes that next to time spent reading and telling stories with his family in his home, his favorite leisure activity is taking his family "into the woods, where we can live for a while near the heart of nature, where no one can disturb or vex us, surrounded by pure air, the trees, the shrubbery, the flowers, and the sweet fragrance that springs from a hundred plants, enjoying the chirp of the crickets and the songs of the birds" (173). He calls this "solid rest" and adds—in wholly Emersonian terms—that when he has the time, a half-hour in his garden at Tuskegee provides a solace very much like the solace he finds in the woods:

> When I can leave my office in time so that I can spend thirty or forty minutes in spading the ground, in planting seeds, in digging about the plants, I feel that I am coming into contact with something that is giving me strength for the many duties and hard places that await me out in the big world. I pity the man or woman who has never learned to enjoy nature and to get strength and inspiration out of it. (173)

Writing specifically about Dougherty County, Georgia, but describing a situation typical of the entire Black Belt, W. E. B. Du Bois abruptly states in *The Souls of Black Folk* (1903) that "there is no leisure class" of African Americans in the American South (94). It is a phrase that sets Washington's description of trips to the woods and dabbling in his garden in stark relief. The folk that Du Bois concerns himself with obviously do not spend their spare time "in spading the ground, in planting seeds, in digging about the plants" for fun. Their contact with the earth is a grinding struggle against soil and a tenant farming system that exhausts tenants and soil alike. In Du Bois's words they experience "toil, like all farm toil," that "is monotonous" with the added impediment that "there are little machinery and few tools to relieve its burdensome drudgery" while the land that they work "groans with its birth-pains, and brings forth scarcely a hundred pounds of cotton to the acre, where fifty years ago it yielded eight times as much" (94, 85). For African Americans in the South, Du Bois argues, nature—writ "soil"—was an oppressive field that could not even be freely navigated because "the free movement of agricultural laborers is hindered by the migration-agent laws" and the more general "peonage system of white patronage [that] exists over large areas" (98, 99).[17]

Published later but still two years before Hurston arrived in Harlem, Jean Toomer's *Cane* (1923) cast Southern space in different terms than those of either Washington or Du Bois. Toomer described it as a traversable space—or at least a space that could be penetrated and exited—and found the place's lush organic environment evocative of African origins. In the novel that made Toomer the darling of the Harlem Renaissance, the South is a region of sawmills and cotton mills that he gives to his readers in the glow of hazy afternoons and after the work-whistles have blown. In "the sawdust glow" and "the velvet pine-smoke air" of dusk, it is a place where men still "go singing" with "race memories of king and caravan, / High-priests, an ostrich, and a juju-man" (12–13). It is a place where, as in "Carma," a dusty road under the right conditions (when "the sun is hammered into a band of gold," when "pine-needles, like mazda, are brilliantly aglow," when "no rain has come to take the rustle from the falling sweet-gum leaves,") can cause a woman to return imaginatively to her ethnic origins—to "a goat path in Africa" (10).

Over the course of three books, *Modernism and the Harlem Renaissance*, *Afro-American Poetics*, and *Workings of the Spirit*, Houston Baker recognizes that Jean Toomer and Zora Neale Hurston were both engaged in spatial projects, but his work consistently suggests that *Cane* was both the catalyst for and, ironically, the a priori fulfillment of the Harlem Renaissance while subtly suggesting that Alain Locke and Richard Wright were correct when they condemned Hurston's work for what they recognized as its abandonment of racial politics. *Cane*, Baker argues, fills the critical gap between Du Bois's *The Souls of Black Folk* and Locke's *The New Negro*. It fulfills Du Bois's vision for a "cultural sound" of blackness while performing the pathbreaking "deformation of mastery" (Baker's term that in this case suggests the blending of an Anglo-American modernist aesthetic project with "the fluid and multiform mask of African ancestry") that makes the Harlem Renaissance possible (*Modernism* 56, 57). For

Baker, the novel is the "*breakthrough*" into unmediated racial awareness that would carry Locke, *The New Negro*, and the Harlem Renaissance in general toward a new sense of black nationalism in the nineteen-twenties (*Afro-American* 101). *Cane*, Baker feels, is an aesthetically masterful text that carries the universal appeal of a "journey of an artistic soul toward creative fulfillment" while also being "unsparing in its criticism of the inimical aspects of black American heritage and resonant in its praise of the spiritual beauty to be discovered there" (17-18).

As he reanimates *Cane*'s centrality in the Harlem Renaissance, Baker reasserts the aesthetic system that was deployed against Hurston, particularly when she published *Their Eyes Were Watching God*. *Cane*, for Baker as it was for Locke and Wright, is what black literature was supposed to be in the first decades of the twentieth century—aesthetically modernist, immanently black, and undeniably cognizant of interracial conflict. The novel is surely valuable for what it says about the worst aspects of "black American heritage," but it would not be recognized as *the* comprehensive expression of the moment if it had not included the the lynchings of Tom Burwell and Mame Lamkins. These two incidents, portrayed as vividly in Toomer's text as lynchings often are in late-twentieth-century histories of lynching, connect the novel to what Baker calls the "disfranchisement, lynchings, crop failures, and general miseries" that defined the South during the period—the very things that Locke, Wright, and, most recently, Hazel Carby, have all accused Hurston of abandoning (*Modernism* 76).[18]

Thus, for Baker, Toomer is a figure who found his artistic breakthrough by navigating the space—"the valleys and lowlands"—"of Blackness" itself while simultaneously working to construct a second "ordered" space or "framework that will contain the black American's complex existence, offer supportive values, and act as a guide for the perspective soul's journey from amorphous experience to a finished work of art" (101, 25). In a third book, *The Workings of the Spirit*, Baker acknowledges—just as I am doing here—that Zora Neale Hurston, too, engaged in spatial work. And while his intent is clearly to redeem Hurston through a discussion of her spatial project, Baker still reasserts her secondary status just as he reestablishes Toomer's centrality in both *Modernism and The Harlem Renaissance* and *Afro-American Poetics*. In the argument that stretches over these three works, Toomer is foundational to the early twentieth century's emerging sense of an African American race spirit, to Harlem's artistic movement, and to the new sense of a black nation that emerged out of Harlem.

Hurston, on the other hand, is credited with creating an image space for black female creativity—certainly an important project, but a provincial one in comparison to that of Toomer, which Baker defines as national and racial in scope. According to Baker in *Workings of the Spirit*,

"Hurston's *Mules and Men* (1935) is a *locus classicus* for black women's creativity" because it accomplishes the "*instantiation* (a word that marks time and suggests place) of the conjure woman as peculiar, imagistic, Afro-American space" (282). Hurston's work, Baker recognizes, involves "seek[ing] a habitation beyond alienation and ancient disharmonies in a land where Africans have been scarred and battered, shackled in long rows on toilsome levees," and he argues that all of this "cultural work" (oddly, it is this term that Baker uses to describe Hurston's art) is performed within the space of *conjure*—"the *Sprit House* of black women's creativity" (304).

Hurston's spatial project, while it does define the conjure woman as a space of healing, was much more ambitious than has been suggested by Baker or any other scholar of Hurston and the Harlem Renaissance. To return to the language Baker uses to describe Toomer's mission, Hurston was interested in instantiating a *livable* rather than a particularly "ordered" space for the practice of everyday black life; she was deeply critical of any kind of "framework" designed to "contain the black American's complex existence"; she was dubious of attempts to "guide" souls toward any particular point; and she was even conflicted over what the term *art* should mean. Hurston had experienced framing, containing, and guiding in Harlem—in her relationships with Fannie Hurst, Annie Nathan Meyer, Charlotte Osgood Mason, Alain Locke, and even Franz Boas—and her return to Florida was in large part a reaction against it. The spatial project she carries out in novels such as *Jonah's Gourd Vine* and *Their Eyes Were Watching God* turns in the opposite direction. It strives to recapture a space that whites had tried (with considerable success) to strip away from African Americans through several decades of violence; it strives to overcome the difficulties of centralized power and enforced homogeneity that attended the idea of black nationality just as they attend nationality in general; and it strives to portray a spatial enmeshment that runs entirely counter to the dominant traditions of white environmental experience.

In the myriad vignettes of African American life that Toomer presents in *Cane*, nothing—or no one—moves. Dusty roads, like the one that Fern spends her days watching, often extend into the distance but no one travels them. When people do move, they go no place in particular, like Carma, whom we find guiding a mule down the Dixie Pike; or they circulate on the fringes of the cane fields and firelight as Bob Stone is circulating when he hears of his lover's infidelity; or they move from a sight of initial violence, as the people of "Blood-Burning Moon" do, to a site more appropriate for a lynching. For those like Kabnis, who enter the South from the outside, the road into the South seems to be the only road, and it only goes back from whence it came.

Jonah's Gourd Vine and *Their Eyes Were Watching God*, by contrast, include characters who traverse broad expanses of space in what are essentially—in the scope of the novels, in the context of Hurston's strained relationship with the cultural center of Harlem, and in the context of the spatial project that she sketches in her letters—acts of mapping and spatial reclamation that work to call Florida into being as a space where a vibrant African American life can be practiced. This all begins in *Jonah's Gourd Vine* as Hurston moves her protagonist, John Pearson, from Macon County, in the east central portion of Alabama, into the Florida panhandle and eventually into the heart of Central Florida where he moves freely between Wildwood, Sanford, Maitland, Eatonville, Oviedo, Orlando, and finally Plant City. *Their Eyes Were Watching God* amplifies the spatial project Hurston had begun in *Jonah's Gourd Vine* by offering a female rather than a male protagonist, by extending the project of spatial control to involve a struggle for the control of the (black) (female) self, and by converting the type of spatial navigation that John Pearson performs into a navigation of blackness (not just a navigation of space) so that the space under reclamation in the novel becomes *blackspace*—a space where blackness can be freely lived and embraced.

Their Eyes Were Watching God, like *Jonah's Gourd Vine*, first moves Southeast, beginning somewhere near Lake City in North Florida, and then moving to Green Cove Springs after Janie meets Joe Starks before then diving Southward into the heart of Central Florida: to Maitland and Eatonville and surrounding towns such as Apopka, Ocala, Altamonte Springs, and Sanford. Eventually, after Janie meets Tea Cake, the novel moves North to Jacksonville and then South once again to the Everglades and Lake Okeechobee, Clewiston, Belle Glade, Palm Beach, Fort Meyers, and Fort Lauderdale.

As Hurston moves Janie across North Florida and then down into the bowels of the state, she uses her character's movements to take possession of the space where African Americans had historically been virtually powerless. From the antebellum period to the early twentieth century, the South was a tight zone of white power within which African Americans had virtually no spatial agency. They could not possess it; they could not traverse it without the threat of violence. Often, they lacked even the ability to control their own bodily space. With Janie, though, Hurston works to transform the historically oppressive space into one where African Americans can live their own vibrant and unfettered lives.[19]

It is in the process of seizing Floridian space that Hurston imagines a new relationship with nature that breaks entirely from the white literary tradition—with all of its tendencies toward abstraction, disengagement, and destruction—that extends from Emerson into the twentieth century. Hurston reveals in the opening sections of *Their Eyes Were Watching God* that the space Janie inhabits has been coded as a site of violence and domination since at least the mid-nineteenth century—the period of her grandmother's youth. During the Civil War, Janie's grandmother sought refuge from her master's wife in a swamp; Janie's mother, Leafy, was raped by her schoolteacher (presumably a white man) in the woods. Whether a refuge or a site of violence, Hurston's nature was part of a very violent milieu. Its rhythms involved desperate flights, rapes, and (although they never actually take place in *Jonah's Gourd Vine* or *Their Eyes*) lynchings like the ones that Toomer describes in *Cane*.

Within the new territory that Hurston marks out for Janie, though, the natural world is coded differently. No longer a site of violence, it is the objective correlative for Janie's personal development, an omnipresent reminder of African spirituality, and a link to the most authentic forms of blackness. Janie lives her life trying to achieve the level of ecstasy that she sees in the world around her from the moment that she comes of age "under a blossoming pear tree" watching "a dust-bearing bee sink into the sanctum of a bloom; the thousand sister-calyxes arch to meet the love embrace and the ecstatic shiver of the tree from root to tiniest branch creaming in every blossom and frothing with delight" (10–11). Each of Janie's relationships—with Logan Killicks, Joe Starks, and Vergible Woods—is initiated as an attempt to fulfill this vision of ideal marriage. In the end, only Vergible Woods, Tea Cake, "could be a bee to a blossom—a pear tree blossom in the spring"; beyond fulfilling this vision of her youth, though, Tea Cake transports Janie to the Everglades, a place Hurston portrays as the highly organic epicenter of all she believed Florida to be (106).

In the Everglades, Janie lives alongside "blacks from all over the South and the Caribbean as well" in what is an unmistakably "Pan-African community," and she finds herself both awash in and central to a welter of explicitly black expression (Wall 189). In "de muck," Hurston writes, "jooks clanged and clamored"; there were "pianos living three lifetimes in one"; there was "dancing fighting, singing, crying, laughing, winning and losing love every hour" (128, 131). Eventually, Janie and Tea Cake's home "was full of people every night. That is, all around the doorstep was full. Some were there to hear Tea Cake pick the box; some came to talk and tell stories, but most of them came to get into whatever game was going on or might go on" (133).

The scene Hurston describes is Harlem without patronage and race leadership and with some measure of financial self-sufficiency.[20] It is black expression unbound, run amuck, and surprisingly democratic. Here, for the first time, Janie could present herself however she wanted—even in the "blue denim overalls and heavy shoes" that she would return to Eatonville wearing—and she "could listen and laugh and even talk some herself if she wanted to. She got so she could tell big stories herself from listening to the rest" (134).

As she moves Janie and Tea Cake into the black community that they find in the Everglades, Hurston fashions their descent into "the muck" as an immersion in an organic blackness. Here in the muck, nature is big, fertile, and black. It is unruly like the place's distinctively black culture, but even more so—it is always at least potentially out of control, it is always essentially uncontrollable, and it is powerful enough to overthrow the systems of exploitation that work to control it. The muck is defined by its "big beans, big cane, big weeds, big everything," and all of its bigness is credited to "dirt so rich and *black* that a half mile of it would have fertilized a Kansas wheatfield" (129; emphasis added). This dirt is physical in a way that surpasses anything in Emerson's oeuvre. It adds its own blackness to the black bodies that work in it so that always, as they "work all day for money, fight all night for love," there is "the rich black earth clinging to bodies and biting the skin like ants" (131).

Janie and Tea Cake are ultimately driven from the Everglades—and Tea Cake eventually dies—when a hurricane hits the Everglades and Lake Okeechobee breaches the dykes and levees that contain it. As tragic as they are, though, the hurricane and the flood are the fulfillment of everything that Janie and Tea Cake had loved about the Everglades. These two catastrophic events bring everything that had always been there in the muck—the power, the unruliness, the recklessness, the elemental force—to its fullest expression.[21] For all the human suffering that ensues, Hurston describes the hurricane and the subsequent flood as the triumph of this nature, which she identifies as an immanently black nature throughout the novel, over white bondage. With the hurricane coming, Okeechobee becomes a restless "monster" that "began to roll and complain" behind "the seawalls" that were used "to chain the senseless monster in his bed" (158). At the height of the hurricane, Hurston writes of the lake that "the monstropolous beast had left its bed. He seized hold of his dikes and ran forward until he met the quarters; uprooted them like grass and rushed on after his supposed-to-be conquerors, rolling the dikes, rolling the houses, rolling the people in the houses along with other timbers. The sea was walking the earth with a heavy heel" (161–62).

After the hurricane, Hurston has largely accomplished her task of redefining the South and Florida as places fit for the performance of African American life and art. When the hurricane ends, Tea Cake is forced to participate—at gunpoint—in the collection and burial of the bodies of storm victims (with the whites receiving proper burials and the blacks receiving mass graves) in Palm Beach; Tea Cake and Janie eventually escape back to the Everglades where Janie ultimately has to kill Tea Cake while he is in a state of rabid insanity; Janie is acquitted of her crime by an all-white judge and jury while she is condemned for her actions in the court of black public opinion; and Janie returns to Eatonville alone.

Although the novel confesses the enduring presence of white power in the Palm Beach episode, and although it offers a harsh critique of Janie's black community in the courtroom scene, the first two-thirds of *Their Eyes Were Watching God* conjure into being just what Hurston had wanted since she announced her plan to buy land on the Indian River in 1929: a space where black life could be lived—and where art could be created—outside of the humiliating patronage systems of Harlem. Hurston was never able to secure the type of permanent institutional support that would allow her to actually create a spatially specific artistic renaissance in the South, but her stories, it must not be forgotten, work to accomplish the same purpose. As Michel de Certeau reminds us stories do have the power to shape our spatial experience, and stories Hurston tells remake the South, and Florida in particular, into an organic and immanently physical space within which a rich and vibrant African American life can be practiced without fear, humiliation, or apology.

Afterword

Ernest Hemingway and American Literature's Legacy of Environmental Disengagement

This project has allowed me to realize two things about the relationship the United States shares with the natural world. The first is that it took (or has taken, depending upon how one views the current status of environmental politics) far too long for a coherent, sustained, and effective environmental movement to develop in the United States. As this book demonstrates, it has been possible to protest the nation's environmental unsustainability since the early nineteenth century, but the transformation of sporadic protest into a unified environmental movement has been hampered by a number of factors. Sometimes the environmental message was unheard or abandoned because the bearers of the message were out of fashion (as was the case with Cooper and Longfellow); sometimes the audience only heard the portions of the message that were convenient to it (as was the case when Emerson's environmental philosophy was narrowed to the parts that suited the purposes of an expansionist and imperialist nation); sometimes real progress toward environmental goals was arrested due to leadership changes and catastrophic human tragedies (such as the end of the Theodore Roosevelt presidency and the world wars that rendered environmental politics less important); sometimes the audience was so afraid of difference that it preemptively silenced the environmental message (as was the case with Cather and Steinbeck).

In the end, James Fenimore Cooper's reservations about the American political system seem to have borne themselves out, at least in the realm of environmental politics. Until at least the late twentieth century (again, if we even want to grant this), national leaders failed to execute a coherent, consistent, and effective environmental policy, and the democratic mass rejected environmental reforms as threats to its privileged concepts of progress, free markets, and individualism.

The second, and more haunting, realization is that the United States has gone—and still goes—to staggering lengths to ignore environmental realities that have been profoundly hard to deny since the early decades of the twentieth century when it became apparent, to anyone who wished to consider it, that North America was not the illimitable, indestructible space that it seemed to be throughout most of the nineteenth century. Cather, Steinbeck, and Hurston worked against the grain of entrenched environmental and spatial politics, but the overwhelming trend of American environmental politics throughout the twentieth century was to maintain faith in nature's limitedness and indomitability against all evidence to the contrary.

Throughout *Environmental Evasion*, I have pointed out that the relationship between American literature and American culture is never the one we want it to be. I have argued that American literature's environmental heroes—Emerson and Thoreau—are not as saintly as we wish they were; I have suggested that "nature's nation" has never been as innocent as the label implies; and I have focused on author after author who approached the natural world in ways that departed from what I have consistently presented as an undesirable norm. I want to conclude this book, however, with a move in the opposite direction. I want to suggest that in Ernest Hemingway we can see American literature and culture pursuing the same goals but in an unfortunate manner. Hemingway's writings consistently deny environmental crisis *even while testifying to its global reality* and providing a stunning demonstration of the evasive environmental politics that prevailed in American literature and culture throughout much of the twentieth century.

Ernest Hemingway was raised to believe in Theodore Roosevelt's program of vigorous outdoor activity and to appreciate nature in the respective spiritual and scientific modes of John Burroughs and Louis Agassiz. His writings—from the beginning to the end of his career—contain such an aptitude for naturalistic observation that critics still agree with Alfred Kazin's judgment that "no nature writer in all American literature save Thoreau has had Hemingway's sensitiveness to color, to climate, to the knowledge of physical energy under heat or cold, that knowledge of the body thinking and moving through a landscape" (334).[1]

Despite his commitment to observation and his penchant for naturalistic description, Hemingway practiced a politics of environmental evasion that is remarkable because of the lengths it goes in *In Our Time* (1925) and *Green Hills of Africa* (1935) to preserve an idea of a perpetually virgin and perpetually available natural world.[2] Even acknowledging the global patterns of environmental destruction that threaten the natural spaces he loves, Hemingway fixes his gaze on a metonym of environmental openness that he casts into perpetuity within the complex form of *In Our Time*, and he suggests in *Green Hills of Africa* that "good country" or "virgin land" will always be available somewhere in the world for those who are willing to pursue a Thoreauvean plan of environmental imperialism.

The Circular Trajectory of Environmental Openness in *In Our Time*

For Hemingway and his characters, nature *needs* to survive for the same reasons that Emerson, Thoreau, and Faulkner all needed it to endure: it is a place where masculinity can be earned, practiced, and reasserted; where those who have been emasculated by the cramp and confinement (and war) of urban (or modern) life can be regenerated; where origins can be experienced; where white fantasies of conquest and dominance can be relived. The natural world serves all of these functions in the stories of *In Our Time*. In "Indian Camp," Nick Adams walks down logging roads and into a camp of Native American lumber workers to undergo an initiation into gendered violence that simultaneously reasserts his father's medical skill and capacity for brutality on the body of a Native American woman.[3] In "The End of Something" Nick breaks up with his first girlfriend while surrounded by second-growth forest and the ruins of an abandoned sawmill, in "Three-Day Blow" he experiments with a form of adult masculinity by getting drunk and reentering the "second-growth forest" with a gun. In "Cross Country Snow," Nick uses the natural world as a retreat from domesticity and a pregnant girlfriend. Finally, in "Big Two-Hearted River," Nick retreats into an isolated and approximately virginal riverbank to recover, presumably, from the trauma of World War I.

As we have long recognized, Hemingway's descriptions of nature throughout *In Our Time* display a naturalist's observational aptitude and scientific perspective.[4] Despite the fact that he can *describe* nature, though, Hemingway consistently refuses to engage environmental loss in the psychological and ethical terms that drove Cather to her dark critique of Jim Burden's conflicted form of nature loving and Steinbeck to all of his (and his characters') attenuated means of environmental preservation. In fact, although he was particularly equipped to see, record, and understand the consequences of the types of environmental destruction he and his works witness, Hemingway actively avoids any admission of environmental fragility, destructibility, or limitability. He accomplishes this in *In Our Time* primarily by constricting his (and Nick's) narrative gaze in "Big Two-Hearted River" and by then casting this story's contrived sense of perpetual environmental openness into both a historical loop that is contained within the stories of *In Our Time* and an unknowable future, both of which are implied by *In Our Time*'s terminal vignette, "L'Envoi."

In her 1926 review of *In Our Time*, Ruth Suckow calls "Big

Two-Hearted River" one of the book's best stories. And she attributes its greatness to the fact that it "is an embodiment in prose" of a very real event of the period—young men going " 'back to nature' " in an effort to slough off the typical "disillusion of youth after the war" (26). The short story itself says nothing explicitly about the war, but as Kenneth S. Lynn recognizes in "The Troubled Fisherman," this has not prevented a powerful body of scholarship from keeping Suckow's interpretation alive. In his 1932 "Ernest Hemingway: Bourdon Gauge of Morale," for instance, Edmund Wilson asserts without any equivocation that "Big Two-Hearted River" expresses a post–World War I malaise and that Hemingway "was the archetypal representative of a war-scarred 'lost generation' " (Lynn 151). Twelve years later, in his introduction to Viking's 1944 *Portable Hemingway*, Malcolm Cowley refreshed the old interpretation by again implying "that Hemingway's fisherman, like Hemingway himself, was a war veteran who was trying to block out fear-ridden recollections of being wounded" by returning to the bosom of nature (Lynn 152). The only significant change in the critical reception of this particular short story since the foundational interpretations of Suckow, Wilson, and Cowley has been a mild deemphasis of World War I. Even within this slight interpretive shift, though, the story remains "a return to origins," a return "to the eternal verities" of a very simplistic and idealized "nature" that offers "harmony and regeneration" (Strychacz 82).

What interests me most with "Big Two-Hearted River," though, are the lengths to which Hemingway and Nick Adams have to go in order to construct an approximately virgin space out of a larger area that bears all of the markings of human destruction and to imagine that this virgin nature will always remain in its current unpenetrated state—particularly considering everything that *In Our Time* itself says about the modern world's particular knack for destroying natural spaces. "Big Two-Hearted River," after all, begins with Nick stepping off of a train into a ravaged landscape. Where the town of Seney had once stood, there was "no town, nothing but the rails and the burned-over country" (133). Nick dismisses the grim fate of the town by thinking that it "was burned, the country was burned over and changed, but it did not matter. It could not all be burned" (134–35). He then walks until he passes out of the burned zone, into a pine forest, and eventually into the area immediately surrounding the part of the river that he wants to fish.

Nick's ultimate destination is a place on the river that bears no physical reminders that in the twentieth century nature is finite, fragile, and threatened. Once there, in the bosom of what is, for all appearances, a "virgin nature," Nick works to "choke" his mind whenever it starts to "work," which includes an effort to suppress his memory of the "years before when he had fished crowded streams, with fly fishermen ahead of him and behind him" where "again and again" he had come upon "dead trout, furry with white fungus, drifted against a rock, or floating belly up in some pool" (142, 149).

Isolated in this patch of river, totally unconcerned with what lies on the fringes of the space he has cordoned off for himself or what his memory may foretell for the river he is enjoying at the moment, Nick moves steadily toward a dark and inscrutable swamp that contains all that he and Hemingway want the natural world to be: a dark, threateningly virginic, and dangerous space that is penetrable to anyone with the requisite skill and desire but suspended in a state of defiant openness. In the final gesture of the story, which closes "Big Two-Hearted River" and the entire sequence of conventional short stories that span *In Our Time*, Nick reflects that "there were plenty of days coming when he could fish the swamp" (156).

By all conventional standards, this is a fairly unproblematic end for both "Big Two-Hearted River" and *In Our Time*'s sequence of major stories, but it is neither such a simple ending nor the end of the book. The end of "Big Two-Hearted River" formally encloses and thereby preserves the state of ecological openness and availability that brought Nick Adams to the river in the first place. Hemingway leaves the iconic swamp suspended in an unpenetrated state of availability and sends its availability forward into an ahistorical future that by the end of the story is clearly being imagined without any thought to the scene around Seney, Nick's memory of ruined rivers, or the patterns of environmental destruction that slip into the earlier stories of *In Our Time*.

The preservation of ecological openness that Hemingway accomplishes with the end of "Big Two-Hearted River" is amplified by the vignette that immediately follows it, "L'Envoi," which is *In Our Time*'s final story of any sort. Filling less than one page like all of the vignettes but bearing a title like only "On the Quai at Smyrna," the terminal story is written in the voice of a Western journalist and describes a deposed Greek king working in his garden as he awaits the judgment of a victorious "revolutionary committee" (157). The vignette ends with the narrator commenting that "Like all Greeks" the king "wanted to go to America" (157). Predictably, "L'Envoi" has been interpreted as a closing gesture that recommends American democracy as the solution to the revolutions that appear throughout *In Our Time*, but, even when politics are excluded from the hermeneutic frame, the story has been generally understood as a relatively conventional act of closure.[5]

Any claim of closure, however, ignores the openness and motion that are implied by the story's title. *Envoi* is one form of the French verb, *envoyer*, "to send," which is "derived from the Latin *inviare*, to send on the way," and that as a noun *envoi* means the *act of sending*, the *thing being sent*, and, oddly, the "the concluding stanza of a ballad that typically serves as a dedication" (Bass xx–xxi).[6]

By its very title, then, "L'Envoi" evokes several key questions: If *In Our Time* is to be sent off, where is Hemingway sending it, and what, precisely, does it contain? To answer the first question first, "L'Envoi" forces *In Our Time* to arch backward upon itself *and* leap forward into an indefinite future, and the message that *In Our Time* transmits is largely a record of violence, revolution, and interpersonal turmoil within which only nature—enclosed and suspended in the state of ecological openness that Hemingway creates in "Big Two-Hearted River"—endures unchanged, unthreatened, and defended from even the idea of obliteration. Thematically, the story that "L'Envoi" tells, with its revolution and Greek king, returns to "On the Quai at Smyrna"—the book's first story, which is also set in Greece during a climactic historical moment—and suggests that *In Our Time*'s thematic concerns constitute a closed cycle without an end. For all of its recursive themes and narratives, however, the final vignette is still an *envoi* and it still jettisons all of *In Our Time*'s narratives of revolution, violence, and virgin nature—as cyclical as they are within the text itself—into the rest of the twentieth century, if not beyond.

Bad Faith in *Green Hills of Africa*

When Hemingway engages the condition of the natural world in his 1935 *Green Hills of Africa*, it is as if he has found the message he cast into the future at the end of *In Our Time* and set about reconfiguring his earlier act of environmental evasion. *In Our Time* betrays an awareness of environmental destruction, looks away from it, and creates an image of perpetually available and pristine natural space that it encloses within its generic structure and sends into the future. *Green Hills of Africa*, on the other hand, acknowledges that environmental degradation is a global phenomenon, looks it plainly in the face, and bluntly disregards it. And while *In Our Time* offers complex aesthetic hedges against the threat of environmental annihilation, *Green Hills of Africa* recommends an environmental imperialism that fulfills, in the worst possible ways, Thoreau's command to encounter wilderness at any cost.

Thoreau writes in *Walden* that "we *need* the tonic of wilderness;" he argues that "we *require* that all things be mysterious and unexplorable, that land and sea be infinitely wild, unsurveyed and unfathomed by us because unfathomable," that "we *must* be refreshed by the sight of inexhaustible vigor, vast and titanic features," and that "[w]e *need* to witness our own limits transgressed" by the natural world (298; emphasis added). As I have already explained, Thoreau suggests that we satisfy this need for nature by turning to "the unexplored forests and meadows" that surround "our village," by exploring the wilderness of the self, and—if nothing else works—by searching for authentic wilderness experience in the four corners of the Earth (298). His call is to be "the Mungo Park, the Lewis and Clark and Frobisher" of the "streams and oceans," the "higher latitudes," and the "whole new continents" *of the self*, and to "go round the world" searching for wilderness only "till you can do better"—until, that is, you can "Explore thyself" (301–302).

The necessity of nature and the necessity of contact with wilderness are just as palpable in Hemingway's work, but, rather than pursuing the type of inquest that Thoreau describes, Hemingway literalizes Thoreau's colonialist metaphors and proceeds as if Thoreau's secondary solution—a global search for wilderness—is a legitimate, justifiable, and sustainable response to American, or Western, environmental destruction. *Green Hills of Africa* is a somber requiem for Africa.[7] It appreciates the continent's beauty, but it records—even shows Hemingway participating in—its destruction. It often speaks of Africa as a rutted, shot-out, and used-up country that the West has driven to the brink of death, but it justifies the course of Western empire and acquiesces to its environmental costs. In the space of two crucial paragraphs, Hemingway admits that he is aware of environmental destruction, that he understands environmental destruction as a symptom of Western imperialism, and that he has no fundamental problem with any of it. He writes that

> a continent ages quickly once *we* come. The natives live in harmony with it. But the foreigner destroys, cuts down the trees, drains the water, so that the water supply is altered and in a short time the soil, once the sod is turned over, is cropped out and, next, it starts to blow away as it has blown away in every old country and as I had seen it start to blow in Canada. (284; emphasis added)

Hemingway clearly states—and without any sense of irony—that "A country was made to be as *we* found it," that "*we* are . . . intruders," and that "*we*" are those who ruin these same countries. In the same breath, though, he argues that this "we" (meaning Americans, presumably) has the right to go "somewhere else as we had always had the *right* to go somewhere else and as we had always gone" (284–85; emphasis added). In his tight interweaving of imperialism and environmental destruction, Hemingway refuses to admit the environmental implications of his own text—that by the mid-twentieth century the perpetual existence of "virgin" lands (or "last good countries") anywhere is supremely tenuous. In the face of all he has written, he simply insists that the same type of "good places" that had "always" been available to "our people" would continue to exist into perpetuity for those willing to seek them out (285).

As I have shown throughout *Environmental Evasion*, authors from Jeremy Belknap and James Fenimore Cooper to Willa Cather and John Steinbeck all recognized, at various moments, that Western expansion could cause massive ecological change and that "a country was made to be as we found it." In her description of Lake Okeechobee straining to break its bonds, Hurston had even suggested several years before Hemingway wrote *Green Hills* that "the earth gets tired of being exploited." At the same time, all of these authors resisted wanton environmental destruction in significant ways. Cather and Steinbeck refused to pursue courses of radical environmental politics, but they still called attention to the absurdities and contradictions of early-twentieth-century American land ethics. Cooper ultimately consigned both Native Americans and the North American environment to destruction, but the narratives he tells *are at least* conflicted over the issues. Jeremy Belknap and Timothy Dwight both delighted in seeing forests fall—they gave instructions on how to properly clear forested land whenever they could—but even they excoriated the type of wastefulness that Hemingway describes, and they were at least pursuing goals that they believed to be just rather than capitulating, as Hemingway is, to processes that they found regrettable.

Beyond their unparalleled acquiescence to environmental exploitation, these two particular paragraphs are remarkable because they demonstrate the profoundly untenable nature of Hemingway's response to environmental destruction. He concedes environmental destruction, asserts a "right" to seize "good country" wherever in the world it may exist, and acts as if it will always exist. He insists, that is, on the type of environmental openness that he formulates in *In Our Time*, and he preserves his faith in it by adopting an Emersonian gaze that takes the portion of the Gulf Stream that flows by Havana as a metonym of environmental health and perpetuity. The Gulf Stream comes to Hemingway in a reverie that he experiences in the process of penetrating "a new country," and despite the fact that *Green Hills of Africa* spends three hundred pages suggesting that no pocket of wilderness is safe from the appearance of Europeans or Americans in Jeeps bearing rifles, the Gulf Stream reassures Hemingway of nature's timelessness, perpetuity, and immutability. "This Gulf Stream," he writes, "has moved, as it moves, since before man . . . since before Columbus," and it "will flow, as it has flowed, after the Indians, after the Spaniards, after the British, after the Americans and after all the Cubans and all the systems of governments . . . are all gone" (150).

The Gulf Stream is for Hemingway what horizons and night skies are for Jim Burden and Alexandra Bergson: a metonym for nature's illimitability, perpetuity, and immunity to human destruction that is always available to neutralize any sense of anxiety over environmental destruction taking place "on the ground." It directs Hemingway's gaze away from the African scene, the "new country" that he is penetrating, and removes the threat of environmental destruction to another global space and an image of environmental inexorability that neutralizes the threat of any ultimate environmental destruction.

Ann Putnam argues in "Memory, Grief, and the Terrain of Desire" that *Green Hills of Africa* is "divided against itself" so that "actions that honor and respect the natural world compete with actions that would destroy it" (99). I would suggest, though, that to whatever degree *Green Hills of Africa* is "divided," it is also in complete control of its own dividedness. It understands the paradoxical environmental ethics that it practices, and it *manages* the palpable absurdity of its tacit but nonetheless constant claim (which runs entirely counter to everything he writes about Africa) that there will always "be another [virgin] country where a man could live and hunt if he had time to live and hunt" (282).

Hemingway recognizes the scope and scale of twentieth-century environmental loss as well as any author in the first half of the twentieth century. Rather than name the void—which, again, is the possibility of environmental exhaustion just as it was for William Cooper in 1810—and subsequently initiate a truth event that could lead to new subjectivities and actual political intervention, Hemingway remains strictly faithful to a simulacral virgin nature and the things—both intellectual and practical—that he must do to maintain its viability. In his formal enclosure and linguistic continuance of environmental openness in *In Our Time* and in his strategic turn toward the Gulf Stream in *Green Hills of Africa*, Hemingway maintains the ahistorical, illimitable, and indestructible simulacrum of nature that has prevailed in American culture and in the American canon against the overwhelming evidence of nature's impending demise and the literary voices that have acknowledged it.

Because of the lucidity with which it testifies to environmental destruction and the frankness with which it denies the seriousness of this same environmental destruction, Hemingway's environmental politics border on the absurd and leaves me wondering how much Hemingway could have really believed in his own reaction to environmental destruction. My intention is not to vilify Hemingway himself (this has been done enough) but to suggest that he offers—as absurd as it is—the purest expression of the evasive environmental politics that endured in American literature and culture until the late twentieth century when literary traditions began to matter less, when "literature" itself became problematic, and when the urgency of environmental crisis finally forced American literature and culture to stop evading environmental politics.

In taking this contradictory environmental politics to its fullest extremes Hemingway seems to anticipate an end for the evasive environmental politics of American literature and culture that is in line with the apocalyptic strand of his modernist era. His tense contradictions seem to ask how long the (hollow) center can hold; they seem to wait in anticipation, as the final stanza of *The Waste Land* waits for rain, for the moment when these contradictions will crack and burst like the towers in Eliot's unreal city.

Notes

Introduction

1. This is obviously a highly condensed description of the work that has been done on the history of environmentalism over the past fifty years, and it smoothes out some of the differences of opinion that have dominated the field. Some of the earliest historians of the movement, such as Samuel P. Hays and Roderick Nash, recognized that late-twentieth-century environmentalism had historical precedents, but they emphasized its difference from the earlier conservationist and preservationist movements that are usually associated with Gifford Pinchot and John Muir, respectively. Others, like Carolyn Merchant in *The Death of Nature*, Max Oelschlaeger in *The Idea of Wilderness*, and Lynn White Jr. in "The Historical Roots of Our Ecologic Crisis," have almost entirely tossed aside the periodizing impulse and crafted narratives that locate the origins of environmental crisis in "Judeo-Christian," or "Abrahamic," land ethics, suggest that these land ethics have become a fundamental symptom of modernity, and trace moments of environmentalist resistance throughout a telescopic historical narrative that extends to the late twentieth century. Still others, such as William Cronon, Jack Davis, Stephen Fox, Robert Gottlieb, Carolyn Merchant (in many works beyond *The Death of Nature*), and Donald Worster have balanced the sharp periodic boundaries and telescopic narratives by accepting some periodizations but focusing on the continuities between periods rather than the differences.

To trace these arguments, see Samuel P. Hays's *Beauty, Health, and Permanence: Environmental Politics in the United States, 1955–1985* (with Barbara D. Hays); *Conservation and the Gospel of Efficiency: The Progressive Conservation Movement, 1890–1920, Explorations in Environmental History*; "From Conservation to Environment: Environmental Politics in the United States since World War II"; and *A History of Environmental Politics Since 1945*; Roderick Nash's *American Environmentalism: Readings in Conservation History*; *The Rights of Nature: A History of Environmental Ethics*; and *Wilderness and the American Mind*; Carolyn Merchant's *The Death of Nature: Women, Ecology, and the Scientific Revolution*; Max Oelschlaeger's *The Idea of Wilderness: From Prehistory to the Age of Ecology*; Lynn White Jr.'s "The Historical Roots of Our Ecologic Crisis"; William Cronon's *Changes in the Land: Indians, Colonists, and the Ecology of New England*; Jack Davis's "Conservation Is Now a Dead Word: Marjory Stoneman Douglas and the Transformation of American Environmentalism"; Stephen

Fox's *The American Conservation Movement: John Muir and His Legacy*; Robert Gottlieb's *Forcing the Spring: The Transformation of the American Environmental Movement*; Carolyn Merchant's *Columbia Guide to American Environmental History*, *Ecological Revolutions: Nature, Gender, and Science in New England*; and "Women of the Progressive Conservation Movement"; and Donald Worster's *American Environmentalism: The Formative Period: 1860–1915*.

For more recent histories that demonstrate the continuing attractiveness of Hays's and Nash's original periodizations of environmentalism, see Kirkpatrick Sale's *The Green Revolution: The American Environmental Movement, 1962–1992* and Phillip Shabecoff's *Earth Rising: American Environmentalism in the 21st Century* and *A Fierce Green Fire: The American Environmental Movement*.

2. Here I am relying heavily on the groundbreaking work of William Cronon's *Changes in the Land* and Carolyn Merchant's *Ecological Revolutions*. For fuller discussions of early resource exhaustion and early conservation measures, please see *Changes in the Land*, particularly pages 82–172, and *Ecological Revolutions*, particularly pages 65–68 and 185–260.

3. The early Massachusetts game laws were particularly ineffective, but they still demonstrate a concern over dwindling deer stocks. It is worth noting that these laws quickly became entrenched in Massachusetts. The state completely suspended hunting for white-tailed deer for three years beginning in 1718 and installed "early game wardens in the 1740s" (Cronon 101). The British government was interested in preserving trees that could be used for masts and the production of pitch and wrote these protections into the 1691 Charter of Massachusetts Bay (Cronon 110). Although I do not have the space to fully discuss it here, the conservation of fish and fish habitats was another major concern in early New England. As soon as mills and mill dams began to appear on rivers and streams in the region, the spawning of fish such as alewives and salmon suffered greatly. This situation led to numerous "Fish Acts" throughout the eighteenth century, which were usually designed to balance the rights of private enterprise, the natural rights of citizens to fish in common waters, and ecological necessities. Peter Kalm discusses the depletion of fish stocks due to mills and mill dams in his *Travels in North America*. For a full discussion of this, see Merchant's *Ecological Revolutions*.

4. While I don't want to sidetrack this introduction again, I think Badiou's language on this issue is valuable. In *Saint Paul*, he describes the conflict between truth events and instituted knowledges like this: "[T]he contemporary world is . . . doubly hostile to truth procedures. This hostility betrays itself through nominal occlusions: where the name of a truth procedure should obtain, another, which represses it, holds sway. The name 'culture' comes to obliterate that of 'art.' The word 'technology' obliterates the word 'science.' The word 'management' obliterates the word 'politics.' The word 'sexuality' obliterates love" (12). As I believe the rest of my argument clearly suggests, in American culture words such as "progress" and "wealth" and perhaps even "natural resources" or "resource management" threaten (or have threatened) to obliterate terms, such as "environmentalism," that are freighted with a mandate for fundamental change. With environmentalism as with the general situation Badiou is describing, nominal occlusion does indeed play a critical role.

I also want to note that the process I am describing here—the process by which a critique of ideologies comes to be perceived as an attack upon the state—is almost exactly the same as the process that theorists such as Jürgen Habermas and Slavoj Žižek recognize as fundamental to the late twentieth century's "new social movements." In his *Theory of Socially Communicative Action*, Habermas argues that late-twentieth-century feminism, environmentalism, and antiwar movements are wholly new types of conflict that threaten the very foundation of the late-twentieth-century welfare state because they cannot be neutralized by the "money and power" "compensations" that the welfare state has traditionally used to ameliorate class conflict. Beyond merely being unresponsive to the welfare state's means of maintaining social control, Habermas suggests, these new political phenomena pose an active threat to late capitalist societies because they critique the economic growth that the welfare state requires to maintain its welfare systems (392–93).

In *Looking Awry*, Slavoj Žižek adds that the subversive nature of these social movements is compounded by the fact that they also demand a rethinking of democracy. While democracy turns people into an agglomeration of abstract, Cartesian subjects, Žižek argues, the "new social movements" are "striving after . . . a fundamental transformation of the entire mode of action and belief, a change in the 'life paradigm' affecting our most intimate attitudes" (164). They offer such changes as "a new attitude toward nature, which would no longer be that of domination but rather that of a dialogic interplay" and a "pluralistic, 'soft,' 'feminine' rationality" rather than the West's traditional "aggressive 'masculine' reason" (164). In the end, Žižek argues, "new social movements" present "a project of radical change in the 'life paradigm' " that "necessarily undermines the very foundations of formal democracy" until "formal democracy and the 'new social movements' " reach an "antagonism" that is "irreducible" (164).

Rather than classifying environmentalism as a new phenomenon, I would suggest that environmental politics, the modern nation-state, and modern democracy have always shared the type of antagonistic relationship that Habermas and Slavoj Žižek identify. For a more extensive discussion of environmentalism and new social movements, please see Philip W. Sutton's *Explaining Environmentalism: In Search for a New Social Movement*.

5. George Perkins Marsh's *Man and Nature* is particularly instructive example of how isolated moments of environmentalist awakening were isolated, independent events rather than points in a continuous progression. In the Foreword to the most recent printing of Marsh's text, William Cronon offers this assessment of the book's importance to the history of American environmental politics:

> It is no exaggeration to say that *Man and Nature* launched the modern conservation movement. . . . [I]t helped provide the impetus for creating the national forests of the United States and played a role in the formation of the vast Adirondack preserve in upstate New York as well. Although today we are more likely to remember Theodore Roosevelt, Gifford Pinchot, and John Muir as the earliest leaders of American conservation, Marsh laid the foundation on which they and

> others constructed the nation's first political movement dedicated to protecting natural resources. (x)

Marsh owes this status to his keen rhetorical skill, his polemic assertions that "man" is an unrelentingly destructive environmental force, his recognition that European colonialism produced environmental ruin, and his desire to mitigate environmental damage. He argues that "[m]an has forgotten that the earth was given to him for usufruct alone, not for consumption"; he argues that "man pursues his victims with recklessness destructiveness" and "unsparingly persecutes, even to extirpation, thousands of organic forms which he cannot consume"; he recognizes that European colonialism has caused "great, and, it is to be feared, sometimes irreparable, injury" to the "virgin earth" that it has worked to subjugate; and he comments on all of this in "the general interests of humanity" so that the "decay" of the natural world may be "arrested" (36, 37, 46).

When Marsh published *Man and Nature* in 1864, the North American environment was being exploited at alarming rates in the names of progress and national expansion with little thought being devoted to the physical condition of the natural world. When Marsh reminds his readers that "man had changed millions of square miles, in the fairest and most fertile regions of the Old World, into the barrenest deserts" and then suggests that this same process is repeating itself in the New World, where "the earth is fast becoming an unfit home for its noblest inhabitants," he reveals the same unspeakable void—the possibility of environmental exhaustion—that had been named much earlier by Kalm and Chastellux and Belknap and Cooper, but his work is clearly not connected to any of those earlier utterances.

In Badiouian terms, *Man and Nature* is certainly an intervention that names the void of the environmental situation of the United States, and because of the book's historical proximity to the national parks movement it is tempting to view this book as Cronon does, as a truth event that incites the whole chain of events that make up the early twentieth century's progressive conservation movement which is identified with preservation, conservation, and urban health initiatives. In the same year that Marsh published *Man and Nature*, Congress granted Yosemite to the State of California as a public park; eight years later, in 1872, Congress would create Yellowstone National Park and embark on the grandest era of national park creation in the history of the United States.

The parks and preserves may in fact be a *consequence* of *Man and Nature*, but in a Badiouian sense (he comments in *Ethics* that "not every novelty is an event"), mere consequences do not necessary amount to acts of fidelity to the original event; consequences do not mean that a truth event or movement is underway. In the case of *Man and Nature* and the progressive conservation movement, the opposite may be true. While *Man and Nature* and the progressive conservation movement stand almost shoulder to shoulder historically, Marsh sees his task as one of education and of sociocultural change. To the extent that his task is one of helping "arrest" the "decay" of the natural world, it can be successful, in Marsh's own words, "only by the diffusion of knowledge on the subject among the classes that, in earlier days, subdued and tilled ground in which they had no vested rights, but who, in our time, own their woods, pastures, and their ploughlands . . . and have, therefore, a strong interest in the protection of their domain against deterioration" (46). It should involve, moreover, "some abatement in the restless love of change which characterizes us, and makes us almost nomads rather than a sedentary people" (280). Considering this, one must ask whether the creation of a national park is faithful to Marsh's intervention or if it constitutes one way to allay environmental anxiety without pursuing the real avenues of truth—education and social change—that could theoretically mitigate further environmental damage everywhere rather than in isolated parks and preserves.

6. Donald Pease offers a helpful summary of the field of American Studies in "New Americanists: Revisionist Interventions into the Canon." Here, Pease offers this list of the field's "master-texts": F. O. Matthiessen's *American Renaissance* (1941); Henry Nash Smith's *Virgin Land* (1950); R. W. B. Lewis's *The American Adam* (1955); Richard Chase's *The American Novel and Its Tradition* (1957); Harry Levin's *The Power of Blackness: Hawthorne, Poe, Melville* (1958); Leslie Fiedler's *Love and Death in the American Novel* (1960); Marius Bewley's *The Eccentric Design* (1963); Leo Marx's *The Machine in the Garden* (1965); Richard Poirier's *A World Elsewhere* (1966); Quentin Anderson's *The Imperial Self* (1971); Sacvan Bercovitch's *American Jeremiad* (1973) (12). As Pease's article develops, he offers this description of how the new criticism (the criticism that becomes known as "New Americanist") has begun to supplant the "cold war" texts: "Smith's *Virgin Land* gives way to Annette Kolodny's *Lay of the Land* and Slotkin's *Fatal Environment*; R. W. B. Lewis's *American Adam* becomes Myra Jehlen's *American Incarnation*, Carolyn Porter's *Seeing and Being*, or Henry Louis Gates's *Figures in Black*; Chase's *American Novel and its Tradition* ends up Russel Resing's *Unusable Past*; Roy Harvey Pearce's *Continuity of American Poetry* translates to Paul Bové's *Deconstructive Poetics*, while Bercovitch's *American Jeremiad* finishes as Frank Lentricchia's *Criticism and Social Change*" (32).

7. Here I am broadly summarizing portions of the spatial theories that Henri Lefebvre articulates in *The Production of Space* and the discussion of spatial practice that Michel de Certeau offers in *The Practice of Everyday Life*. I will return to these theories in subsequent chapters of *Environmental Evasion*.

Chapter 1. Ralph Waldo Emerson, Henry David Thoreau, and the Formation of American Literature's Core Environmental Values

1. The fame that Emerson generated during his own lifetime drastically outpaced his book sales until well into the 1850s. He achieved his remarkable status by essentially exporting himself to Europe, where he gained a significant amount of popularity while aligning himself with Thomas Carlyle; importing himself back into the United States as a home-grown author who was something of a rage in England; and lecturing—first to New England lyceums and then to Young Men's Associations as far West as Cincinnati. For a full account of Emerson's rise to prominence see Mary Kupiec Cayton's "The Making of an American Prophet:

Emerson, His Audiences, and the Rise of the Culture Industry in Nineteenth-Century America" and Richard F. Teichgraeber's *Sublime Thoughts/Penny Wisdom: Situating Emerson and Thoreau in the American Market.* While they generally focus upon his critical reception rather than his relationship with his audience, Sarah Ann Wider's *The Critical Reception of Emerson: Unsettling all Things* and Charles E. Mitchell's *Individualism and Its Discontents: Appropriations of Emerson, 1880–1950* contribute to this subject as well.

2. Terms such as "virgin nature" and "mother nature" are so prevalent in both casual and academic discourse that they can seem banal if not completely meaningless. Louise Westling, though, offers a concise history of the gendering of nature in *The Green Breast of the New World: Landscape, Gender, and American Fiction* that reinforces just how long North American nature has been understood as a virginal or maternal force rather than an antagonistic demonic power. Westling identifies two divergent "views of the feminine in European culture" that she defines as "that of the pure virginal or maternal source of life and comfort, and that of the demonic witch," but she argues—for the very reason that I have left it out of my list of gendered appellations—that beyond the Puritan era American culture is worried very little by notions of howling wilderness or figurations of nature as "demonic witch" (36). She argues later that the any sort of demonic female wilderness would have been rather remote to Emerson in New England where by the early nineteenth century, "deforestation . . . was almost complete, and the . . . Indians were equally devastated, reduced to small bands of ragged paupers by European disease, colonial appropriation of land and natural resources, and ecological transformation that made traditional subsistence impossible" (45). Merchant engages this same issue of nature's gender in *Ecological Revolutions* when she explains that in the 1830s "speeches made to farmers at local societies for promoting agriculture routinely drew on female earth rhetoric" (203).

3. Numerous scholars have already noted that Emerson had a problem with the female. He conflated femininity with nature, devalued them both, and demonstrated all of this by deconstructing the legacy of his one-time confidant, Margaret Fuller, who had offered counterinterpretations of nature, femininity, and female nature before her early death in 1850. For fully developed discussions of this issue, see Stephanie Smith's *Conceived by Liberty: Maternal Figures and Nineteenth-Century American Literature*; Louise Westling's *The Green Breast of the New World: Landscape, Gender, and American Fiction*; Dorothy Berkson's " 'Born and Bred in Different Nations': Margaret Fuller and Ralph Waldo Emerson"; and Lindsey Traub's "Woman Thinking: Margaret Fuller, Ralph Waldo Emerson, and the American Scholar."

Emerson's obsession with natural science is an equally well understood phenomenon among scholars. Emerson regarded science as a messianic force capable of wedding the visible to the invisible, and it made such a strong impression on him when he visited the Paris Muséum d'Histoire Naturelle in 1833 that he proclaimed he would become a naturalist. From 1833 on, Emerson wrote as a scientist, and he equated his own organization of thought and language with the organizing and classifying work of natural scientists.

As a historical phenomenon, though, natural science is not as neutral, innocent, or apolitical as it seems at first glance. Natural science codifies a dominant masculinist orientation toward the natural world, and it is politically inseparable from imperialist enterprise. It offered Emerson the hyper-masculinist and imperialist philosophical system that would ultimately manifest itself in *Nature* as he defines the natural world away from femininity and destructibility and toward an illimitable, permanent, and perpetually available field that serves the ideological ends of empire.

The natural science Emerson encountered at the Muséum d'Histoire Naturelle was, in the words of Lee Rust Brown, "one of the Old World's most complex and capable means of coming to adequate terms with the outlandishness of the New," which Europe was uncovering, of course, through exploration and colonization (97). And the methodology of natural science consisted of "selecting, eviscerating, and hollowing" out objects belonging to "visible nature" (the form of nature always gendered female) into abstract (and therefore masculine and more valuable) "intellectual horizons" (97).

At the Paris Muséum, the place that had such a life-shaking impact on Emerson, natural science had achieved a "severe aesthetic fulfilled in . . . sequences of glass-doored armoires lining the . . . galleries and . . . in the subordinated, pagelike surfaces of the formal gardens" where "all nature . . . yielded itself to the conceptual graphics of outline, series, and hierarchy" (Brown 65). It was a place where feminine nature, including raw materials and exotic specimens procured from the New World through the actions of empire, was splayed out, pinned down, stuffed, mapped, and classified; a place where the staunchly antifeminine Enlightenment science of those such as Francis Bacon found its most perfect embodiment.

Emerson admired the Paris Muséum because it wedded the physical and the abstract, but it was also a site of the "aggressive-defensive activity" of empire: along with the physical and the abstract it fused the gender politics of the Enlightenment with European imperialism while helping create the image of the naturalist that Emerson ultimately became for American literature and culture—the "bourgeois subject simultaneously innocent and imperial, asserting a harmless hegemonic vision that instills no apparatus of domination" (Pratt 34).

For the most recent descriptions of Emerson's relationship with natural science, see Laura Dassow Walls's *Emerson's Life in Science: The Culture of Truth* and Lee Rust Brown's *The Emerson Museum: Practical Romanticism and the Pursuit of the Whole*. For earlier interpretations of Emerson's engagement with science, see Leon Chai's *The Romantic Foundations of the American Renaissance*; H. H. Clark's "Emerson and Science"; Elizabeth A. Dant's "Composing the World: Emerson and the Cabinet of Natural History"; Harold Fromm's "Overcoming the Oversoul: Emerson's Evolutionary Existentialism"; B. L. Packer's *Emerson's Fall: A New Interpretation of the Major Essays*; David Robinson's "Emerson's Natural Theology and the Paris Naturalists: Towards a Theory of Animated Nature"; and Carl F. Strauch's "Emerson's Sacred Science."

For more fully developed critiques of natural science and science in general, see Carolyn Merchant's *The Death of Nature*; Donna Haraway's *Mod-*

est_Witness@Second_Millennium. FemaleMan©_Meets_Oncomouse™; Max Oelschlaeger's *The Idea of Wilderness*; the essays of Fritjof Capra, George Sessions, and Arne Naess that are collected in Sessions's *Deep Ecology for the 21st Century*; and Louise Westling's *The Green Breast of the New World*.

Two distinct families of criticism have posed these arguments about Emerson's justification of American industrial capitalism and imperialism. For discussions of Emerson's legitimization of American industrial economics, see Maurice Gonnaud's *An Uneasy Solitude: Individual and Society in the Work of Ralph Waldo Emerson*; Len Gougeon's *Virtue's Hero: Emerson, Antislavery, and Reform*; Howard Horwitz's *By Law of Nature: Form and Value in Nineteenth-Century America*; Barbara Packer's "The Transcendentalists"; Carolyn Porter's *Seeing and Being: The Plight of the Participant Observer in Emerson, James, Adams, and Faulkner*; and John Carlos Rowe's *At Emerson's Tomb: The Politics of Classic American Literature*. For discussions of Emerson's imperialism, see Eric Cheyfitz's *The Poetics of Imperialism: Translation and Colonization from* The Tempest *to* Tarzan; and "A Common Emerson: Ralph Waldo Emerson in an Ethnohistorical Context"; Jenine Abboushi Dallal's "American Imperialism UnManifest: Emerson's 'Inquest' and Cultural Regeneration"; Paul Giles's "Transnationalism and Classic American Literature"; and Brady Harrison's "The Young Americans: Emerson, Walker, and the Early Literature of American Empire."

4. I am slightly modifying the language that Steven Rendall uses in his translation of *The Practice of Everyday Life*. De Certeau, via Rendall, most often uses the word *stories* in his discussion of the creation and modification of spatial practices, and in some places he discusses a particular type of story—the story of spatial mapping that is centered around the navigation of a particular space (to use my own examples rather than de Certeau's, be it urban in the guise of J. Alfred Prufrock's experience in London or rural in the fashion of Tess Durbeyfield's navigation of Thomas Hardy's rural Wessex in *Tess of the D'Urbervilles*). I find, however, that de Certeau oscillates freely between the specific genre of spatial mapping stories and stories in general and that he often invokes "story" with such generality that it would not take him out of context to substitute "narrative" for "story" as I do in this paragraph. As I hope is apparent by this point in my argument, I find that Emerson's work—which is, of course, much more easily classified as "narrative" rather than "story"—an exceptional narrative intervention into spatial practice that should not be kept from de Certeau's theoretical concerns on the basis of generic classifications that are slippery even in de Certeau's own text.

5. Bloom's collection is entitled *Ralph Waldo Emerson* (1985), and "Mr. America" appears as its untitled introduction; Buell's collection is entitled *Ralph Waldo Emerson: A Collection of Critical Essays* (1993), and "Mr. America" appears as "Emerson: Power at the Crossing"; and Porte and Morris's collection is *The Cambridge Companion to Ralph Waldo Emerson* (1999), and the spirit of "Mr. America" is kept alive—recast, in fact, to meet new challenges to Emerson's positive heritage—in the volume's preface and introduction. I mention these collections of essays with some hesitation. They present nothing new or groundbreaking, after all, but as texts intended for the use of Emerson initiates

they seem an exceptional site for the construction—or maintenance—of Emerson's status as a positive icon of American literature and culture.

6. Pease, Giamatti, and Updike are not the only ones who approached Emerson from a revisionist perspective during the early 1980s, but they are the ones who elicited the strong and sustained reaction from Emerson's defenders. Likewise, Bloom was not the only critic to react strongly to what he interpreted as Emersonian heresy. Eric Cheyfitz rankled the Emerson institution twice, first with *The Trans-Parent: Sexual Politics in the Language of Emerson* in 1981 and then with *The Poetics of Imperialism: Translation and Colonization from* The Tempest *to* Tarzan in 1991, which introduces the thesis about Emerson's imperialism that Cheyfitz develops more fully in "A Common Emerson: Ralph Waldo Emerson in an Ethnohistorical Context" (2003) and sets the stage for the more recent arguments posed by Brady Harrison and Jenine Abboushi Dallal.

In 1984, the same year that Bloom published "Mr. America" for the first time, Lawrence Buell issued his own reaction to the new arrivals in Emerson studies, and he reached similar conclusions in rhetoric that, though strident in its own right, did not quite contain the totalizing force of Bloom's reaction. In "The Emerson Industry in the 1980s: A Survey of Trends and Achievements," Buell considers Cheyfitz's work worthy of some merit, but he characterizes it as a "clever" rather than "learned" book that follows a "relatively slapdash pursuit of its ultimate goal," which is, of course, an interrogation of Emerson's relationship with gender (131). Similarly, Buell confronts Pease as an example of "deconstructionist criticism" whose "Emerson, *Nature*, and the Sovereignty of Influence" "runs the risk of hypostasisization"; it is a "fruitful" line of criticism that is, by implication, more "inevitable" than original or otherwise valuable (133–34). In the introduction to his collection of Emerson scholarship, Porte does not name him, but he unequivocally contests the approach that Cheyfitz uses in *The Poetics of Imperialism*: "Emerson would have nothing to do with an American civilization, so-called, willing to cover its crimes with cries of manifest destiny and America first. . . . [He] was a severe critic of an America capable of invading Mexico, oppressing blacks, and denying women equal rights" (11).

7. Cayton offers a very concise discussion of the misinterpretation and misapplication of Emerson by the merchant-class audiences that funded, publicized, and attended his lectures after the waning of the initial New England lyceum movement. Cayton draws a crucial distinction between the initial lyceum movement, which was "begun by John Holbrook in 1829 to promote dissemination of useful information, discussion, and debate," and the "Young Men's Associations" that began to supersede the lyceums by 1840 (83). The Young Men's Associations were different from the lyceums in several ways: they were more deliberately intended to "inculcate certain moral values," they were "intimately linked to city boosters and businesspeople" in ways that lyceums were not, and their reliance upon traveling lecturers cultivated a culture of celebrity (86). One of Cayton's central theses is that Emerson's later audiences, which cared less about the actual substance of Emerson's speeches than they did about experiencing a bonafide celebrity, had already begun to excise the cultural criticism from Emerson's lectures to hear only the parts that seemed to support or legitimize their commercial desires.

For a much broader look at the uses to which Emerson has been put, see Charles E. Mitchell's *Individualism and its Discontents: Appropriations of Emerson, 1880–1950.*

8. Thoreau's current fame is completely unrelated to the status he enjoyed during his lifetime and throughout the late nineteenth and early twentieth centuries. As Buell explains thoroughly in *Environmental Imagination*, Thoreau's readership and book sales were incredibly small compared to his more successful contemporaries, and they only improved significantly through the determined, long-term marketing efforts of Ticknor and Fields and, later, Houghton, Mifflin. From the 1880s until 1906, when the company published Thoreau's collected writings, Houghton, Mifflin repeatedly dropped Thoreau's name in the introductions to new pieces of nature writing from writers such as Charles Dudley Warner, Frank Bolles, and John Burroughs and placed his "comparatively descriptive and scientific, nonmystical, and non-pugnacious essays" in anthologies designed for classroom use (Buell 346–47).

In 1880, Thoreau's publishers had sold 3,695 copies of *Walden* since it was first published in 1854, 3,528 of *Cape Cod* since 1865, and 3,263 of *The Maine Woods* since 1864 (Buell 348). By that date, according to Buell, none of Thoreau's books "had achieved an average sale of more than 200 copies annually; in the 1890s, the firm sold only 310 copies of its first edition of Thoreau's collected works, the ten-volume Riverside edition; and the "Walden" edition of 1906 was not reprinted for decades" (Buell 349). The new publicity that Houghton, Mifflin initiated in the 1880s did help Thoreau's position, but only modestly. His sales quadrupled, according to Buell, but "his annual thousands were dwarfed by Emerson's ten thousands, not to mention Longfellow's hundred thousands" (342).

Because of its concision and the attention it grants to Ticknor and Fields/Houghton, Mifflin, I am particularly fond of Buell's interpretation of Thoreau's publication history. For other accounts, however, see Wendell Glick's *The Recognition of Henry David Thoreau*; Michael Meyer's *Several More Lives to Live: Thoreau's Political Reputation in America*; Michael Meyer and Walter Harding's "Thoreau's Reputation"; Raymond R. Borst's *Henry David Thoreau: A Reference Guide, 1835–1899*; Gary Scharnhorsts's *Henry David Thoreau: A Case Study in Canonization*; and Robert Sattelmeyer's "Walden: Climbing the Canon."

9. Buell, Oelschlaeger, and Botkin are hardly the only scholars to valorize Thoreau as the preeminent nineteenth-century philosopher of nature. For other declarations of Thoreau's exceptionality as an early environmentalist and visionary ecological thinker, see Philip Cafaro's "Thoreau's Virtue Ethics in *Walden*" and "Thoreau's Environmental Ethics in *Walden*"; Robert Kuhn McGregor's *A Wider View of the Universe: Henry Thoreau's Study of Nature*; Oelschlaeger's "Environment and the 21st Century: A Thoreauvian Interlude"; Scott Russell Sanders's "Speaking a Word for Nature"; William Rossi's "Thoreau's Transcendental Ecocentrism"; and Donald Worster's *Nature's Economy: A History of Ecological Ideas* and "Thoreau and the American Passion for Wilderness."

In recent criticism, the saintly status that Oelschlaeger has bestowed upon Henry David Thoreau has rarely been challenged. Andrew McMurry and James McKusick have worked against the grain to reinstate Emerson as the central figure of environmental thought in American literature, and only Ira Brooker, Paul Giles, and Karl Kroeber have extended any sort of postcolonialist critique into Thoreau's work or suggested that the Emersonian-Thoreauvian tradition of environmental writing overwrites or obscures alternative traditions. Writing against the cult of "St. Henry," Brooker suggests that Thoreau imperializes Walden Pond by converting it into an intellectual commodity that he sold to the masses as a wilderness lifestyle and sensibility, while Giles recognizes such patterns of intellectual commodification as part of an overarching tendency in Thoreau's writing to "to sublimate historical and political conflicts into a narrative conflating nation with nature" that, when Thoreau's attention turns to the natural world, he continues Emerson's imperialist environmental vision (Giles, 69). To Brooker and Giles, Kroeber adds that Thoreau's institutional power obscures an "un-Thoreauvian tradition of nature writing" made up of authors such as William Bartram, Susan Fenimore Cooper, Aldo Leopold, and Rachel Carson, that is "more scientifically oriented, more scientific in mode, and more focused on long-term, noncyclic natural changes" (313).

Chapter 2. James Fenimore Cooper, Canon Formation, and American Literature's Erasure of Environmental Anxiety

1. For a more extensive discussion of Emerson's relationship with Greeley, see Richard F. Teichgraeber's *Sublime Thoughts/Penny Wisdom: Situating Emerson and Thoreau in the American Market*. Teichgraeber explains that at least until the middle of the nineteenth century Greeley was Emerson's chief promoter in American popular culture. Greeley felt it was his responsibility to educate the public on emerging American writers, and in the case of Emerson he accomplished this by issuing reviews of Emerson's works before they had attracted any public attention or noticeable success. Greeley-edited publications, beginning with the *New Yorker* and continuing with the daily and weekly editions of the *Tribune*, provided a steady stream of reviews and notices that in effect served to rationalize Emerson's reputation well before any of his publications had gained any significant commercial success. . . . [Greeley provided] the continuing publicity needed to make and keep Emerson's name and writings visible in American culture at large. (211)

2. Jonathan Arac has accurately described "Fenimore Cooper's Literary Offences" as an attempt to remove literature from history and politics. For his full interpretation of Twain's essay, see "Nationalism, Hypercanonization, and *Huckleberry Finn*."

3. When Twain issued his essay in 1895, George Santayana had already earned his BA at Harvard in 1882 and was working toward the PhD and faculty appointment he would earn from the same institution in 1889. Five years later, in 1904, Van Wyck Brooks enrolled at Harvard, and T. S. Eliot followed in 1906. Before Santayana emigrated to Great Britain in 1912, he had made lasting impressions on Brooks, who graduated in 1907, and Eliot, who, after earning his BA in 1910 and his MA in 1911, had begun working toward the PhD in philosophy that he would never complete. For a full discussion of the relationships that Santayana,

Brooks, and Eliot shared, see Frank Lentricchia's *The Modernist Quartet*, which situates Santayana, John Dewey, William James, and Josiah Royce as chief influences of T. S. Eliot, Ezra Pound, Wallace Stevens, and Robert Frost.

4. William Charvat's discussion of Cooper in *The Profession of Authorship in America: 1800–1870* is still a foundational study of Cooper's commercial success and his understanding of both his audience and the nuances of the nineteenth-century publishing industry. James D. Wallace's *Early Cooper and His Audience*, however, offers a longer and more comprehensive analysis.

5. While William Cooper often garners a passing mention in James Fenimore Cooper's critical biographies, as is the case in Donald A. Ringe's standard *James Fenimore Cooper*, he has received very little sustained attention since Robert Spiller's *Fenimore Cooper: Critic of His Times* and the second volume of Vernon Louis Parrington's *Main Currents in American Thought*. Wayne Franklin's *The New World of James Fenimore Cooper* is one notable exception to this trend.

6. By the very theoretical rubric that she establishes at the beginning of her text, in which no form of environmentalism can play any part in any pre-contemporary text, Tichi prevents herself from finding anything but failure in Cooper's skeptical view of the American project of environmental modification. In staging her argument, Tichi uses scenes from *The Chainbearer* and *Wyandotte* to argue that Cooper has no essential problem with the destruction of wilderness but that the central thrust of his engagement with national expansion concerned who would authorize "the use of the American axe" (172). Tichi's use of *The Chainbearer* and *Wyandotte* to suggest that Cooper "really" supports the clearing of wilderness allows her to flatten out the environmental tensions of the Leatherstocking series and reduce any sense of environmental anxiety in these novels to a discussion of class. In a similar manner, she uses Cooper's bitterly satirical description of apocalyptic environmental disaster in *The Crater* (1847) (in which a massive earthquake swallows up the entire nation and all of its agrarian improvements) to condemn *all* of his environmental criticism as ridiculous.

In accusing Tichi of burying Cooper's environmental anxieties in a discussion of class, I do not want to be misunderstood. My goal is not to merely replace her theoretical rubric with my own environmentally sympathetic approach. The real problem of Tichi's argument is that it drastically reduces the environmental problems that Cooper engages in *The Pioneers* and the other novels of the Leatherstocking series by transforming what is clearly a multivocal discussion of land ethics into a single narrative of cultural and political power that does not explain, as I will in the rest of this chapter, that the federalism of Cooper and Marmaduke Temple is significantly different from earlier federalist discussions of the environment.

7. As I explained in the Introduction, it is quite rare to find a historian of environmentalism who periodizes environmentalism as a wholly unique late-twentieth-century movement. In fact, only Kirkpatrick Sale, in *The Green Revolution*, makes such an argument. The question of every other historian is not whether or not environmentalism possesses a history but where its origins lie and how it is to be periodized. Some of the earliest historians of environmentalism, such as Samuel P. Hays and Roderick Nash, recognized that late-twentieth-century

environmentalism had historical precedents, but they emphasized its difference from the earlier conservationist and preservationist movements. This prevailing mode of environmentalist historiography, which limits itself largely to the history of environmentalism in the United States, is perfectly comfortable extending the history of environmental crisis and corresponding forms of dissent to the colonial period. For a more complete description of the history of environmentalism, see the Introduction.

8. When I discuss William Cooper and James Fenimore Cooper in close proximity, I will refer to James as "Fenimore Cooper."

9. Belknap's *History of New Hampshire* is a clear antecedent to Dwight's *History of New England and New York*—Dwight refers to it repeatedly throughout his text. The fact that Cooper would have been familiar with his father's *A Guide in the Wilderness* is rather obvious considering the paternal connection, but the fact that Cooper's 1838 *The Chronicles of Cooperstown*, is a deliberate revision of his father's *Guide* and stands as further evidence of a sustained intellectual engagement with the earlier text.

It is also easy to downplay Cooper's engagement with Timothy Dwight. Cooper was quite young when he attended Yale College—he was admitted at the age of thirteen and he was expelled for mischief at sixteen—and he publicly downplayed the impact of his formal education. During his presidency, however, Yale was in almost every way Dwight's college, and it seems that it would have been impossible to attend it during this period without coming into some sort of contact with him. He taught classes, preached sermons, and presided over public student disciplinary courts like the one that expelled Cooper from Yale after his junior year. Although we have no evidence that Cooper ever said or wrote anything about Dwight, he did strive to maintain contact with several of his Yale professors, particularly Benjamin Silliman, whose hiring was one of the most important events of Dwight's tenure. The first volume of Parrington's *Main Currents* contains a concise overview of Timothy Dwight, but Robert Spiller's *Fenimore Cooper* offers the best description of Dwight's Yale and Cooper's engagement with it. Spiller discusses Cooper's relationship with Silliman, but the best evidence of the relationship are Cooper's letters to the professor, which have been collected in James Franklin Beard's edition of *The Letters and Journals of James Fenimore Cooper*.

10. For a detailed examination of how this particular type of elevated, panoramic gaze became commonplace in late-eighteenth and early-nineteenth-century American culture, see Donald A. Ringe's *The Pictorial Mode: Space and Time in the Art of Bryant, Irving, and Cooper*.

11. Belknap believes that deforestation will have a beneficial moderating effect on the climate. It is worth nothing, I believe, that Belknap is so far from condemning the clearing of forested land that he spends a great deal of the third book of his *History* describing the most efficient methods of clearing land. The rural economy promoted by Belknap combines the particularly American problem of clearing forested land and draining bogs with established practices of European agriculture such as fertilizing cultivated fields with animal manure and planting grass in old fields to restore their fertility.

12. As Swann and Rans both recognize, the fishing laws that Judge Temple has procured from the legislature allow fishing when the fish of Lake Otsego are spawning, which is actually when fishing causes the worst ecological damage.

13. Natural history is not the only science that Cooper critiques. He also places the science of surveying in the vanguard of American expansionism in *The Prairie* and *The Deerslayer* before devoting an entire novel to it in *The Chainbearer*.

Chapter 3. Henry Wadsworth Longfellow, United States National Literature, and the American Canon's Erasure of Material Nature

1. There was a fourth time that Longfellow presented this argument, but I have not listed it here. After publishing "The Literary Spirit of Our Country" in *The United States Literary Gazette* in 1824, he repeated the spirit of this piece in his 1826 Bowdoin commencement oration, "Our Native Poets." "Our Native Poets" made its way into print shortly after Longfellow gave the address, but it is most accessible today as it is reprinted in Thomas Wentworth Higginson's *Henry Wadsworth Longfellow*, a biography that was printed in 1902. It has not been reprinted since. Because "Our Native Poets" is largely a recapitulation of "The Literary Spirit of Our Country," I will not devote any significant attention to it in this chapter.

2. Two of the figures I mention here are important, but for brevity's sake I will not discuss them directly in this chapter. James Russell Lowell was a key supporter of Longfellow's vision of American literature, and he is even more important now because he has been used (in my opinion, misread) in the last half of the twentieth century to actually discredit the types of literary environmental determinism that interested Longfellow. Shortly after Longfellow published *Kavanagh*, Lowell published a review essay in the *North American Review* that thoroughly supported Longfellow's position on American national literature—almost point by point. Lowell's essay has not attracted tremendous critical attention in quite some time, but Tichi has argued that the essay attacks those who thought "that a great national literature would come largely from the 'rolling rivers, dark & green woods, boundless meadows, and majestic peaks' of the American landscape" (151). Tichi explains that this particular passage is directed primarily at Timothy Dwight's *The Columbiad*, but her treatment of the essay as a whole suggests that Lowell may have also meant to discredit the types of claims that I am recognizing in Longfellow's work. This is simply not the case. The main objective of Lowell's essay is to support Longfellow's claims in *Kavanagh* that a national genius must be born—and born out of a European tradition that, like Longfellow, he did not want American literature to abandon—before it can be molded by an environment. Lowell implicitly accepts the fact that a genius, once born, can be molded by an environment.

In addition to Lowell, I will not directly discuss Duyckinck in this chapter. I include him here as a way to quickly expand what I mean by "Young Americans" beyond the highly esoteric figure of Cornelius Mathews. We remember Duyckinck much more readily today than Mathews, of course, because he was Melville's editor and chief promoter, he was linked with almost every mid-nineteenth-century author that we now consider significant, and he was one of the most powerful editors of the century. Duyckinck, in short, was much more poised and well connected than Mathews, but he shared his friend's vision for a national American literature. Between 1840 and 1842, Duyckinck and Mathews collaborated on *Arcturus: A Journal of Books and Opinions*, which, like the *Niagara* that Hathaway proposes in Longfellow's *Kavanagh*, was launched with the explicit purpose of cultivating an American national literature that was much more patriotic and nativist than what Longfellow envisioned.

3. Any discussion of Longfellow's literary manifestoes is rare, but the types of limiting analysis I mention here may be found in Eric Carl Link's "American Nationalism and the Defense of Poetry" and Van Wyck Brooks's *The Flowering of New England*. Link's essay essentially forgets Longfellow's other manifestoes as it claims that "The Defence of Poetry" is "the principal document that sets forth Henry Wadsworth Longfellow's views of poetry," while *The Flowering of New England* claims that the same essay amounted to "sufficiently mild words with which to announce an era"; that "twenty other poets and orators were saying the same things. Longfellow spoke for them all and only spoke with more authority because, with his chair at Harvard, he had an ampler sounding-board behind him" (Link Section II; Brooks 154). For a more extensive treatment of Longfellow's manifestoes, see Cecil B. Williams's *Henry Wadsworth Longfellow*, and for a brief general overview of the aesthetic system that Longfellow presents in these manifestoes, without Brooks's condescension, see Lawrence Buell's *New England Literary Culture: From Revolution Through Renaissance*, especially pages 44–45.

4. For this argument in its fully developed form, see Eric Carl Link's "American Nationalism."

5. Although it sympathizes with Mathews, supports his literary nationalism, and joins in his critique of internationalist literary figures such as Longfellow, Perry Miller's *The Raven and the Whale* still offers one of the most thorough treatments of Mathews's role in the nineteenth-century debates over U.S. literary nationalism. For a more recent discussion of Mathews and his circle, see Edward L. Widmer's *Young America: The Flowering of Democracy in New York City*. Both Miller and Widmer acknowledge that Longfellow's *Kavanagh* is a direct engagement with Cornelius Mathews. Beyond Miller and Widmer, numerous scholars have written about the role that Young Americans played in nineteenth-century American imperialism. For two recent arguments in this vein, see Brady Harrison's "The Young Americans: Emerson, Walker, and the Early Literature of American Empire" and Jenine Abboushi Dallal's "American Imperialism UnManifest."

6. The similarities between Churchill and Longfellow and Hathaway and Mathews are quite stark. So stark, in fact, that in *The Raven and the Whale*

Perry Miller refers to these characters as "Churchill-Longfellow" and "Hathaway-Mathews" (252).

7. As all of Longfellow's standard biographies have acknowledged, Longfellow never traveled into the (near or far) West, and he never actually saw the Mississippi; his ability to describe the West depended upon artistic renderings of the West, particularly John Banvard's panorama of the Mississippi, which he saw on display in Boston on December 19, 1846. For descriptions of Longfellow's experience with this panorama and discussions of its effect on Longfellow as he composed *Evangeline*, see Samuel Longfellow's *Life of Henry Wadsworth Longfellow*; Cecil B. Williams's *Henry Wadsworth Longfellow*; and Charles C. Calhoun's *Longfellow: A Reconsidered Life.*

8. Here and in the rest of my citations of Longfellow's poetry, I list page numbers rather than line numbers because each of the volumes of poetry I quote do not list line numbers.

9. Virginia Jackson offers an excellent reading of Longfellow's treatment of Native Americans and Native American languages in "Longfellow's Tradition; or, Picture-Writing a Nation." Jackson explains that Longfellow was as well informed as possible about Native American languages and cultures—largely through a close engagement with Henry Schoolcraft's work on these subjects—but that he still conceded the eventual disappearance of these people, their languages, and their cultures. "*Hiawatha*," Jackson recognizes, "actively joins the American campaign to 'disappear' native cultures by appealing to chronicle genocide passively as a fait accompli," and it thus participates in the same narrative of "Vanishing Americans" that Lora Romero identifies while discussing James Fenimore Cooper's work in her *Home Fronts: Nineteenth-Century Domesticity and Its Critics.*

10. To explain this shift in attitudes about the environment, Shawn Loewen, in "The New Canaan: Abundance, Scarcity, and the Changing Climate of Nature Writing in Nineteenth-Century America," writes that over the course of the nineteenth century the "dominant conception of nature" in the United States shifted from "a discourse of abundance" to a "discourse of scarcity" (98).

11. I mention that Catlin's letter is published in a New York newspaper because it is quite easy to imagine such documents as entirely out of touch with their time and place. This newspaper publication is even more important because it predates the letter's appearance in a book by eight years. It was eventually included in two volumes of letters published in 1841: the volume I cite, *North American Indians: Being Letters and Notes on Their Manners, Customs, and Conditions, Written During Eight Years' Travel Amongst the Wildest Tribes of Indians in North America, 1832–1839*, and the less long-titled *Letters and Notes on the Manners, Customs, and Condition of the North American Indians.*

Catlin's call for the creation of "*magnificent park*" is recognized by Roderick Nash in *American Environmentalism*, and by a multitude of National Park Service Internet sites, as the first such plea. I would be remiss, however, if I did not briefly mention (as do Nash and the other historians, but not the park service) that Catlin's vision of a national park would enclose "[races of] man and [species of] beast" that both exist under similar threats of extinction; that is, the park would contain the threatened buffalo as well as "the native Indian in his classic attire, galloping his wild horse, with sinewy bow, and shield, and lance" (Catlin 293, 294–95). The plan is patently racist and complicit in the processes of nineteenth-century American continental expansionism and imperialism. As Mark David Spence comments in *Disposessing the Wilderness: Indian Removal and the Making of the National Parks*, "Catlin's vision of 'classic' Indians grossly ignored the cultural dynamism of native societies, and his park would have created a monstrous combination of outdoor museum, human zoo, and wild animal park" (11). Catlin's conflation of Native Americans and native biota under the specter of extinction, however, is rather commonplace in the nineteenth-century United States.

12. For recent discussions of these claims of plagiarism, see Virginia Jackson's "Poe, Longfellow, and the Institution of Poetry"; Kent P. Ljungquist's "The 'Little War' and Longfellow's Dilemma: New Documents in the Plagiarism Controversy of 1845"; Meredith McGill's "Poe, Literary Nationalism, and Authorial Identity"; and Edward J. Piacentino's. "The Poe-Longfellow Plagiarism Controversy: A New Critical Notice in The Southern Chronicle."

13. The process of feminization that both Santayana and Brooks identify in mid-to-late-nineteenth-century American culture is precisely the type of feminization that Ann Douglas makes the subject of her famous *Feminization of American Culture*. Although I feel that Douglas's text warrants no real explication here, I do find it interesting to see the ways that her argument extends the critical efforts of early-twentieth-century male critics who were explicitly afraid of, and worked against, the power of femininity in American (and American male) culture.

14. Brooks's dismissal of Longfellow in the texts that I am discussing here is powerful in its own right, but it is important to note that much of Brooks's critique of Longfellow came to be reprinted in works that were published later in the twentieth century, keeping his interpretation of Longfellow in circulation long after Brooks's initial texts had gone out of print. The particular passage I quote here is part of a larger idea that Brooks republishes verbatim in *Our Literary Heritage: A Pictorial History of the Writer in America* (1956), fully twenty years after he initially offered the sentiment in *The Flowering of New England*. The larger passage that makes it into the later work reads like this: "In later days, when other fashions came, when the great wheel of time had passed beyond them, one saw these poems in another light. They seemed to lack finality and distinction, whether in thought or phrase. But no one could quite forget their dreamy music, their shadowy languor, their melodious charm, their burden of youthful nostalgia" (*Flowering* 168).

15. Muir began publishing in these journals in 1890 and continued to do so until his death; the Yosemite, General Grant, and Sequoia national parks were created in the same year. Muir and Johnson founded the Sierra Club in 1892; Pinchot became the director of the Division of Forestry in 1898 and would hold the post under presidents McKinley and Roosevelt before resigning from Taft's administration in 1910. The Audubon Society was formed in 1905, and Muir's battle for the Hetch Hetchy began in 1909; it continued until 1913, when the construction of the Hetch Hetchy Dam was approved by Congress. Muir died the next year, in 1914. These events are discussed in virtually every history of

environmentalism. Although the Muir-Pinchot debates, which I am focusing on with this list, only represent one form of environmentalism (that which focuses on saving "wild" spaces), it stands out as one of the most public environmental debates of the early twentieth century. Muir's battle to save Hetch Hetchy gripped national print media in a way that would only be matched fifty years later in the controversy surrounding Rachel Carson's *Silent Spring*. For more about these events, see Fox's *The American Conservation Movement*; Gottlieb's *Forcing the Spring*; Hays's *Conservation and the Gospel of Efficiency*; Nash's *Wilderness and the American Mind* and *Readings in Conservation History*; Shabecoff's *A Fierce Green Fire*; and Worster's *American Environmentalism*. For particularly insightful treatments of the Hetch Hetchy debate, specifically see Fox and Nash's *Wilderness and the American Mind*.

16. While I am interested in the ways that Whitman himself engaged the natural world, I cannot fully engage this subject in this chapter—even in this book. My concern here is primarily with what Whitman became in Brooks's critical rendering. For one of the first ecocritical investigations of Whitman's work, however, see M. Jimmie Killingsworth's *Walt Whitman and the Earth: A Study in Ecopoetics*.

17. In "The Genteel Tradition in American Philosophy," Santayana declares that egocentrism and anthropocentrism are two of the primary flaws of the genteel tradition. In his own words, Santayana writes that America's genteel "systems are egotistical; directly or indirectly they are anthropocentric, and inspired by the conceited notion that man, or human reason, or the human distinction between good and evil, is the center and pivot of the universe" (64). It is this very manifestation of genteel ideology that prevents Santayana from declaring Emerson a writer of the first rank; Emerson's "love and respect for nature" is perverted in Santayana's opinion: "Nature . . . is precious because it is his own work, a mirror in which he looks at himself and says (like a poet relishing his own verses), 'What a genius I am! Who would have thought there was such stuff in me?' " (53).

In a passage that has made him famous among Deep Ecologists, Santayana argues that the only real cure for American gentility is unmediated contact with the natural world:

> [Anthropocentrism and Egocentrism are] what the mountains and the woods should make you at last ashamed to assert. From what, indeed, does the society of nature liberate you, that you find it so sweet . . . it is the yoke of this genteel tradition itself, your tyrant from the cradle to the grave, that these primeval solitudes lift from your shoulders. They suspend your forced sense of your own importance not merely as individuals, but even as men. They allow you, in one happy moment, at once to play and to worship, to take yourselves simply, humbly, for what you are, and to salute the wild, indifferent, noncensorious infinity of nature. (62–64)

When I claim that Longfellow's environmental vision resisted anthropo- and egocentrism, I am specifically referring to *Evangeline* and *The Song of Hiawatha*, which, with the occasional moment when nature darkens with Evangeline's mood, generally do not project human problems or motivations onto the natural world.

Chapter 4. Willa Cather and John Steinbeck, Environmental Schizophrenia, and Monstrous Ecology

1. A version of this chapter has been previously published in the *Journal of American Culture* as "Why Isn't He So Green?: John Steinbeck's Monstrous Ecology." It appears here with the permission of the *Journal of American Culture* and Blackwell Publishing.

2. Histories of environmental politics ordinarily draw significant distinctions between preservation and conservation. Preservation is ordinarily associated with John Muir, and it emphasizes saving natural spaces based on aesthetics or inherent rights to existence. Conservation is most often associated with Gifford Pinchot and emphasizes the "wise use" of natural resources. While these differences are significant, my primary concern in this chapter is to illustrate the pervasiveness of environmental politics—under whatever name—in the early twentieth century.

3. Rosowski is not the only figure to read Cather in a the context of the conservation movement. For recent work in this vein see Joseph Urgo's "*My Ántonia* and the National Parks Movement."

4. The figures I am presenting here are made possible by the *New York Times*'s searchable archive, which is freely available on the newspaper's Web site.

5. The governors were not excited about the prospect of mandatory meetings with the president. Roosevelt had already steered this convention with a fairly firm grip upon the wheel, and the governors did not want similar conventions to serve as a way for the president to influence the states in ways that circumvented the Congress. The governors' decision to meet without the president was a reaction to these concerns.

The resolution passed by the participants of this convention, as reported by the *Times,* reads as follows:

> We commend the wise forethought of the President in sounding the note of warning as to the waste and exhaustion of the natural resources of the country and signify our high appreciation of his action in calling this conference to consider the same, and to seek remedies therefore through the co-operation of the Nation and the States.
>
> We agree that this co-operation should find expression in suitable action by the Congress within the limits of and co-extensive with the National jurisdiction of the subject, and, complementary thereto by the Legislatures of the several States within the limits of and co-extensive with their jurisdiction.
>
> We declare the conviction that in the use of our natural resources States are interdependent and bound together by ties, by National benefits, responsibilities, and duties.

We agree in the wisdom of future conferences between the President, members of Congress, and the Governors of the States regarding the conservation of our natural resources, with the view of continued co-operation and action on the lines suggested. And to this end we advise that from time to time, as in his judgment may seem wise, the President call the Governors of the States, members of Congress, and others, into conference. We agree that further action is advisable to ascertain the present condition of our natural resources and to promote the conservation of the same. And to that we recommend the appointment by each State a commission on the conservation of natural resources, to co-operate with each other and with any similar commission on behalf of the Federal Government.

To Continue Forest Policies

We urge the continuation and extension of forest policies adapted to secure the husbanding and renewal of our diminishing timber supply, the prevention of soil erosion, the protection of headwaters, and the maintenance of the purity and navigability of the streams. We recognize that the private ownership of forest lands entails responsibilities in the interests of all the people, and we favor the enactment of laws looking to the protection and replacement of privately owned forests.

We recognize in our waters a most valuable asset of the people of the United States, and we recommend the enactment of laws looking to the conservation of water resources for irrigation, water supply, power, and navigation, to the end that navigable and course *[sic]* streams may be brought under complete control and fully utilized for every purpose. We specially urge on the Federal Congress the immediate adoption of a wise, active, and thorough waterway policy, providing for the prompt improvement of our streams and conservation of their water sheds required for the uses of commerce and the protection of the interests of our people.

We recommend the enactment of laws looking to the prevention of waste in the mining and extraction of coal, oil, gas, and other minerals with a view to their wise conservation for the use of the people, and to the protection of human life in the mines.

Let us conserve the foundations of our prosperity. ("Governors to Meet by Themselves")

6. The *Times* covered the results of the National Conservation Commission's study in eight articles between December 8 and December 12, 1908. While the North American Conference on Conservation was Roosevelt's last conservation conference, at least for a moment he had other plans. At this conference, he actually proposed another one that he hoped to hold the next year. He wanted it to be a broadly international conference, and he wanted to hold it at The Hague in September 1910. Despite his enthusiasm, the conference never took place. For a full report of the president's plans, see "World Conference on Conservation."

7. See "Platform Drafted for the Convention," "Full Text of Taft Platform," "Roosevelt Policies Must Go On," and "Mr. Taft's Speech."

8. Between 1901 and 1914, Houghton published *Our National Parks* (1901), *Stickeen* (1909), *My First Summer in the Sierra* (1911), and *The Story of My Boyhood and Youth* (1913). In the decade after his death, Houghton also released *Travels in Alaska* (1915), *A Thousand Mile Walk to the Gulf* (1917), *Steep Trails* (1918), Jeannie C. Carr's collection of Muir's letters, *Letters to a Friend; Written to Mrs. Eliza S. Carr, 1866–1879* (1915), and William F. Badè's *The Life and Letters of John Muir* (1924).

9. In *The American Conservation Movement: John Muir and His Legacy*, Stephen R. Fox explains that Charles Eliot, Frederick Law Olmstead Jr., Ethan Hitchcock, Enos Mills, Ellen Glasgow, journalist Henry Watterson, and Henry Fairfield Osborn all supported Muir's cause, and he also explains that before the Hetch Hetchy argument was closed "The *Outlook*, *Nation*, *Independent*, *World's Work*, *Collier's*, the New York *Times*, *Tribune*, and *World*, and a hundred or so other newspapers and magazines opposed the project" (Fox 143, 145). Eliot was the president of Harvard College from 1869 to 1909, Olmstead was the prominent urban planner who designed New York City's Central Park, Ethan Hitchcock was the Secretary of the Interior under Presidents McKinley and Roosevelt from 1899 to 1907, Mills was a wilderness protection advocate, Glasgow was a novelist and an acquaintance of Cather's, Watterson was the editor the Louisville *Courier-Journal* from 1869 to 1919 who won a Pulitzer Prize in 1918 for editorials supporting the U.S. entrance into World War I, and Henry Fairfield Osborn was a paleontologist and eventual president of the American Museum of Natural History. It is unclear how well Cather knew Glasgow, but the two authors would have been aware of each other. Elizabeth Sargent writes that she "never heard [Cather] mention" Glasgow, but Glasgow attended the 1933 Pulitzer Prize banquet where Cather delivered a public address that was broadcast on NBC Radio (198). For a list of attendees and two slightly different transcripts of the speech, see Brent Bohlke's *Willa Cather in Person* (168–70) and the online Willa Cather Archive, which also offers an audio recording of the speech under the title "Cather's 1933 Radio Speech."

10. M. Catherine Downs has recently argued that Cather was deeply engaged in her journalistic work and that she even participated in the magazine's muckraking tradition when she rewrote Georgine Milmine's *The Life of Mary Baker G. Eddy* for *McClure's*. Downs is certainly correct when she explains that Cather's experience as a journalist shaped her writing style, but, when it comes to her

opinion of muckraking, it is difficult to overturn James Woodress's longstanding claim that Cather "had no interest in muckraking, found social reformers very dull people, [and] took the dimmest possible view of literature that had a message" (*Life and Art* 123).

11. Cather was offering these comments during the later years of her career when she felt embattled against the newer generation of (largely modernist) writers and critics. It would be easy to claim that her disavowal of politics is simply the function of her mood during these years, but she claims, at least, that she held these opinions much earlier in her career as she was writing her most enduring novels. While she argues in "Escapism" that the novel is the wrong medium for social activism, she also poses a secondary argument that reformers would be better served if they would "follow the method of the pamphleteers" (970). "Only by that method," she argues, "can these subjects be seriously and fairly discussed. And the people who are able to do anything toward improving such conditions will read only such a discussion" (970).

12. The bluntest discussion of nostalgia in Cather's work is in Granville Hicks's "The Case against Willa Cather" (1933). The essay claims that "Miss Cather . . . is concerned with" a "past era, and she looks back on it with nostalgia"; she "has simply projected her own desires into the past: her longing for heroism, her admiration for natural beauty, her desire—intensified by pre-occupation with doubt and despair—for the security of an unquestioned faith" (139, 145). Hicks's essay is also a notable example of the gender-based attacks that Cather was subjected to throughout the 1930s. The demeaning "Miss Cather" in the passage I have quoted here reappears consistently throughout "The Case against Willa Cather." For discussions of Cather's critics that reach beyond the scope of Cather's standard biographies, see Deborah Carlin's *Cather, Canon, and the Politics of Reading* and Joan Acocella's *Willa Cather and the Politics of Criticism*. For an incisive reevaluation of Cather's use of nostalgia, see Sarah Wilson's " 'Fragementary and Inconclusive' Violence: National History and Literary Form in *The Professor's House*." The essay argues that Cather was aware of and manipulated the nostalgia that runs through her texts. Writing, as her title suggests, in the context of *The Professor's House*, Wilson claims Cather understood that a "colonial gaze" was building new "national histories" out of Native American cultures in the Southwest, knew that nostalgia was playing a critical role in this process of national myth-making, and believed—as "Tom Outland's Story" attests—that nostalgia was ultimately an evasion of "social and intellectual responsibility" that was "profoundly unsuited . . . to the brokering of a flexible and inclusive community" (Wilson 578, 586, 584).

13. It is in these sections of the novel that Alexandra often elevates the present into the realm of epic history and offers her most blatant erasure of the imperialist activity that predicated her own Westward movement. Both of these nostalgic moves are quite obvious in her declaration that

> [f]or the first time, since that land emerged from the waters of geologic ages, a human face was set toward it with love and yearning. It seemed beautiful to her, rich and strong and glorious. Her eyes drank in the breadth of it, until her tears blinded her. Then the Genius of

> the Divide, the great, free spirit which breathes across it, must have bent lower than it ever bent to a human will before. The history of every country begins in the heart of a man or a woman. (42)

14. The impact of the prairie on Cather's sense of self has been discussed at length. See, for instance, Sharon O'Brien's *Willa Cather*, especially the third chapter, "Transplanting." For Cather's own description of the "erasure of personality" that she experienced upon entering the "country as bare as a piece of sheet iron," see "Willa Cather Talks of Work."

15. With these lines, Cather is explicitly describing Carl Linstrum's view of the place as a boy, but she seems to be speaking on a much more general level. She echoes the idea of the prairie as "the great fact" several pages later in a description of another character—John Bergson. Here, as he lies dying and thinking about the land that he has died trying to bring to order, he ends his reverie thinking, "and then the grass," essentially repeating the phrase that Cather attributes to Carl earlier—that prairie or the grass is "the great fact" or the enigmatic essence of the place (14).

16. It is in rapturous moments such as these that Cather—blurring the lines between her control of the narrative and the emotions running through Alexandra—creates the most imperialist moment of the novel, which I have quoted in note 11.

17. Cather wrote a different introduction for the 1926 edition of *My Ántonia* that does not directly undercut Jim Burden's authority. The primary reason for the change was to grant the novel a greater degree of subtlety. For a fuller discussion of the introduction, see Jean Schwind's "The Benda Illustrations to *My Ántonia*: Cather's 'Silent' Supplement to Jim Burden's Narrative."

18. The fact that the grass in this gravesite has never been cut is so important to Jim that he repeats it, almost verbatim, much later in the narrative. Upon another visit to the place, he writes that he and Ántonia "sat down outside the sagging wire fence that shut Mr. Shimerda's plot off from the rest of the world. *The tall red grass had never been cut there.* It has died down in winter and come up in the spring until it was as thick and shrubby as some tropical garden-grass" (239; emphasis added).

19. The standard source of information about Steinbeck's scientific lineage is Richard Astro's *John Steinbeck and Edward F. Ricketts: The Shaping of a Novelist*. James C. Kelley's "John Steinbeck and Ed Ricketts: Understanding Life in the Great Tide Pool," however, offers a very helpful update to Astro's work.

20. Steinbeck published *Sea of Cortez* with Ed Ricketts in 1941. The text included a narrative of the ecological expedition they made into the Gulf of California in addition to a catalog of the area's marine life. The narrative portion of *Sea of Cortez* was republished without the scientific apparatus as *The Log from the Sea of Cortez* in 1951. From this point forward, I will only refer to the *Log* because it is still in print and it contains the narrative portion of the original project that interests me.

21. See Hedgpeth, Timmerman, and Gladstein and Gladstein.

22. Ingebretsen's "Monster-Making" offers a concise theory of monstrosity that he develops further in *At Stake: Monsters and the Rhetoric of Fear in Public Culture*. For other scholars who follow Ingebretsen's course, see Fred Botting's

Making Monstrous: Frankenstein, *Criticism, Theory*; Jeffrey Cohen's *Monster Theory: Reading Culture*; Judith Halberstam's *Skin Shows: Gothic Horror and the Technology of Horror*; Marie-Hélène Huet's *Monstrous Imagination*; and Karyn Michele Valerius's *Misconceptions: Monstrosity and the Politics of Interpretation in American Culture from the Antinomian Controversy to Biotechnology.*

23. For more on the spread of natural science museums, see the first chapter of *Environmental Evasion* and the resources I mention there in addition to Susan Sheets-Pyenson's *Cathedrals of Science: The Development of Colonial Natural History Museums during the Late Nineteenth Century*. The process of scientific/taxidermic preservation that Doc pursues in *Cannery Row* and *Sweet Thursday* is precisely the type of preservation that went into the African Hall exhibit in the American Museum of Natural History that opened in 1936. In large part, African Hall was made possible by the technologically innovative taxidermist Carl Akeley, who killed the animals that would eventually be displayed in the hall during the 1920s. As Donna Haraway tells the story in "Teddy Bear Patriarchy," Akeley was driven, almost monomaniacally, to kill and preserve the silverback gorillas that would become the centerpiece of African Hall because he "feared the gorilla would be driven to extinction before it was adequately known to science" (34). In Haraway's language, Akeley regarded taxidermy as a type of "scientific knowledge" that "canceled death; only death before knowledge was final, an abortive act in the natural history of progress" (34). When taxidermied specimens made it onto display they became cultural agents that Akeley and his contemporaries believed could heal the ills of the modern world. As Haraway explains it, the American Museum of Natural History, African Hall, and Akeley's specimens were intended to function as "a medical technology, a hygienic intervention" against decadence (55). Both Steinbeck and Akeley understood that this form of preservation was an inadequate response to the destruction of biological life. Akeley, as Mariana Torgovnick puts it, was "an active gorilla conservationist," and he worked to create the Virtunga Wildlife preserve in Africa (58). Penelope Bodry-Sanders's *Carl Akeley: Africa's Collector, Africa's Savior* offers a more sympathetic reading of Akeley, and Torgovnick offers her own interpretation of the man's life as she reviews Bodry-Sanders's book in "Stuffed Animals." For more elaborate descriptions of events at the American Museum of Natural History, see Stephen T. Asma's *Stuffed Animals and Pickled Heads: The Culture and Evolution of Natural History Museums*; Joseph Wallace's *A Gathering of Wonders: Behind the Scenes at The American Museum of Natural History*; and Douglas J. Preston's *Dinosaurs in the Attic: An Excursion into the American Museum of Natural History.*

24. In this letter Steinbeck is expressing the same Malthusian overpopulation thesis that is featured in Fairfield Osborn's *Our Plundered Planet* and William Vogt's *Road to Survival*, both of which were published in 1948, well before this essay. While Hedgpeth recognizes the similarities of Osborn's and Vogt's texts to passages in *Travels with Charley*, no hard evidence exists, in Robert J. DeMott's *Steinbeck's Reading* or elsewhere, that Steinbeck had read these books. As Hedgpeth recognizes, *Road to Survival* was a Book of the Month Club book and the likelihood of Steinbeck's at least casual contact with it is highly probable (304).

25. Although scholars have constantly suggested that Steinbeck knew nothing of Rachel Carson, he does allude to "uninhibited spraying" in *America and Americans*, which seems a rather direct echo of Carson's work (377). It is a fleeting moment, though, and no other evidence exists to suggest that Steinbeck was particularly engaged with Carson even though *Silent Spring* was being published serially in the *New Yorker* in 1961, while Steinbeck was writing *Travels with Charley,* and published as a book in 1962, well before he wrote *America and Americans*. In her synopsis of the attacks that were launched against Carson, Linda Lear writes that Carson was defamed as "a hysterical woman whose alarming view of the future could be ignored . . . a 'bird and bunny lover,' a woman who kept cats and was therefore clearly suspect . . . a romantic 'spinster' who was simply overwrought about genetics . . . in short, a woman out of control" (xvii).

Chapter 5. Zora Neale Hurston, the Power of Harlem, and the Promise of Florida

1. For recent examinations of Faulkner's understanding of the environment and his engagement with environmental problems, see Lawrence Buell's "Faulkner and the Claims of the Natural World"; Wiley C. Prewitt Jr.'s "Return of the Big Woods: Hunting and Habitat in Yoknapatawpha"; Bart Welling's "A Meeting with Old Ben: Seeing and Writing Nature in Faulkner's *Go Down, Moses*"; and Judith Bryant Wittenberg's "*Go Down, Moses* and the Discourse of Environmentalism." For all of these critics, *Go Down, Moses* is Faukner's most important discussion of the environment, but other—and earlier—texts also engage the problem of the natural world. Faulkner establishes that the natural world is very important to his idea of masculinity in his 1929 novel *Sartoris* (*Sartoris* was heavily edited before its original publication, and it was reissued in 1973 in its original form as *Flags in the Dust*), and he offers several important comments on nature in lectures he delivered at the University of Virginia (which are collected in *Faulkner in the University*) and in an essay entitled "Mississippi" (which is included in his *Essays, Speeches, and Public Letters*).

2. *Fire!!* was primarily the work of Hurston, Langston Hughes, and Wallace Thurman, but a much larger circle of artists had some bearing on the ultimate shape of the short-lived journal (only one issue was ever printed). This larger group, which Hurston and her friends called the "Niggerati" included Bruce Nugent, Aaron Douglas, John P. Davis, Helene Johnson, Dorothy West, Gwendolyn Bennett, Augusta Savage, Countee Cullen, Harold Jackman, and Dorothy Peterson (Hemenway 43).

3. Both Valerie Boyd and Robert Hemenway report that Hurston arrived in Harlem with "a dollar and fifty cents in her purse" (Boyd 93). Boyd offers a concise description of the rent and salary situation that Hurston would have faced in Harlem: "Harlem's rents were twelve to thirty dollars a month higher than in other areas of the city, although black New Yorkers earned lower salaries than their white counterparts. In the mid-1920s, thirty dollars was a significant chunk of money, equal to about $300 today. Still, a 1924 Urban League study found that

Negroes paid from 40 percent to 60 percent higher rents than white people for the same class of apartments—and segregated housing practices did not give black folks the option to just move out of Harlem and into more affordable New York neighborhoods. As a result, the average Harlem resident spent an astonishing 40 percent of his or her income on rent" (94–95). Here and throughout this chapter I rely upon Robert Hemenway's *Zora Neale Hurston: A Literary Biography* and Valerie Boyd's *Wrapped in Rainbows: The Life of Zora Neale Hurston* for information about Hurston's life. Where I rely specifically on a particular biography, or where they differ, I will be specific about the source of my information.

4. Hurston understood, perhaps better than anyone else involved in the Harlem Renaissance, that the patronage system required performances of dependence, and the type of abjection I am identifying here is precisely the type of sentiment that Hurston knew she could manipulate in order to get the funding she needed. The degree to which Hurston was in control of her own situation has been a subject of debate for more than thirty years. In *Harlem Renaissance* (1971), for instance, Nathan Huggins acknowledges that in the opinion of Louise Thompson (a close friend of Hurston's and a fellow employee of Charlotte Osgood Mason), Hurston was actively manipulating her patrons (130). Basing his judgment largely on Thompson's opinion, Huggins suggests Hurston's relationship with her primary patron was the expression of a flaw in Hurston's character. She had, Huggins believed, an innate "dependency" that made it easy for her to be "the exuberant pagan that pleased her white friends" (130). More recent critics, such as Tiffany Ruby Patterson, Ralph D. Story, and M. Genevieve West, though, insist that what Huggins perceives as pandering was in fact Hurston's canny ability to manage the people she needed to manage so that she could perform her artistic and anthropological work at a time when no other means of self-support were available to black female artists (or non-PhD-holding anthropologists, for that matter).

5. Boas was disappointed with the end results of Hurston's first anthropological mission and Hurston stood before him even more humiliated because of all he had done to make the trip possible in the first place.

6. Hurston describes this psychic connection in *Dust Tracks on a Road*, stating that "both Max Eastman and Richmond Barthe" also shared a similar connection with Mason (128). Cheryl Wall adds that Alain Locke and Hall Johnson also "testified to psychic experiences with their benefactor," but, perhaps most important of all, Wall also recognizes that "[w]hatever other powers she possessed, and Charlotte Mason believed devoutly that they were telepathic, the power to write checks was paramount" (154).

7. For another discussion of Hurston's relationship with Mason and patronage in general, see West's *Zora Neale Hurston and American Literary Culture*. West recognizes that Hurston must have seen Mason as "the only source of funding available" (46). She wanted to continue her anthropological research, West explains, and, lacking any advanced degrees, "she could hardly have expected continuing financial support from foundations or scientific societies" (West, 46).

8. Du Bois believed that African American art should be propagandistic and fundamentally disagreed with Alain Locke's "idea that 'Beauty rather than Propaganda should be the object of Negro literature and art' " (Lorini 160). His

quarrel, of course, was not with Locke alone—he resisted the entirety of what Barbara Foley calls the "culturalist" turn of black art in the early twentieth century, which included much of the art that was produced during the Harlem Renaissance. For a full treatment of Du Bois's aesthetic, see Alessandra Lorini's " 'The Spell of Africa is Upon Me': W. E. B. Du Bois's Notion of Art as Propaganda." For a much broader discussion of early-twentieth-century African American race politics and the ways that aesthetic arguments involved politics, see Barbara Foley's *Spectres of 1919: Class and Nation in the Making of the New Negro.*

9. Walter White was a civil rights worker who served as executive director of the NAACP from 1931 until his death in 1955.

10. Stewart E. Tolnay and E. M. Beck's A *Festival of Violence: An Analysis of Southern Lynchings, 1882–1930* is currently the definitive record of Southern lynching, and I rely heavily upon it throughout the next several pages. Other texts that have proven invaluable to my understanding of lynching in the South include *Without Sanctuary: Lynching Photography in America,* by Allen, Als, Lewis, and Litwack; *At the Hands of Persons Unknown,* by Philip Dray; *Lynchings: Extralegal Violence in Florida during the 1930s,* by Walter T. Howard; " 'Whitewash' in Florida: The Lynching of Jesse James Payne and Its Aftermath," by Jack E. Davis; "Rosewood and America in the Early Twentieth Century," by David R. Colburn; and "Booker T. Washington's Tour of the Sunshine State, March 1912," by David H. Jackson.

11. The most well-known example of "legal lynching" is the Scottsboro case that took place in Alabama between 1931 and 1937. As Leon T. Howard summarizes this case, "In 1931 white southerners in Alabama convicted nine black youths of raping two white women, and sentenced eight of them to death. Although, as events proved, the evidence and facts clearly indicated innocence, white authorities carried out a series of 'legal lynchings' by repeatedly convicting and sentencing these victimized young men (even though higher courts of appeal kept overturning these convictions)" (22).

12. For a fuller account of the Ocoee riot, see Tiffany Ruby Patterson's *Zora Neale Hurston and a History of Southern Life.*

13. The Neale and Shoemaker lynchings attracted intense national attention because they were singularly brutal events at a moment when lynching had become rare enough to once again attract attention and because one of them involved the lynching of a white man who had not been accused of a crime (22). In the first of these events, which happened in 1934 in Greenwood, Florida (roughly seventy miles northwest of Tallahassee or thirty-five miles southeast of Dothan, Alabama), Claude Neal was arrested as a suspect in the murder of an eighteen-year-old white girl, Lola Cannidy, stolen from police custody, and tortured before being killed, mutilated, and partially dismembered. Before the lynching ever happened, members of the mob announced their plans to media outlets in Dothan, the news eventually reached the Associated Press, and it became a national story shortly before Neal was killed.

Joseph Shoemaker was beaten nearly to death and left to die in 1935. He was discovered and treated for his wounds but still died several days later. Shoemaker and the two other men who were attacked along with him (they survived the incident) "were guilty only of being socialists and activists" (Howard 81). Shoemaker may have been a socialist, but the political projects that he was pursuing in Tampa were not radical in any shocking sense. As Howard explains, he was a New Deal democrat who found himself in life-threatening trouble because he was simultaneously challenging the city's corruption and making ill-advised statements that overstated his socialism. According to Howard, his most "serious error in judgement was reflected in his bold, provocative statement that 'the biggest cooperative enterprise in the United States is the post office. Is this communism? If so, we want more of it' " (81).

The Shoemaker lynching drew the ire of The Socialist Party of America and the American Civil Liberties Union, Florida newspapers, and scores of smaller organizations and individuals (Howard 83); Neal's lynching, publicized as it was even before it took place, "galvanized antilynching forces," became the centerpiece of Water White's push for stronger federal antilynching laws, and even polarized the White House (Howard 64–65). White exchanged letters with Eleanor Roosevelt on a fairly regular basis, and according to Howard he "exerted great pressure on the White House over the Neale incident . . . largely through Eleanor" (65). White asked Eleanor and President Roosevelt to "make a public statement denouncing lynchings in light of the recent horrible instance 'involving Neal' " (65). According to a note that she sent to the president, Eleanor was in favor of the idea, but the president found the subject too volatile and went no farther than pledging support for antilynching legislation.

14. Kaplan also discusses Hurston's gun. As is my own inclination, Kaplan is less convinced than Hemenway that Hurston got the gun after having a knife drawn on her while she was working and collecting stories at the Everglades Cypress Lumber Company, which was near Loughman, Florida. Kaplan rightly suggests that Hurston must have felt exposed to any number of dangers because of the sheer oddity of her situation: she was "traveling in blistering heat, sleeping in her car when 'colored' hotel rooms couldn't be had, defending herself against jealous women, putting up with bedbugs, lack of sanitation, and poor food in some of the turpentine camps, sawmills, and phosphate mines she visited. Evidently, she cut an unusual figure: a single, black woman, driving her own car, toting a gun, sometimes passing for a bootlegger, offering prize money for the best stories and 'lies' " (52).

15. Hurston's letters suggest that this sense of Florida as a personal artistic haven was particularly strong in the late 1930s. In an August 1937 letter to Henry Allen Moe, for instance, Hurston wrote, from Haiti, that "as soon as I land in New York and talk to you and Lippincott I shall head for Florida to polish off this volume. . . . I cant do so well here because now the material is engulfing me" (Kaplan 404). Projecting a stronger sense of the economic factors that sent Hurston to work in the South, she wrote to Carl Van Vetchen in February 1938, from Matiland, Florida, that she had "ducked off down here for two reasons. One reason was that I just had to come, and the other was that I wanted to. I had to come because I could not stay in New York until I had made some more money. And I knew that I could get some as soon as I hand in the script for the book on Haiti. Then too, I wanted to come and get it out of the way so that I

could get back to work on FAN THE LADY. Having the tail end of the book hanging over my head was ruining my entire life. I could not work very fast in New York so I ran down here to finish it quick" (Kaplan 412–13).

16. Hurston's letter to Jones offers her fullest explanation of exactly what went wrong at Bethune-Cookman. She explains that "I found it impossible to do anything worthwhile for (A) student body of only 226 and the same students were needed for all the Choral groups, Major athletics, social groups, various dramatic groups at the same time" (317). Beyond the difficulties posed by the student body, Hurston reports that President Bethune placed ridiculous demands upon her while refusing to offer her any administrative support when she needed it and that her work was constantly underfunded (Kaplan 317–18).

17. In her recent "Shades of Darkness: Race and Environmental History," Carolyn Merchant declares that the field of environmental history has come to recognize that "slavery and soil degradation are interlinked systems of exploitation, and deep-seated connections exist between the enslavement of human bodies and the enslavement of the land" (37).

18. In *Cane*, the lynchings of Tom Burwell and Mame Lamkins occur in "Blood-Burning Moon" and "Kabnis," respectively. In the first story, Bob Stone attacks Tom Burwell and is eventually killed by him, and then Tom is attacked by a mob, dragged to an abandoned factory where he is tied to a stake, and burned alive. Toomer offers the scene in gruesome detail: "Now Tom could be seen within the flames. Only his head, erect, lean, like a blackened stone. Stench of burning flesh soaked the air. Tom's eyes popped. His head settled downward. The mob yelled" (34). Mame Lamkins is killed in the street for attempting to hide her husband when the mob was hunting for him. As with the earlier lynching, Toomer offers this one in grim detail: "They killed her in th street, an some white man seein th risin in her stomach as she lay there soppy in her blood like any cow, took an ripped her belly open, an the kid fell out. It was living; but a nigger baby aint supposed t live. So he jabbed his knife in it an stuck it t a tree. An then they all went away" (90).

19. For a full discussion of how navigation or circumlocution can allow a person to take control of a particular place, see Michel de Certeau's discussion of this issue in *The Practice of Everyday Life*. In de Certeau's terms, this amounts to an "*appropriation* of the topographical system," and such appropriations allow people to "found," "authorize," or "open" a "legitimate *theater* for practical *actions*" (de Certeau 97, 123–25). While Hurston's reclamation of space in *Jonah's Gourd Vine* and *Their Eyes Were Watching God* is what de Certeau calls an "appropriation of the topographical system," it is also what Deleuze and Guattari refer to as an act of "reterritorialization": an act of seizing and becoming enmeshed within the "milieus and rhythms" of a particular location (*Thousand Plateaus* 314). For Deleuze and Guattari, space becomes a territory when a social body gains control of, and inhabits, the space's "milieus and rhythms," which is another way of describing what Henri Lefebvre calls the "unlimited multiplicity or uncountable set of social spaces which we refer to generically as 'social space' " (86). For Deleuze and Guattari, just as for Lefebvre, space is multilayered and historical. It begins with a bedrock physical or ecological space upon which layer after layer of social

spaces (in Lefebvre's terms) or milieus (in Deleuze and Guattari's terms)—racial space, economic space, national space, etc.—have been stacked.

20. Although it is fairly easy to deconstruct the situation that Janie and Tea Cake find in the Everglades (after all, they are performing seasonal work, they are living in company housing, and they are essentially migrant workers), the wages that workers like them received were perceived as fairly lucrative by such prominent figures as Bishop Henry McNeal Turner. David H. Jackson writes that Turner "believed that Florida was a 'paradise' for blacks and a place where they could make a lot of money," ostensibly doing precisely the type of work that Janie and Tea Cake perform in *Their Eyes Were Watching God* (255).

21. For a fuller discussion of how these events mark the culmination of what Janie and Tea Cake like about the Everglades, see Philip Joseph's "The Verdict from the Porch: Zora Neale Hurston and Reparative Justice."

Afterword

1. Susan F. Beegel discusses Hemingway's spiritual and scientific engagements with nature in "Hemingway as a Naturalist." Her essay traces Hemingway's upbringing in Oak Hall, Illinois, and all of the figures—including his mother and father, Theodore Roosevelt, John Burroughs, Louis Agassiz, Carl Akeley, and Jack London—who influenced his environmental thinking. Beegel finds Hemingway a remarkable naturalist and praises his particularly keen powers of scientific observation. Although my interpretation of Hemingway's contributions to American Literature's vision of the natural world is decidedly more negative than Beegel's, her work on the origins of his environmental commitments is invaluable. Terry Tempest Williams quotes this passage from Kazin in her keynote address to the Seventh International Hemingway Conference and thoroughly agrees with his assessment of Hemingway's aptitude as a naturalist. Although they do not state it as plainly, all of the eighteen essays that are included with Williams's keynote address in Robert E. Fleming's *Hemingway and the Natural World* take Hemingway's exceptionality as a nature writer more or less for granted.

2. For the sake of clarity, I believe it is worth mentioning at the outset that *In Our Time* is a collection of loosely related short stories with a particularly complex history. The text as we have it today is composed of two narrative strands—one that features relatively conventional short stories, many featuring Nick Adams, and another composed of "chapters" (titled with roman numerals, printed with italicized text, and never longer than a single page) that critics often describe as "interchapters" or "vignettes" (which is how I will refer to them)—that critics have described as a collection of short stories, a short story cycle, a " 'fragmentary novel,' " and even a "cubist anatomy" (Brogan 31). The publication history of the book is also quite complex. For a full discussion of this issue, please see Michael Reynolds's *Hemingway: The 1930s*, "A Brief Biography," and "Ernest Hemingway's *In Our Time*" in addition to Peter A. Smith's "Hemingway's 'On the Quai at Smyrna' and the Universe of 'In Our Time.'"

3. "Indian Camp" plays a central role in the feminist backlash against Hemingway that Judith Fetterley initiated in *The Resisting Reader*. Fetterley's argument, staged in the context of *A Farewell to Arms* but essentially about Hemingway's oeuvre in general, holds that if "we weep at the end of" *A Farewell to Arms* "all our tears are ultimately for men, because in the world of *A Farewell to Arms* male life is what counts. And the message to women reading this classic love story . . . is clear and simple: the only good woman is a dead one, and even then there are questions" (71).

While *A Farewell to Arms* is the primary subject of the chapter she devotes to Hemingway, Fetterley opens her argument by claiming that "Indian Camp," with its "guilt for the attitudes men have toward women and guilt for the consequences to women of male sexuality," is a prototype for the later novel. Hemingway scholarship has struggled to find new directions since Fetterley delivered what Mark Spilka calls her "devastating" and "relentless" critique, but this is largely because her work identified sexist and masochistic elements in Hemingway's writings that *had always* been there, that everyone *had always known* to be there, and that, therefore, no one—especially those who wanted to resist Fetterley's reading—could defend in good faith ("Repossessing" 245).

Fetterly's brief treatment of "Indian Camp" is a case in point. In her summary of the story's action, Fetterley writes that "a little boy watches his father perform a contemptuous and grotesque Caesarean section on an Indian woman" (46). Fetterley's language is strong here as it is elsewhere in her larger argument, but it does capture exactly what happens in the story, which is surely part of the reason that her work has been difficult to move beyond. Since the early 1980s, critics have simply ignored the problems that Fetterly identifies in Hemingway's work; they have rejected the guilt that Hemingway lovers feel in the face of her critique and alternately decided to "read Hemingway *with* guilt" (Spilka 236); they have recapitulated Fetterley's critique; and, in rare instances that have produced some of the best Hemingway scholarship of the past thirty years, they have redeemed Hemingway through the same feminist mode of critique that Fetterley deployed in the first place.

For arguments that represent the more or less overt ways that critics have struggled against Fetterley's reading, see Robert Scholes's *Textual Power: Literary Theory and the Teaching of English*, which, published just five years after *The Resisting Reader*, operates as if Fetterley's critique had never been uttered, and Frederick Busch's "Reading Hemingway Without Guilt," which simply suggests that lovers of Hemingway ignore the problems identified by Fetterley. For an example of how critics have simply maintained the terms of Fetterley's argument, see Robert Scholes and Nancy Comley's *Hemingway's Genders: Rereading the Hemingway Text*, and for arguments that work to redeem Hemingway from a feminist perspective, see Rose Marie Burwell's *Hemingway: The Postwar Years and the Posthumous Novels*; Margaret D. Bauer's "Forget the Legend and Read the Work: Teaching Two Stories by Ernest Hemingway"; Robert Spilka's "Repossessing Papa: A Narcissistic Meditation for Literary Throwbacks"; and Joyce Wexler's "E. R. A. for Hemingway: A Feminist Defense of *A Farewell to Arms*."

4. For a discussion of Hemingway's observational aptitude and scientific perspective, see Beegel's "Eye and Heart: Hemingway's Education as a Naturalist."

5. For David J. Leigh, "L'Envoi" "throws an ironic shadow over the entire movement of Nick Adams's education into disillusionment," for Strychacz it constitutes an acquiescence to "the inversions and chaotic displacements" that riddle the entire book, and for Linda W. Wagner it "completes the emptiness of the collection" by universalizing Nick Adams's limitations and disillusionment (134, 84, 123–24).

6. I do not want to sidetrack this chapter with a discussion of Derrida, but Hemingway's "L'Envoi" should bring Derrida's *The Post Card* to mind for anyone who has read it. In *The Post Card*, which I have mentioned in my discussion of Emerson, Derrida replaces the dominant metaphor of knowledge as library or static archive with his metaphor of the "Great Telematic Network" where all knowledge is always moving, always dynamic, and only available for interpretation at momentary posts, or stopping points, in its activity of circulation (Derrida, 27). In the "Great Telematic Network," Derrida explains, every *envoi* cast into the "Great Telematic Network" is subject to the terrors of loss and interception, to all of the potentialities of linguistic, historical, and interpretive play, and to the extension of the text beyond itself, its own history, and its author. At the very least, invoking the *envoi* constitutes an opening-up rather than narrative closure or an insular hermeneutic system.

7. Since its initial publication, critics have recognized *Green Hills of Africa* as a self-indulgent book in which Hemingway gives free rein to his masculinist posturing and his disdain for politically engaged critics such as Granville Hicks and Malcolm Cowley. For a discussion of the battle with his critics that Hemingway carries out in *Green Hills*, see Robert W. Trogdon's " 'Forms of Combat': Hemingway, The Critics, and *Green Hills of Africa*."

Works Cited

Acocella, Joan. *Willa Cather and the Politics of Criticism*. Lincoln: U of Nebraska P, 2000.

Alcott, Bronson. *Ralph Waldo Emerson: An Estimate of his Character and Genius in Prose and Verse*. 1882. Philadelphia: Albert Saifer, 1968.

Allen, James, and Hilton Als, Congressman John Lewis, and Leon F. Litwack. *Without Sanctuary: Lynching Photography in America*. New Mexico: Twin Palms, 2000.

Anderson, Jill. " 'Be Up and Doing': Henry Wadsworth Longfellow and Poetic Labor." *Journal of American Studies* 37:1 (2003): 1-15.

Arac, Jonathan. "Nationalism, Hypercanonization, and *Huckleberry Finn*." *National Identities and Post-Americanist Narratives*. Ed. Donald E. Pease. Durham: Duke UP, 1994.

Asma, Stephen T. *Stuffed Animals and Pickled Heads: The Culture and Evolution of Natural History Museums*. New York: Oxford UP, 2001.

Astro, Richard. *John Steinbeck and Edward F. Ricketts: The Shaping of a Novelist*. Minneapolis: U of Minnesota P, 1973.

Badiou, Alain. *Being and Event*. 1988. Trans. Oliver Feltham. New York: Continuum, 2005.

———. *Ethics: An Essay on the Understanding of Evil*. 1993. Trans. Peter Hallward. New York: Verso, 2001.

———. *Saint Paul: The Foundation of Universalism*. 1997. Trans. Ray Brassier. Stanford: Stanford UP, 2003.

Baer, Ulrich. "*Writing for an Endangered World*" (Book Review). *Library Journal* 126:7 (2001): 92.

Baker, Houston A. Jr. Afro-American Poetics: Revisions of Harlem and the Black Aesthetic. Madison: U of Wisconsin P, 1988.

Baker, Houston A. *Modernism and the Harlem Renaissance*. Chicago: U of Chicago P, 1987.

———. *Workings of the Spirit: The Poetics of Afro-American Women's Writing*. Chicago: U of Chicago P, 1991.

Barnes, Will C. "Gifford Pinchot, Forester." *McClure's Magazine* (1893–1926) July 1908 31:3: 319–27.

Bauer, Margaret D. "Forget the Legend and Read the Work: Teaching Two Stories by Ernest Hemingway" *College Literature* 30:3 (2003): 124–37.

Beard, James Franklin, ed. The *Letters and Journals of James Fenimore Cooper.* (6 vols.) Cambridge: Harvard UP, 1960–68.

Beegel, Susan F. "Eye and Heart: Hemingway's Education as a Naturalist." Wagner-Martin, *A Historical Guide.* 53–92.

———, ed. *Hemingway's Neglected Short Fiction, New Perspectives.* Tuscaloosa: U of Alabama P, 1989.

———, Susan Shillinglaw, and Wesley N. Tiffney Jr., eds. *Steinbeck and the Environment: Interdisciplinary Approaches.* Tuscaloosa: U of Alabama P, 1997.

Belknap, Jeremy. *The History of New Hampshire.* 3 vols. (1784, 1791, 1792) Boston: Bradford and Read, 1813.

Benjamin, Walter. *The Origin of German Tragic Drama.* 1963. Trans. John Osborne. New York: Verso, 1998.

Berkson, Dorothy. " 'Born and Bred in Different Nations': Margaret Fuller and Ralph Waldo Emerson." *Patrons and Protégées: Gender, Friendship, and Writing in Nineteenth Century America.* Ed. Shirley Marchalonis. New Brunswick: Rutgers UP, 1988. 3–30.

Bloom, Harold. "Mr. America." *New York Review of Books.* 31:18 (1984). Online edition. 4 numbered sections. <http://www.nybooks.com/articles/5651>. Accessed 2 March 2005. Rpt. as "Emerson: Power at the Crossing." *Poetics of Influence.* Ed. John Hollander. New Haven: Charles Schwab, 1988. 309–23. Rpt as "Emerson: Power at the Crossing" in Buell. *Ralph Waldo Emerson* 148–58. Also rpt as "Introduction" in *Ralph Waldo Emerson.* Ed. Harold Bloom. Modern Critical Views. New York: Chelsea House, 1985.

———. *Ralph Waldo Emerson.* Ed. Harold Bloom. Modern Critical Views. New York: Chelsea House, 1985.

Bodry-Sanders, Penelope. *Carl Akeley: Africa's Collector, Africa's Savior.* New York: Paragon, 1991.

Bohlke, Brent, ed. *Willa Cather in Person: Interviews, Speeches, and Letters.* Lincoln: U of Nebraska P, 1986.

Borst, Raymond R. *Henry David Thoreau: A Reference Guide, 1835–1899.* Boston: Hall, 1987.

Botkin, Daniel. *No Man's Garden: Thoreau and a New Vision for Civilization and Nature.* Washington: Island, 2000.

Botting, Fred. *Making Monstrous: Frankenstein, Criticism, Theory.* New York: St. Martin's, 1991.

Boyd, Valerie. *Wrapped in Rainbows: The Life of Zora Neale Hurston.* New York: Scribners, 2003.

Brogan, Jacqueline Vaught. "Hemingway's *In Our Time*: A Cubist Anatomy." *The Hemingway Review* 17:2 (1998): 31–46.

Brooker, Ira. *Midwest Quarterly: A Journal of Contemporary Thought* 45:2 (2004): 137–54.

Brooks, Van Wyck. *America's Coming-of-Age.* 1915. New York: Huebsch, 1924.

———. *Three Essays on America.* New York: Dutton, 1934.

———. *The Flowering of New England: 1815–1865*. 1936. Rev. Ed. New York: World Publishing, 1946.

———, and Otto L. Bettman. *Our Literary Heritage: A Pictorial History of the Writer in America*. New York: Dutton, 1956.

Brown, Lee Rust. *The Emerson Museum: Practical Romanticism and the Pursuit of the Whole*. Cambridge: Harvard UP, 1997.

Buell, Lawrence. "The Emerson Industry in the 1980's: A Survey of Trends and Achievements." *ESQ* 30:2 (1984): 117–36.

———. *The Environmental Imagination: Thoreau, Nature Writing, and the Formation of American Culture*. Cambridge: Harvard Belknap, 1995.

———."Faulkner and the Claims of the Natural World." Kartiganer and Abadie. 1–18.

———. *The Future of Environmental Criticism: Environmental Crisis And Literary Imagination*. Malden: Blackwell, 2005.

———. "Introduction." *Selected Poems*. By Henry Wadsworth Longfellow. New York: Penguin, 1988.

———. *New England Literary Culture: From Revolution Through Renaissance*. Cambridge: Cambridge UP, 1986.

———, ed. *Ralph Waldo Emerson: A Collection of Critical Essays*. Englewood Cliffs: Prentice-Hall, 1993.

———. *Writing for an Endangered World : Literature, Culture, and Environment in the U.S. and Beyond*. Cambridge : Harvard Belknap, 2001.

Burwell, Rose Marie. *Hemingway: The Postwar Years and the Posthumous Novels*. New York: Cambridge UP, 1996.

Busch, Frederick. "Reading Hemingway Without Guilt." *New York Times Book Review* 12 January 1992: 1, 17–19.

Cafaro, Philip. "Thoreau's Virtue Ethics in *Walden*." *The Concord Saunterer* 8 (2000): 23–47.

———. "Thoreau's Environmental Ethics in *Walden*" *The Concord Saunterer* 10 (2002): 17–63.

Calhoun, Charles C. *Longfellow: A Reconsidered Life*. Boston: Beacon, 2004.

———. "The Multicultural Longfellow." *Chronicle of Higher Education* 50:37 (5/21/04): 102.

Carby, Hazel V. "The Politics of Fiction, Anthropology, and the Folk." *Their Eyes Were Watching God: A Casebook*. Ed. Cheryl Wall. New York: Oxford UP, 2000.

Carlin, Deborah. *Cather, Canon, and the Politics of Reading*. Amherst: U of Massachusetts P, 1992.

Carson, Rachel. *Silent Spring*. 1962. Boston: Houghton, Mariner, 2002.

Cather, Willa. "Cather's 1933 Radio Speech." *The Willa Cather Archive*. Multimedia. Audio. *<http://cather.unl.edu/multimedia/index.html>*. 26 Sept. 2005.

———. *My Ántonia*. 1918. New York: Penguin, 1994.

———. *O Pioneers!*1913. New York: Bantam, 1989.

———. "Escapism." 1936. *Willa Cather: Stories, Poems, and Other Writings*. New York: Library of America, 1992. 968–73.

———. "The Novel Demeuble." 1938. *Willa Cather: Stories, Poems, and Other Writings*. New York: Library of America, 1992. 834–37.

———. "Willa Cather Talks of Work." 1913. *The Kingdom of Art: Willa Cather's First Principles and Critical Statements, 1893–1896*. Lincoln: U of Nebraska P, 1966.

Cayton, Mary Kupiec. "The Making of an American Prophet: Emerson, His Audiences, and the Rise of the Culture Industry in Nineteenth-Century America." *American Historical Review* 92 (1987): 598–620. Rpt in Buell, *Ralph Waldo Emerson*. 77–100.

Chai, Leon. *The Romantic Foundations of the American Renaissance*. Ithaca: Cornell UP, 1987.

Charvat, William. *The Profession of Authorship in America, 1800–1870*. Ed. Matthew J. Bruccoli. Ohio State UP, 1968.

Chase, Richard. *The American Novel and Its Tradition*. 1957. Baltimore: Johns Hopkins UP, 1987.

Chastellux, Jean François, Marquis de. *Travels in North-America in the Years 1780–81–82*. New York: 1828.

Cheyfitz, Eric. "A Common Emerson: Ralph Waldo Emerson in an Ethnohistorical Context." *Ninteenth-Century Prose* 31:1/2 (2003): 250–81.

———. *The Poetics of Imperialism: Translation and Colonization from* The Tempest *to* Tarzan. 1991. Expanded ed. Philadelphia: U of Pennsylvania P, 1997.

———. *The Trans-Parent: Sexual Politics in the Language of Emerson*. Baltimore: Johns Hopkins UP, 1981.

Clark, H. H. "Emerson and Science." *Philological Quarterly* 10 (1931): 225–60.

Cohen, Jeffrey Jerome, ed. *Monster Theory: Reading Culture*. Minneapolis: U of Minnesota P, 1996.

Colburn, David R. "Rosewood and America in the Early Twentieth Century." *The Florida Historical Quarterly* 76:2 (1997): 175–92.

Cooper, James Fenimore. *The Letters and Journals of James Fenimore Cooper*. (6 vols.). Ed. James Franklin Beard. Cambridge: Harvard UP, 1960–68.

———. *The Deerslayer*. 1841. Albany: State U of New York P, 1985.

———. *The Last of the Mohicans*. 1826. New York: Signet, 1980.

———. *The Pathfinder: Or The Inland Sea*. 1840. New York: Penguin, 1989.

———. *The Pioneers, Or the Sources of the Susquehanna; A Descriptive Tale*. 1823. Albany: State U of New York P, 1980.

———. *The Prairie*. 1827. New York: Penguin, 1987.

Cooper, William. *A Guide in the Wilderness: Or the History of the First Settlements in The Western Counties of New York with Useful Instructions to Future Settlers*. 1810. Freeport, NY: Books for Libraries, 1970.

Crews, Frederick. "Whose American Renaissance?" *New York Review of Books* 35:16 (1988).

Cronau, Rudolf. "A Continent Despoiled." *McClure's Magazine* (1893–1926) Apr 1909 32:6: 639–48.

Cronon, William. *Changes in the Land: Indians, Colonists, and the Ecology of New England*. 1983. New York: Hill and Wang, Farrar, 2003.

———. Foreword. *Man and Nature*. 1864. Ed. David Lowenthal. Seattle: U of Washington P, 2003. ix–xii.

Dallal, Jenine Abboushi. "American Imperialism UnManifest: Emerson's 'Inquest' and Cultural Regeneration." *American Literature* 73:1 (2001): 47–83.

Dant, Elizabeth A. "Composing the World: Emerson and the Cabinet of Natural History." *Nineteenth-Century Literature* 44 (1989): 18–44.

Davis, Jack. "Conservation Is Now a Dead Word: Marjory Stoneman Douglas and the Transformation of American Environmentalism." *Environmental History* 8:1 (2003): 53–76.

Davis, Jack E. " 'Whitewash' in Florida: The Lynching of Jesse James Payne and Its Aftermath." *The Florida Historical Quarterly* 68:3 (1990): 277–98.

De Certeau, Michel. *The Practice of Everyday Life*. Trans. Steven Rendall. Berkeley: U of California P, 1988.

De Crèvecoeur, J. Hector St. John. *Letters from an American Farmer and Sketches of Eighteenth-Century America*. 1782. New York: Penguin, 1986.

Decker, Jeffrey Louis. "Disassembling the Machine in the Garden, Antihumanism and the Critique of American-Studies." *New Literary History* 23:2 (1992): 281–306.

Deleuze, Gilles, and Félix Guattari. *Anti-Oedipus: Capitalism and Schizophrenia*. Trans. Robert Hurley, Mark Seem, and Helen R. Lane. Minneapolis: U of Minneapolis P, 2003.

———. *A Thousand Plateaus: Capitalism and Shizophrenia*. Trans. Brian Massumi. Minneapolis: U of Minneapolis P, 2003.

———. *Kafka: Toward a Minor Literature*. 1975. Trans. Dana Polan. Minneapolis: U of Minneapolis P, 1986.

DeMott, Robert J. *Steinbeck's Reading: A Catalogue of Books Owned and Borrowed*. New York: Garland, 1984.

Derrida, Jacques. *The Post Card: From Socrates to Freud and Beyond*. Trans. Alan Bass. Chicago: U of Chicago P, 1987.

Dixon, Melvin. *Ride Out the Wilderness: Geography and Identity in Afro-American Literature*. Chicago: U of Chicago P, 1987.

Douglas, Ann. *The Feminization of American Culture*. New York: Knopf, 1977.

Downs, M. Catherine. *Becoming Modern: Willa Cather's Journalism*. Selinsgrove: Susquehanna UP, 1999.

Dray, Philip. *At the Hands of Persons Unknown: The Lynching of Black America*. New York: Random, 2002.

Du Bois, W. E. B. *The Souls of Black Folk*. 1903. New York: Norton, 1990.

Dwight, Timothy. *Travels in New England and New York*. 4 Vols. 1821–22. Cambridge: Belknap, Harvard, 1969.

Emerson, Ralph Waldo. "Nature." *Essays, Second Series*. In *Essays: First and Second Series*. Ed. Joel Porte. New York: Vintage, Library of America, 1990.

———. *Nature*. 1836. *The Collected Works of Ralph Waldo Emerson*. Vol 1: Nature, Addresses, and Lectures. Ed. Robert Spiller, Alfred Ferguson, et al. Cambridge: Belknap, Harvard UP, 1971. 7–45.

Evans, Constantine. "Fenimore Cooper's Libel Suits." *Syracuse University Library Associates Courier* 27:2 (1992): 47–74. Rpt online at the James Fenimore

Cooper Society Web site. <http://www.oneonta.edu/external/cooper/articles/other/1992other-evans.html>. June 14, 2005.

Faulkner, William. *Faulkner in the University*. Ed. Frederick Gwynn and Joseph Blotner. Charlottesville: U of Virginia P, 1959.

———. *Flags in the Dust*. Ed. Douglas Day. New York: Vintage: Random, 1974.

———. *Go Down, Moses*. 1942. New York: Vintage, 1990.

———. "Mississippi." *Essays, Speeches and Public Letters*. Ed. James B. Meriwether. New York: Random, 1963. 11–43.

Felton, C. C. "Simms's *Stories and Reviews*." *North American Review* 63:2 (1846): 357–81.

Fetterly, Judith. *The Resisting Reader: A Feminist Approach to American Fiction*. Bloomington: Indiana UP, 1977.

Fiedler, Leslie A. *Love and Death in the American Novel*. 1960. Rev. Ed. New York: Stein, 1966.

———. *Waiting for The End*. 1964. New York: Delta, 1964.

Fitzgerald, F. Scott. *The Great Gatsby*. 1925. New York: Scribner, 1995.

Fleming, Robert E., ed. *Hemingway and the Natural World*. Moscow: U of Idaho P, 1999.

Fletcher, Angus. "Whitman and Longfellow: Two Types of the American Poet." *Raritan: A Quarterly Review* 10:4 (1991 Spring): 131–45.

Foley, Barbara. *Spectres of 1919: Class and Nation in the Making of the New Negro*. Urbana: U of Illinois P, 2003.

Fox, Stephen R. *The American Conservation Movement: John Muir and His Legacy*. Madison: U of Wisconsin P, 1981.

Foucault, Michel. *The Order of Things: An Archaeology of the Human Sciences*. 1966. New York: Vintage, Random House, 1994.

Franklin, Wayne. *The New World of James Fenimore Cooper*. Chicago: U of Chicago P, 1982.

French, Warren. "How Green Was John Steinbeck?" Beegel, Shillinglaw, and Tiffney. 281–92.

Fromm, Harold. "Overcoming the Oversoul: Emerson's Evolutionary Existentialism." *The Hudson Review* 57:1 (2004): 71–95.

"Full Text of Taft Platform." *New York Times Archive 1851–1980*. 16 June 1908. 15 Aug. 2008. <http://query.nytimes.com/search/query?srchst=p>.

Fuller, Margaret. "American Literature: Its Position in the Present Time, and Prospects for the Future." *Papers on Literature and Art*. 1846. Facsimilie. New York: AMS, 1972. 122–59.

Gartner, Matthew. "Becoming Longfellow: Work, Manhood, and Poetry." *American Literature: A Journal of Literary History, Criticism, and Bibliography* 72:1 (2000): 59–86.

Giles, Paul. "Transnationalism and Classic American Literature." *PMLA* 118:1 (2003): 62–77.

Gioia, Dana. "Longfellow in the Aftermath of Modernism." *The Columbia History of American Poetry*. Ed. Jay Parini and Brett C. Millier. New York: Columbia UP, 1993. 64–96.

Gladstein, Clifford Eric, and Mimi Reisel Gladstein. "Revisiting the Sea of Cortez with a "Green Perspective." Beegel, Shillinglaw, and Tiffney. 161–75.

Glick, Wendell. *The Recognition of Henry David Thoreau: Selected Criticism Since 1848*. Ann Arbor: U of Michigan P, 1969.

Glotfelty, Cheryll. Introduction. *The Ecocriticism Reader: Landmarks in Literary Ecology*. Ed. Glotfelty and Harold Fromm. Athens: U of Georgia P, 1996.

Godden, Richard. "Pioneer Properties, or 'What's in a Hut?' " *James Fenimore Cooper: New Critical Essays*. Ed. Robert Clark. London: Vision 1985. 121–42.

Gonnaud, Maurice. *An Uneasy Solitude: Individual and Society in the Work of Ralph Waldo Emerson*. Trans. Lawrence Rosenwald. Princeton: Princeton UP, 1981.

Gottlieb, Robert. *Forcing the Spring: The Transformation of the American Environmental Movement*. Washington: Island, 1993.

Gougeon, Len. *Virtue's Hero: Emerson, Antislavery, and Reform*. Athens: U of Georgia P, 1990.

"Governors Cheer Roosevelt's Talk." *New York Times Archive 1851–1980*. 16 May 1908. 15 Aug. 2008. <http://query.nytimes.com/search/query?srchst=p>.

"Governors to Meet at the White House." *New York Times Archive 1851–1980*. 10 May 1908. 15 Aug. 2008. <http://query.nytimes.com/search/query?srchst=p>.

"Governors to Meet by Themselves." *New York Times Archive 1851–1980*. 16 May 1908. 15 Aug. 2008. <http://query.nytimes.com/search/query?srchst=p>.

Gruesz, Kirsten Silva. "Feeling for the Fireside: Longfellow, Lynch, and the Topography of Poetic Power." *Sentimental Men: Masculinity and the Politics of Affect in American Culture*. Ed. Mary Chapman and Glenn Hendler. Berkeley: U of California P, 1999. 43–63.

Habermas, Jürgen. *The Theory of Communicative Action*. "Volume 2: Lifeworld and System: A Critique of Functionalist Reason." 1981. Trans. Thomas McCarthy. Boston: Beacon, 1987.

Hagemann, E. R. " 'Only Let the Story End as Soon as Possible': Time-and-History in Ernest Hemingway's *In Our Time*. *Critical Essays on Hemingway's* In Our Time. Ed. Michael S. Reynolds. Boston: Hall, 1983. 52–59.

Halberstam, Judith. *Skin Shows: Gothic Horror and the Technology of Horror*. Durham: Duke UP, 1995.

Haraway, Donna. *Modest_Witness@Second_Millennium.FemaleMan©_Meets_Oncomouse™: Feminism and Technoscience*. New York: Routledge, 1997.

———. "Teddy Bear Patriarchy: Taxidermy in the Garden of Eden, New York City, 1908–1936." *Primate Visions: Gender, Race, and Nature in the Modern World*. New York: Routledge, 1989. 26–58.

Haralson, Eric L. "Mars in Petticoats: Longfellow and Sentimental Masculinity." *Nineteenth-Century Literature* 51:3 (1996): 327–56.

Harding, Walter, and Michael Meyer. *The New Thoreau Handbook*. New York: New York UP, 1980.

Harrison, Brady. "The Young Americans: Emerson, Walker, and the Early Literature of American Empire." *American Studies* 40:3 (1999): 75–97.

Hays, Samuel P. *Conservation and the Gospel of Efficiency: The Progressive Conservation Movement, 1890-1920.* New York: MacMillan, 1969.

———. *Explorations in Environmental History.* Pittsburgh: U of Pittsburgh P, 1998.

———. "From Conservation to Environment: Environmental Politics in the United States since World War II." *Environmental Review* 6 (Fall 1982): 14–29.

———. *A History of Environmental Politics Since 1945.* Pittsburgh: U of Pittsburgh P, 2000.

Hays, Samuel P., and Barbara D. Hays. *Beauty, Health, and Permanence: Environmental Politics in the United States, 1955–1985.* New York: Cambridge UP, 1987.

Hedgpeth, Joel W. "John Steinbeck: Late-Blooming Environmentalist." Beegel, Shillinglaw, and Tiffney. 293–309.

Hemenway, Robert. *Zora Neale Hurston: A Literary Biography.* Urbana: U of Illinois P, 1977.

Hemingway, Ernest. *In Our Time.* 1925. New York: Scribners, 1996.

———. *Green Hills of Africa.* 1935. New York: Simon, Touchstone, 1996.

Hicks, Granville. "The Case Against Willa Cather." *Willa Cather and Her Critics.* Ed. James Schroeter. Ithaca: Cornell UP, 1967. 139–47. Rpt from *English Journal* (November 1933).

Higginson, Thomas Wentworth. *Henry Wadsworth Longfellow.* American Men of Letters. Boston: Houghton, 1902.

Holmes, Oliver Wendell. *Ralph Waldo Emerson.* American Men of Letters. Boston: Houghton, Riverside, 1885.

Horwitz, Howard. *By Law of Nature: Form and Value in Nineteenth-Century America.* New York: Oxford UP, 1991.

Howard, Walter T. *Lynchings: Extralegal Violence in Florida during the 1930s.* Selinsgrove: Susquehanna UP, 1995.

Huet, Marie-Hélène. *Monstrous Imagination.* Cambridge: Harvard UP, 1993.

Huggins, Nathan Irvin. *The Harlem Renaissance.* New York: Oxford UP, 1971.

Hurston, Zora Neale. *Dust Tracks On A Road.* 1942. New York: Harper, 1991.

———. *Jonah's Gourd Vine.* 1934. New York: Harper, 1990.

———. *Mules and Men.* 1935. New York: Harper, 1990.

———. *Their Eyes Were Watching God.* 1937. New York: Harper, 1990.

———. *Zora Neale Hurston: A Life in Letters.* Ed. Carla Kaplan. New York: Anchor, Random, 2003.

Ingebretsen, Edward J. "Monster-Making: A Politics of Persuasion." *Journal of American Culture* 21:2 (1998): 25–34.

———. *At Stake: Monsters and the Rhetoric of Fear in Public Culture.* Chicago: U of Chicago P, 2001.

Irmscher, Christoph. "Longfellow Redux." *Raritan: A Quarterly Review* 21:3 (2002): 100-29.

Jackson, David H. Jr. "Booker T. Washington's Tour of the Sunshine State, March 1912." *The Florida Historical Quarterly* 81:3: 254–78.

Jackson, Virginia. "Longfellow's Tradition: Or, Picture-Writing a Nation." *Modern Language Quarterly: A Journal of Literary History* 59:4 (1998):471–96.

———. "Poe, Longfellow, and the Institution of Poetry." *Poe Studies/Dark Romanticism: History, Theory, Interpretation* 33:1-2 (2000): 23–28.

Jameson, Fredric. *Postmodernism: Or, The Cultural Logic of Late Capitalism.* 1991. Durham: Duke UP, 2003.

Johnson, Rochelle. Introduction. *Rural Hours.* By Susan Fenimore Cooper. Ed. Rochelle Johnson and Daniel Patterson. Athens. U of Georgia P, 1998. ix–xxii.

———. "Walden, Rural Hours, and the Dilemma of Representation." *Thoreau's Sense of Place: Essays in American Environmental Writing.* Ed. Richard J. Schneider. 179–93.

Joseph, Philip. "The Verdict from the Porch: Zora Neale Hurston and Reparative Justice." *American Literature* 74:3 (2002): 455–83.

Kalm, Peter. *Peter Kalm's Travels in North America.* The English Version of 1770. Trans. and ed. Adolph B. Benson. 2 Vols. 1937. New York: Dover, 1966.

Kaplan, Amy. "A Call for a Truce." *American Literary History* 17:1 (2005): 141–47.

Kartiganer, Donald M., and Ann J Abadie, eds. *Faulkner and the Natural World: Faulkner and Yoknapatawpha, 1996.* Jackson: U of Mississippi P, 1999.

Kazin, Alfred. *On Native Grounds: An Interpretation of Modern American Prose Literature.* 1942. New York: Harvest, Harcourt, 1995.

Kelly, James C. "John Steinbeck and Ed Ricketts: Understanding Life in the Great Tide Pool." Beegel, Shillinglaw, and Tiffney. 27–42.

Kelly, William P. *Plotting America's Past: Fenimore Cooper and the Leatherstocking Tales.* Carbondale: Southern Illinois UP, 1983.

Killingsworth, M. Jimmie. *Walt Whitman and the Earth: A Study in Ecopoetics.* Iowa City: U of Iowa P, 2004.

Kimes, William F., and Maymie B. Kimes. *John Muir: A Reading Bibliography.* Fresno: Panorama West, 1986.

Kinnamon, Keneth. "Hemingway and Politics." *The Cambridge Companion to Hemingway.* Ed. Scott Donaldson. New York: Cambridge UP, 1996.

Kolodny, Annette. *The Lay of the Land: Metaphor as Experience and History in American Life and Letters.* Chapel Hill: U of North Carolina P, 1975.

Konvitz, Milton R, ed. "Preface." *The Recognition of Ralph Waldo Emerson: Selected Criticism Since 1837.* Ann Arbor: U of Michigan P, 1972.

Kroeber, Karl. *Ecological Literary Criticism: Romantic Imagining and the Biology of Mind.* New York: Columbia UP, 1994.

Kuklick, Bruce. "Myth and Symbol in American Studies." *American Quarterly* 24 (1972): 435–50. Rpt in *Locating American Studies: The Evolution of a Discipline.* Baltimore: Johns Hopkins UP, 1999. 71–90.

Lawrence, D. H. *Studies in Classic American Literature.* 1923. New York: Penguin, 1990.

Lear, Linda. "Introduction." *Silent Spring.* 1962. Boston: Houghton, Mariner, 2002.

Lefebvre, Henri. *The Production of Space.* 1974. Trans. Donald Nicholson Smith. Malden: Blackwell, 1991.

Leigh, David J., S. J. "*In Our Time*: The Interchapters as Structural Guides to a Psychological Pattern." *Critical Essays on Hemingway's* In Our Time. Ed. Michael S. Reynolds. Boston: Hall, 1983. 130–37.

Lentricchia, Frank. *Modernist Quartet.* New York: Cambridge UP, 1994.

Leopold, Aldo. *A Sand County Almanac.* 1949. New York: Oxford UP, 2001.

Leverenz, David. *Manhood and the American Renaissance.* Ithaca: Cornell UP, 1989.

Link, Eric Carl. "American Nationalism and the Defense of Poetry." *Southern Quarterly: A Journal of the Arts in the South*, 41:2 (2003): 4 sections. 4 March, 2004. <http://vnweb.hwwilsonweb.com/hww>.

———. "Canon Formation and Marginality." *Essays in Arts and Sciences* 28 (1999): 17–33.

Lipsitz, George. "Our America." *American Literary History* 17:1 (2005): 135–47.

Lisca, Peter. *The Wide World of John Steinbeck.* New Brunswick: Rutgers UP, 1958. New York: Gordian, 1981.

Ljungquist, Kent P. "The 'Little War' and Longfellow's Dilemma: New Documents in the Plagiarism Controversy of 1845." *Resources for American Literary Study* 23:1 (1997): 28–57.

Locke, Alain. Untitled review of *Their Eyes Were Watching God. Opportunity* (1 June 1938). Rpt in *Zora Neale Hurston: Critical Perspectives Past and Present.* Ed. Henry Louis Gates Jr. and K. A. Appiah. New York: Amistad, 1993. 18.

Loewen, Shawn. "The New Canaan: Abundance, Scarcity, and the Changing Climate of Nature Writing in Nineteenth-Century America." *ISLE: Interdisciplinary Studies in Literature and Environment* 8:1 (2001): 97–114.

Longfellow, Henry Wadsworth. "The Defence of Poetry." *The North American Review* 34:74 (1832): 56–78.

———. *Evangeline.* In *Selected Poems.* Ed. Lawrence Buell. New York: Penguin, 1988.

———. *Kavanagh: A Tale.* Boston: Ticknor, Reed, and Fields, 1849. *Longfellow: Poems and Other Writings.* New York: Penguin, Library of America, 2000. 703–90.

———. "The Literary Spirit of Our Country" *The United States Literary Gazette.* 1 April 1824. 24–28. Rpt in *Poems and Other Writings.* New York: Library of America, 2000. 791–95.

———. "Our Native Writers." In Higginson. 30–36.

———. *The Song of Hiawatha.* In *Poems and Other Writings.* New York: Library of America, 2000.

Longfellow, Samuel. *The Life of Henry Wadsworth Longfellow.* 2 Vols. Boston: Ticknor, 1886.

Lowell, James Russell. "Longfellow's *Kavanagh*: Nationality in Literature." *North American Review* 61:1 (1849): 196–215.

Lynch, Ann T, "Bibliography of Works by and about John Muir, 1869–1978," *Bulletin of Bibliography* 36:2: 71–80.

Lynn, Kenneth S. "The Troubled Fisherman." *New Critical Approaches to the Short Stories of Ernest Hemingway*. Ed. Jackson J. Benson. Durham: Duke UP, 1990.

Marsh, George Perkins. "Address to the Agricultural Society of Rutland County." 1847. *Online Research Center: George Perkins Marsh, Special Collections, Bailey/Howe Library, University of Vermont*. 1 June 2007. <http://bailey2.uvm.edu/specialcollections/pub-agsocaddr.html>.

———. *Man and Nature*. 1864. Ed. David Lowenthal. Seattle: U of Washington P, 2003.

Marx, Leo. *The Machine in the Garden: Technology and the Pastoral Ideal in America*. 1964. New York: Oxford UP, 2004.

———. "On Recovering the 'Ur' Theory of American Studies." *Literary History* 17:1 (2005): 118–34.

Mathews, Cornelius. "Nationality in Literature." *American Literature, American Culture*. Ed. Gordon Hunter. New York: Oxford UP, 1999. Rpt from *The United States Magazine, and Democratic Review* 20:105 (1847): 264–73.

Matthiessen, F. O. *American Renaissance: Art and Expression in the Age of Emerson and Whitman*. 1941. New York: Oxford UP, 1968.

McGill, Meredith. "Poe, Literary Nationalism, and Authorial Identity." *The American Face of Edgar Allan Poe*. Ed. Shawn Rosenheim and Stephen Rachman. Baltimore: Johns Hopkins UP, 1995.272–304.

McGregor, Robert Kuhn. *A Wider View of the Universe: Henry Thoreau's Study of Nature*. Urbana: U of Illinois P, 1997.

McKusick, James. *Green Writing: Romanticism and Ecology*. New York: St. Martin's, 2000.

McMurry, Andrew. *Environmental Renaissance: Emerson, Thoreau, and the Systems of Nature*. Athens. U of Georgia P, 2003.

Merchant, Carolyn. *The Columbia Guide to American Environmental History*. New York: Columbia UP, 2002.

———. *The Death of Nature: Women, Ecology, and the Scientific Revolution*. 1980. New York: Harper, 1990.

———. *Ecological Revolutions: Nature, Gender, and Science in New England*. Chapel Hill: U of North Carolina P, 1989.

———. "Shades of Darkness: Race and Environmental History." *Environmental History* 8:3 (2003): 380–94.

———. "Women of the Progressive Conservation Movement." *Environmental Review* 8 (Spring 1984): 57–86.

Meyer, Michael. *Several More Lives to Live: Thoreau's Political Reputation in America*. Westport: Greenwood, 1977.

Miller, Perry. "The Romantic Dilemma in American Nationalism and the Concept of Nature." *Nature's Nation*. Cambridge: Belknap, Harvard UP, 1967. Rpt from *Harvard Theological Review* 48:4 (1955): 239–53.

———. *The Raven and the Whale: Poe, Melville, and the New York Literary Scene*. 1956. Baltimore: Johns Hopkins UP, 1997.

Mitchell, Charles E. *Individualism and Its Discontents: Appropriations of Emerson,1880–1950*. Amherst: U of Massachusetts P, 1997.

"Mr. Taft's Speech." *New York Times Archive 1851–1980*. 22 Aug. 1908. 15 Aug. 2008. <http://query.nytimes.com/search/query?srchst=p>.

Nash, Roderick, ed. *American Environmentalism: Readings in Conservation History*. New York: McGraw-Hill, 1990.

———. *The Rights of Nature: A History of Environmental Ethics*. Madison: U of Wisconsin P, 1989.

———. *Wilderness and the American Mind*. 1967. New Haven: Yale UP, 1970.

Newman, Lance. *Our Common Dwelling: Henry Thoreau, Transcendentalism, and the Class Politics of Nature*. New York: Palgrave, 2005.

Norwood, Vera. *Made from This Earth: American Women and Nature*. Chapel Hill: U of North Carolina P, 1993.

O'Brien, Sharon. *Willa Cather: The Emerging Voice*. New York: Oxford UP, 1987.

Oelschlaeger, Max. *The Idea of Wilderness: From Prehistory to the Age of Ecology*. New Haven: Yale UP, 1991.

———. "Environment and the 21st Century: A Thoreauvian Interlude." *The Concord Saunterer* 8 (2000): 3–14.

Osborn, Fairfield. *Our Plundered Planet*. Boston: Little, Brown, 1948.

Packer, B. L. *Emerson's Fall: A New Interpretation of the Major Essays*. New York: Continuum, 1982.

Packer, Barbara. "The Transcendentalists." *The Cambridge History of American Literature*. Vol 2. Eds. Sacvan Bercovitch and Cyrus Patel. New York: Cambridge UP, 1995. 329–604.

Parrington, Vernon Louis. *Main Currents in American Thought: An Interpretation of American Literature from the Beginnings to 1920*. 3 Vols. New York: Harcourt, 1927.

Patterson, Tiffany Ruby. *Zora Neale Hurston and a History of Southern Life*. Philadelphia: Temple UP, 2005.

Pease, Donald E. "New Americanists: Revisionist Interventions into the Canon." *boundary 2* 17:1 (1990): 1–37. Rpt in *Revisionist Interventions into the Americanist Canon*. Ed. Donald E. Pease. Durham: Duke UP, 1994. 1–37.

———. "Emerson, Nature, and the Sovereignty of Influence." *boundary 2* 8:3 (1980): 43–74.

Piacentino, Edward J. "The Poe-Longfellow Plagiarism Controversy: A New Critical Notice in The Southern Chronicle." *Mississippi Quarterly: The Journal of Southern Culture* 42:2 (1989): 173–82.

"Platform Drafted for the Convention." *New York Times Archive 1851–1980*. 8 June 1908. 15 Aug. 2008. <http://query.nytimes.com/search/query?srchst=p>.

Porte, Joel, and Saundra Morris, eds. *The Cambridge Companion to Ralph Waldo Emerson*. Cambridge: Cambridge UP, 1999.

Porter, Carolyn. *Seeing and Being: The Plight of the Participant Observer in Emerson, James, Adams, and Faulkner*. Middletown: Wesleyan UP, 1981.

Pratt, Mary Louise. *Imperial Eyes: Travel Writing and Transculturation*. New York: Routledge, 1992.

Preston, Douglas J. *Dinosaurs in the Attic: An Excursion into the American Museum of Natural History*. New York: St. Martin's, 1986.

Prewitt, Wiley C. Jr. "Return of the Big Woods: Hunting and Habitat in Yoknapatawpha." Kartiganer and Abadie. 198–221.

Putnam, Ann. "Memory, Grief, and the Terrain of Desire: Hemingway's *Green Hills of Africa*." *Hemingway and the Natural World*. Ed. Robert E. Fleming. Moscow: U of Idaho P, 1999. 165–74.

Radway, Janice A. "What's in a Name? Presidential Address to the American Studies Association, 20 November 1998." *American Quarterly* 51:1 (1999): 1–32.

Rans, Geoffrey. *Cooper's Leather-Stocking Novels: A Secular Reading*. Chapel Hill: U of North Carolina P, 1991.

Reising, Russell. *Loose Ends: Closure and Crisis in the American Social Text*. Durham: Duke UP, 1996.

Reynolds, Michael. *Critical Essays on Ernest Hemingway's* In Our Time. Boston: Hall, 1983.

———. *Hemingway: The 1930s*. New York: Norton, 1997.

———. "Hemingway's *In Our Time*: The Biography of a Book." *Modern American Short Story Sequences: Composite Fictions and Fictive Communities*. Ed. J. Gerald Kennedy. New York: Cambridge UP, 1995. 35–51.

———. "Ernest Hemingway 1899–1961: A Brief Biography." Wagner-Martin, *A Historical Guide* 15–50.

Ringe, Donald A. *James Fenimore Cooper*. Updated Ed. Boston: Twayne, Hall, 1988.

———. *The Pictorial Mode: Space and Time in the Art of Bryant, Irving, and Cooper*. Lexington: UP of Kentucky, 1971.

Robinson, David "Emerson's Natural Theology and the Paris Naturalists: Towards a Theory of Animated Nature." *Journal of the History of Ideas* 41 (1980): 69–88.

Robinson, E. Arthur. "Conservation in Cooper's The Pioneers." *PMLA* 82:7 (1967): 564–78.

Romero, Lora. *Home Fronts: Nineteenth-Century Domesticity and Its Critics*. Durham: Duke UP, 1997.

"Roosevelt Invites Governors to Meet." *New York Times Archive 1851-1980*. 20 Feb. 1909. 15 Aug. 2008. <http://query.nytimes.com/search/query?srchst=p>.

"Roosevelt Policies Must Go On." *New York Times Archive 1851-1980*. 23 June 1908. 15 Aug. 2008. <http://query.nytimes.com/search/query?srchst=p>.

Rosowski, Susan J. "Willa Cather's Ecology of Place." *Western American Literature* 30:1 (1995): 37–51.

Rossi, William. "Thoreau's Transcendental Ecocentrism." *Thoreau's Sense of Place: Essays in American Environmental Writing*. Ed. Richard J. Schneider. Iowa City: U of Iowa P, 2000. 28–43.

Rowe, John Carlos. *At Emerson's Tomb: The Politics of Classic American Literature.* New York: Columbia UP, 1997.

Ryan, Melissa, "The Enclosure of America: Civilization and Confinement in Willa Cather's *O Pioneers!*" *American Literature* 72:2 (2003): 275–303.

Sale, Kirkpatrick. *The Green Revolution: The American Environmental Movement, 1962–1992.* New York: Hill and Wang, 1993.

Sanders, Scott Russell. "Speaking a Word for Nature." *The Ecocriticism Reader: Landmarks in Literary Ecology.* Ed. Cheryll Glotfelty and Harold Fromm. 182–95.

Santayana, George. *The Genteel Tradition: Nine Essays by George Santayana.* Ed Douglas L. Wilson. Lincoln: Bison, U of Nebraska P, 1998.

———. "Genteel American Poetry." In *The Genteel Tradition.* 72–76. Rpt. from *New Republic* III: 30 (May 29, 1915).

———. "The Genteel Tradition in American Philosophy." In *The Genteel Tradition.* 37–64. rpt from *University of California Chronicle* 13:4 (October 11, 1911).

———. "The Moral Background" In *The Genteel Tradition.* 77–98. Rpt from *Character and Opinion in the United States* (1920).

Sattelmeyer, Robert. "Walden: Climbing the Canon." *Nineteenth-Century Prose* 31:2 (2004): 12–29.

Scharnhorst, Gary. *Henry David Thoreau: A Case Study in Canonization.* Columbia: U of South Carolina P, 1993.

Schwind, Jean. "The Benda Illustrations to *My Ántonia*: Cather's 'Silent' Supplement to Jim Burden's Narrative. *PMLA* 100:1 (1985): 51–67.

Sessions, George, ed. *Deep Ecology for the 21st Century: Readings on the Philosophy and Practice of the New Environmentalism.* Boston: Shambhala, 1995.

Shabecoff, Phillip. *Earth Rising: American Environmentalism in the 21st Century.* Washington, DC: Island, 2000.

———. *A Fierce Green Fire: The American Environmental Movement.* Washington: Island, 2003.

Sheets-Pyenson, Susan. *Cathedrals of Science: The Development of Colonial Natural History Museums during the Late Nineteenth Century.* Montreal: McGill-Queen's UP, 1988.

Shillinglaw, Susan. "Introduction." *Cannery Row.* By John Steinbeck. New York: Penguin, 1994.

Slotkin, Richard. *The Fatal Environment: The Myth of the Frontier in the Age of Industrialization 1800–1890.* New York: Atheneum, 1985.

Smith, Henry Nash. *Virgin Land: The American West as Symbol and Myth.* 1950. Cambridge: Harvard UP, 1978.

Smith, Peter A. "Hemingway's 'On the Quai at Smyrna' and the Universe of 'In Our Time." *Studies in Short Fiction* 24:2 (1987); 159–62.

Smith, Stephanie A. *Conceived by Liberty: Maternal Figures and Nineteenth-Century American Literature.* Ithaca: Cornell UP, 1994.

Spilka, Mark. "Repossessing Papa: A Narcissistic Meditation for Literary Throwbacks." *Rereading Modernism: New Directions in Feminist Criticism.* Ed. Lisa Rado. New York: Garland, 1994. 231–52.

Spiller, Robert. *Fenimore Cooper: Critic of His Times*. New York: Russell, 1963.

Steinbeck, John. *America and Americans*. 1966. *America and Americans and Selected Nonfiction*. Ed. Susan Shillinglaw and Jackson J. Benson. New York: Viking, 2002. 331–404.

———. "Let's Go After the Neglected Treasures Beneath the Seas." *Popular Science* (September 1966), 84–87.

———. *Cannery Row*. 1945. New York: Penguin, 1994.

———. *The Grapes of Wrath*. 1939. New York: Penguin, 1999.

———. "I am a Revolutionary." *America and Americans and Selected Nonfiction*. Ed. Susan Shillinglaw and Jackson J. Benson. New York: Viking, 2002. 89–90.

———. *The Log from the* Sea of Cortez. 1951. New York: Penguin, 1995. Partial rpt. of *Sea of Cortez*. 1941.

———. *Of Mice and Men*. 1937. New York: Bantam, 1984.

———. *Sweet Thursday*. 1954. New York: Bantam, 1972.

———. *To a God Unknown*. 1933. New York: Penguin, 1995.

———. *Tortilla Flat*. 1935. New York: Penguin, 1986.

———. *Travels with Charley*. 1962. New York: Penguin, 1986.

Story, Ralph. "Patronage and the Harlem Renaissance: You Get What You Pay For." *College Language Association Journal* 32:3 (1989): 284–95.

Stout, Janis. *Willa Cather: The Writer and Her World*. Charlottesville: UP of Virginia, 2000.

Strauch, Carl F. "Emerson's Sacred Science." *PMLA* 73:3 (1958): 237–50.

Strychacz, Thomas. "*In Our Time*, Out of Season." *The Cambridge Companion to Hemingway*. Ed. Scott Donaldson. New York: Cambridge UP, 1996.

Suckow, Ruth. "Short Stories of Distinction." *Register* [Des Moines, Iowa], 12 September 1926. Rpt. in Reynolds, *Critical Essays*. 26.

Sutton, Philip. *Explaining Environmentalism: In Search of a New Social Movement*. Burlington: Ashgate, 2000.

Swann, Charles. "Guns Mean Democracy: *The Pioneers* and the Game Laws." *James Fenimore Cooper: New Critical Essays*. Ed. Robert Clark. Ipswich: Vision, 1985. 96–120.

Teichgraeber, Richard F III. *Sublime Thoughts/Penny Wisdom: Situating Emerson and Thoreau in the American Market*. Baltimore: Johns Hopkins UP, 1995.

Thoreau, Henry David. *Walden*. Walden *and Other Writings*. Ed. Brooks Atkinson. New York: Modern Library-Random House, 1992. 1–312.

———. "Walking." Walden *and Other Writings*. 627–63.

Tichi, Cecelia. *New World, New Earth: Environmental Reform in American Literature from the Puritans through Whitman*. New Haven: Yale UP, 1979.

Timmerman, John H. "Steinbeck's Environmental Ethic: Humanity in Harmony with the Land." Beegel, Shillinglaw, and Tiffney. 310–22.

"To Guard Our Resources." *New York Times Archive 1851-1980*. 9 June 1908. 15 Aug. 2008. <http://query.nytimes.com/search/query?srchst=p>.

Tolnay, Stewart E., and E. M. Beck. *A Festival of Violence: An Analysis of Southern Lynchings, 1882–1930*. Chicago: U of Illinois P, 1995.

Tompkins, Jane. *Sensational Designs: The Cultural Work of American Fiction, 1790–1860.* New York: Oxford UP, 1985.

Toomer, Jean. *Cane.* 1923. New York: Liveright, 1993.

Torgovnick, Marianna. "Stuffed Animals." *Transition* 0:54 (1991): 59–67.

Traub, Lindsey. "Woman Thinking: Margaret Fuller, Ralph Waldo Emerson, and the American Scholar." *Soft Canons: American Women Writers and Masculine Tradition.* Ed. Karen L. Kilcup. Iowa City: U of Iowa P, 1999.

Twain, Mark. "Fenimore Cooper's Literary Offences." 1895. January 14, 2005. <http://etext.lib.virginia.edu/railton/projects/rissetto/offense.html>.

Urgo, Joseph. "*My Ántonia* and the National Parks Movement." *Cather Studies* 5:1 (2003): 44–63.

Valerius, Karyn Michele. *Misconceptions: Monstrosity and the Politics of Interpretation in American Culture from the Antinomian Controversy to Biotechnology.* Diss. SUNY Stony Brook 2000.

Vogt, William *Road to Survival.* New York: William Sloane, 1948.

Waggoner, Hyatt H. *American Poets: From the Puritans to the Present.* Boston: Houghton, 1968.

Wagner, Linda W. "Juxtaposition in Hemingway's *In Our Time.*" *Critical Essays on Ernest Hemingway's In Our Time.* Ed. Michael S. Reynolds. Boston: Hall, 1983. 120–29.

Wagner-Martin, Linda. *Ernest Hemingway: Seven Decades of Criticism.* East Lansing: Michigan State UP, 1998.

———, ed. *A Historical Guide to Ernest Hemingway.* New York: Oxford UP, 2002.

Wall, Cheryl. *Women of the Harlem Renaissance.* Bloomington: Indiana UP, 1995.

Wallace, James D. *Early Cooper and His Audience.* New York: Columbia UP, 1986.

Wallace, Joseph. *A Gathering of Wonders: Behind the Scenes at The American Museum of Natural History.* New York: St. Martin's, 2000.

Walls, Laura Dassow. *Emerson's Life in Science: The Culture of Truth.* Ithaca: Cornell UP, 2003.

Washington, Booker T. *Up From Slavery.* 1901. In *Three Negro Classics.* New York: Avon, 1999.

Weisbuch, Robert. "Post-Colonial Emerson and the Erasure of Europe." Porte and Morris. 192—217.

Welling, Bart H. "A Meeting with Old Ben: Seeing and Writing Nature in Faulkner's *Go Down,Moses.*" *Mississippi Quarterly* 55:4 (2002): 461–96.

Welliver, Judson C. "The National Water Power Trust." *McClure's Magazine* (1893–1926) May 1909 33:1: 35–39.

West, M. Genevieve. *Zora Neale Hurston and American Literary Culture.* Gainesville, U of Florida P, 2005.

Westling, Louise. *The Green Breast of the New World: Landscape, Gender, and American Fiction.* Athens: U of Georgia P, 1996.

Wexler, Joyce. "E. R. A. For Hemingway: A Feminist Defense of *A Farewell to Arms. Georgia Review* 35 (Spring 1981): 111–23.

White, Lynn Jr. "The Historical Roots of Our Ecologic Crisis." *Science* 10 Mar. 1967: 1203–07.

Wider, Sarah Ann. *The Critical Reception of Emerson: Unsettling all Things.* Rochester: Camden, 2000.

Widmer, Edward. *Young America: The Flowering of Democracy in New York City.* New York: Oxford UP, 1999.

Williams, Cecil B. *Henry Wadsworth Longfellow.* New York: Twayne, 1964.

Williams, Terry Tempest. " 'Hemingway and the Natural World' Keynote Address, Seventh International Hemingway Conference." *Hemingway and the Natural World.* Ed. Robert E. Fleming. Moscow: U of Idaho P, 1999. 7–17.

Willis, Lloyd. "Henry Wadsworth Longfellow, United States National Literature, and the Canonical Erasure of Material Nature." *American Transcendental Quarterly* 20:4 (2006): 629–46.

———. Why Isn't He So Green?: John Steinbeck's Monstrous Ecology." *The Journal of American Culture* 28:4 (2005): 357–67.

Wilson, Douglas L., ed. *The Genteel Tradition: Nine Essays by George Santayana.* By George Santayana. 1967. Lincoln: Bison, U of Nebraska P, 1998.

Wilson, Sarah. " 'Fragmentary and Inconclusive' Violence: National History and Literary Form in *The Professor's House.*" *American Literature* 75:3 (2003): 571–99.

Wittenberg, Judith Bryant. "*Go Down, Moses* and the Discourse of Environmentalism." *New Essays on* Go Down, Moses. Ed. Linda Wagner-Martin. New York: Cambridge UP, 1996. 49–71.

Wolfe, Alan. "Anti-American Studies." *The New Republic,* 10 Feb. 2003: 25–32.

Woodberry, George Edward. *Ralph Waldo Emerson.* New York: Macmillan, 1907.

Woodress, James. *Willa Cather: Her Life and Art.* New York: Pegasus, 1970.

"World Conference on Conservation." *New York Times Archive 1851-1980.* 20 Feb. 1909. 15 Aug. 2008. <http://query.nytimes.com/search/query?srchst=p>.

Worster, Donald, ed. *American Environmentalism: The Formative Period: 1860–1915.* New York: Wiley, 1973.

———. *Nature's Economy: A History of Ecological Ideas.* Cambridge: Cambridge UP, 1977.

———. "Thoreau and the American Passion for Wilderness." *The Concord Saunterer* 10 (2002): 5–14.

Wright, Richard. "Between Laughter and Tears." *New Masses* (5 October 1937). Review of *Their Eyes Were Watching God.* Rpt in *Zora Neale Hurston: Critical Perspectives Past and Present.* Ed. Henry Louis Gates Jr. and K. A. Appiah. New York: Amistad, 1993. 16–17.

Žižek, Slavoj. *Looking Awry: An Introduction to Jacques Lacan through Popular Culture.* Cambridge: MIT P, 1991.

Index

Abbey, Edward, 91
abstract space, 26–27
abstraction, 16, 22, 25, 26, 27, 55, 63, 76, 120
Africa, 3, 16, 32, 34–35, 131–33, 158 n23
Akeley, Carl, 158 n 23, 164 n1
Alcott, Bronson, 19
Allee, W. C., 90
American Museum of Natural History, 98, 155 n9, 158 n 23
American Studies, 11, 12, 13, 139 n6
anxiety, 4, 6, 7, 33, 37, 46, 84, 103, 111, 133, 139 n5, 146 n6
astronomy, as space, as symbol, as metonym, 24, 25, 27, 35, 84, 101
Austin, Mary, 75

Badiou, Alain, 10–11, 136 n 4, 138 n5
Baker, Houston, 117–19
Barnard College, 105
Belknap, Jeremy, 4, 6–10, 43–45, 132, 138, 147 n9, 147 n11
Benjamin, Walter, 66–67, 147 n9
Bethune, Mary McCleod, 114, 163 n16
Bethune-Cookman College, 113–14, 163 n 16
Brooks, Van Wyck, 14–15, 28, 38–43, 52, 55, 68–75, 145–46 n3, 149 n3, 151 n13, 152 n 16; works: *America's Coming of Age*, 28, 40, 69, 71–73; *Three Essays on America*, 69, *The Flowering of New England*, 70, 149 n3, 151 n14
Bloom, Harold, 19, 29–30, 142 n5, 143 n 6
Brown, Lee Rust, 51, 141 n3
Bryant, William Cullen, 20, 55
Buell, Lawrence, 30, 35, 142 n5, 143 n6, 144 n8 and n9, 149 n3

Carson, Rachel, 5, 17, 101–102, 145 n9, 152 n15, 159 n25
Cather, Willa, 1, 3–4, 11, 14–17, 21, 74–77, 79–86, 89–90, 101, 103, 125–27, 132, 153 n3, 155 n9, 156 n10, 157 n14; works: *My Ántonia*, 2, 79, 81–83, 85–86, 89, 153 n3, 157 n17, *O Pioneers!*, 79, 81–89; "The Novel Démeublé," 17, 80
Catlin, George, 64–65, 150–51 n11
Chase, Richard, 39, 50–51, 139 n6
Chastellux, Marquis de, 4, 6–8, 10–11, 138
Cheyfitz, Eric, 30, 142 n3, 143 n6
Climate change, 6, 22, 147 n11, 150 n10
Belknap on 147, n11
Communism, 94, 162 n13
Conservation, 4–5, 42, 71, 75–80, 86, 90, 135 n1, 136 n2, 136 n3, 137 n5, 138 n5, 147 n7, 153 n2, 153 n3, 154 n5, 155 n6, 155 n9, 158 n23
Cooper, James Fenimore, 4, 10–11, 14, 20–21, 37–53, 55–56, 64–66,

Cooper, James Fenimore *(continued)* 68–69, 72, 125, 132–33, 138 n5, 145 n9, 146 n4, 146 n5, 146 n6, 147 n8, 147 n9, 148 n13, 150 n9, works: *The Chainbearer*, 146 n6, 148 n13; *The Deerslayer*, 48–52, 148 n12; *The Last of the Mohicans*, 48–52; *The Pathfinder*, 52; *The Pioneers*, 42, 44, 47–48, 64, 146 n6; *The Prairie*, 46, 48–52; *The Spy, 48; Wyandotte*, 146 n6
Cooper, Susan Fenimore, 10, 145 n9
Cooper, William, 14, 43–47, 50, 133, 146 n5, 147 n8
Cowley, Malcolm, 128, 166 n7
Crèvecoeur, J. Hector St. John, 41, 43
Cronon, William, 4–6, 135 n1, 136 n2, 136 n3, 137–38 n5

deforestation, 5, 44–45, 140 n2, 147 n11
Deleuze, Gilles and Felix Guattari, 82, 163–164 n19
Derrida, Jacques, 28, 30, 166 n6
Du Bois, W. E. B., 107, 115–17
Duyckink, Evert, 56, 59, 61, 148–49 n2
Dwight, Timothy, 4, 6–8, 10, 14, 21, 41, 43–47, 49–50, 132, 147n9, 148 n2

Earth Day, 5
Ecocriticism, 5, 13
Ecology/ecological, 3, 13, 15, 33, 35, 42, 47, 75–76, 80, 84, 89–103, 129–30, 132, 135–36 n1, 140 n2, 142 n3, 144 n9, 148 n12p
Eliot, T. S., 38, 134
Emerson, Ralph Waldo, 4, 14–16, 19–32, 35–41, 51–52, 55–57, 62–63, 65–66, 68, 76, 82–83, 90, 101, 103, 116, 120, 122, 125–27, 144 n9, 145 n1, 152 n17; and celebrity, 27, 31, 143 n7; fame and reputation, 139–40 n1, 140 n2, 143 n5, 143 n6; and women, p 140 n3; and natural science, 140–41n 3; and imperialism p 142, n 3; lecturing, lecture reception, and audience reactions, 143, n7; works: "Circles," 19; "Earth-Song," 20; "Hamatreya," 20; "The Method of Nature," 20; "Nature," 23–24; *Nature*, 20–27, 37–38, 55, 141 n3; "Woodnotes," 20
Emersonian gaze, 132
Environment, 4, 6, 8, 11, 13–15, 19, 22, 26, 33–35, 38–39, 42–43, 48, 57–59, 61–66, 71–74, 82–83, 85, 89, 91, 99, 102, 112, 116, 117, 132, 135 n1, 138 n5, 139 n6, 146 n6, 148 n2, 150 n10, 159 n1
environmental activism, 11, 16, 89, 93, 101
environmental gaze, 23–25, 31, 63, 68, 74, 82, 87–88
Environmental politics, 2, 4–5, 8, 10–15, 38, 42–43, 53, 56, 73–74, 76–77, 79–80, 101, 125–26, 132–34, 135 n1, 137 n4, 137 n5, 153 n2
Environmentalism, 5, 9–10, 13, 30, 35, 92, 97, 135 n1, 136–37 n4, 146 n6, 146–47 n7, 150 n11, 152 n15, 159 n1
expansionism, expansionist, 9–10, 19–21, 43–44, 48, 50–51, 55, 88, 91, 125, 132, 138 n5, 146 n6, 148 n13, 151 n11
Exxon Valdez, 5

Faulkner, William, 1, 3, 11, 15, 103, 127, 142 n3, 159 n1; works: *Flags in the Dust*, 159 n1; *Go Down Moses*, 3, 103, 159 n1
federal government, United States, 76, 154 n5
Federalism/federalist, 14, 38, 41, 43, 45–48, 50, 52–53, 55, 64, 146 n6
Felton, C(ornelius), C(onway), 56, 59–60
Fiedler, Leslie, 14, 28, 39, 50, 52, 139 n6

Fire!!, 103, 107, 159 n2
Florida, 16, 103–104, 106–107, 109–16, 119–23, 161–62 n10, 162 n14, 162 n15, 164 n20
forest, 7–8, 21, 23, 45–46, 48, 64, 66–67, 77, 127–28, 154 n5
Foucault, Michel, 51
Franklin, Benjamin, 40–41
Fuller, Margaret, 14, 55, 68, 140 n3

game laws, 42, 47, 136, n 3
genteel, the, 69, 72, 74
genteel tradition, 28, 39–40, 55, 69, 71–72, 152 n17
Giamatti, Bartlett, 28–30, 143 n6
Glotfelty, Cheryl, 13
Gore, Albert, 5
Great Migration, 16, 104, 110
Greeley, Horace, 37, 145 n1
Green, Paul, 114

Habermas, Jürgen, 137 n4
Harlem, 16, 103, 104, 108–109, 112–14, 115, 118–21, 123, 159–60 n3
Harlem Renaissance, 16, 103, 105, 107, 114, 117–19, 160 n4, 161 n8
Hemingway, Ernest, 2–3, 11, 15–16, 21, 74, 125–34, 164 n1, 164 n2, 165 n3, 166 n4, 166 n6, 166 n7; works: *Green Hills of Africa*, 3, 16, 126, 130–33, 166 n7; *In Our Time*, 3, 16, 126–33, 139 n5, 164 n2; "Indian Camp," 127, 165 n3; "Three-Day Blow," 127; "Cross Country Snow," 127; "Big Two-Hearted River," 127–30; "L'Envoi," 127, 129–30; "On the Quai at Smyrna," 129–30, 164 n2
Hetch Hetchy Valley, 71, 79, 151–52 n15, 155 n9
Holmes, Oliver Wendell, 19, 71
Hughes, Langston, 103, 106–109, 112–13, 159 n2
Hurst, Fanny, 105–106, 119
Hurston, Zora Neale, 15–16, 21, 74, 102–23, 126, 132, 159 n2, 160 n3, 162 n14, 162 n15, 163 n16, 164 n21; works: *Dust Tracks on a Road*, 107, 160 n6; *Jonah's Gourd Vine*, 116, 119–21, 163 n19; "Spunk," 105; *Their Eyes Were Watching God*, 109–10, 116–23, 163 n19, 164 n 20

Imperialism, 7, 14, 16, 20–21, 25, 30, 32–35, 38, 47–48, 50–53, 55, 74, 81, 125, 127, 130–31, 139 n6, 141–42 n3, 143 n6, 145 n9, 149 n5, 151 n11, 156 n13, 157 n16
Indian River: 112–13, 115, 123
Irving, Washington, 55, 68

Jeffers, Robinson, 20
Jehlen, Myra, 6, 139 n6
Johnson, Charles S., 103, 108–109

Kalm, Peter, 6, 8, 10–11, 136 n3, 138 n5
Kolodny, Annette, 12, 42–43, 139 n6

Lawrence, D. H., 14, 39, 41, 50, 143 n6
Lefebvre, Henri, 25–27, 139 n7, 163–64 n19
Leverenz, David, 71
Lewis and Clark, 32, 52, 131
Locke, Alain, 106–10, 112–14, 117–19, 161 n8. Works: *The New Negro,* 114, 117–18
Longfellow, Henry Wadsworth, 4, 14–15, 20, 28, 55–74, 80, 125, 144 n8, 148–52; works: "Defence of Poetry," 56–58, 149 n3; *Evangeline*, 15, 56, 62–63, 65–68, 150 n7, 152 n17; *Kavanagh*, 56–57, 59–63, 148 n2, 149 n5; "The Literary Spirit of Our Country," 56–60, 63, 148–49 n1; "Our Native Poets," 148 n 1; *The Song of Hiawatha*, 15, 56, 62, 64, 67, 152 n17
Love Canal, 5

Lowell, James Russell, 15, 56, 148–49 n2
Lynching, 110–11, 118–19, 121, 161 n10, 162 n13, 163 n18

Marsh, George Perkins, 4, 11, 64–65, 137–39 n5
Marx, Leo, 12, 29, 39, 41, 139 n6
Mason, Charlotte Osgood, 105–10, 113–14, 119, 160 n4, 160 n6, 160 n7
Mathews, Cornelius, 14, 15, 56–57, 59–62, 68, 149 n2, 149 n5, 149–50 n6
Matthiessen, F. O., 28, 39–40, 62–63, 139 n6
McClure's, 77, 79–80, 155 n10
Merchant, Carolyn, 4–5, 135 n1, 136 n2, 136 n3, 140 n2, 141 n3, 143 n7, 163 n 17
Meyer, Annie Nathan, 105, 119
Miller, Perry, 4–5, 8, 149 n5, 150 n 6
Modernism, 13, 38–39, 63, 71, 74–75, 117–18, 134, 146 n3, 156 n11
Monstrosity, 92–95, 98–101, 157–58 n22
Morris, Saundra, 30, 142 n5
Muir, John, 4, 11, 71, 75, 79, 135–36 n1, 137 n5, 151 n15, 152 n15, 153 n2, 155 n8, 155 n9

nationalism, 9, 38, 50, 56–57, 59, 62118, 142 n3, 149 n3, 149 n5
national parks, 71, 76, 138 n8, 151 n11, 151 n15, 153 n3, 155 n8
natural science, 21, 51, 52, 98, 140–41 n3, 158 n23
natural space, 16–17, 20, 25–27, 32, 48–49, 63, 126, 128, 130, 153 n2
nature and gender, 140 n2
Nature Writing, 144 n8, 145 n9
new social movements, 137 n4
New York, 6, 8, 37, 59, 77, 79–80, 90, 98, 104, 107–10, 137 n5, 150 n11, 155 n9, 159–60 n3, 162–63 n15
New York Times, 77–78, 153 n4, 155 n9
New York Tribune, 37
New Yorker, 159 n25
nostalgia, 70, 81, 84, 104, 110, 151 n14, 156 n12, 156 n13

Ocoee, 111–12, 161 n12
Oelschlaeger, Max 35, 135 n1, 142 n3, 144 n9
Opportunity, 103, 105, 108–109

panorama, 8, 44, 61, 63, 66, 88–89, 147 n10, 150 n7
patronage, 16, 103–105, 109, 117, 121, 123, 160 n4, 160 n7
Pease, Donald, 28–30, 139 n6, 143 n6
Pinchot, Gifford, 4, 11, 71, 79, 151–52 n15, 153 n2
Poe, Edgar Allan, 28, 39–40, 55, 68, 151 n12
Porte, Joel, 30, 142 n5, 143 n6
Pratt, Mary Louise, 51–52, 141 n3
Preservation, 71, 75–76, 86, 95, 97–99, 101, 127, 129, 135 n1, 138 n5, 147 n7, 153 n2, 158 n23
Progressive Era, 75–76

radicalism, figures of and reactions to, 3, 10–11, 75–76, 82, 90–95, 96, 100–101, 132, 137 n4, 162 n13
Ricketts, Ed 90, 95, 98, 157 n19, 157 n20
Ritter, William Emerson 90
Rollins College 113–15
Roosevelt, Eleanor 162 n13
Roosevelt, Theodore 4, 77–80, 125–26, 137 n5, 151 n15, 153 n5, 155 n6, 155 n7, 155 n9, 164 n1

Sale, Kirkpatrick 5, 136 n1
Santayana, George, 14–15, 19, 28, 38–41, 43, 52, 55, 68–69, 71–75, 145–46 n3. Works: "The Genteel

Tradition in American Philosophy," 28, 39, 69, 71, 152 n17; "Genteel American Poetry," 69; "The Moral Background," 69
schizophrenia, 75, 76, 80–82, 89
sentimentality, "the sentimental" 2, 4–5, 12, 58, 68, 76, 80, 109, 151 n14, 160 n4
Smith, Henry Nash, 11, 39, 41, 139 n6
Socialism/socialist, 94, 162 n13
South, American, 16, 103–104, 109–12, 115–23, 161 n10, 162 n15
spatial practice, 26, 27, 139 n7, 142 n4
Steinbeck, John 2–4, 11, 14–16, 21, 74–76, 89–101, 103, 125–27, 132, 157 n19, 157 n20, 158 n23, 158 n24, 129 n25; works: *America and Americans*, 3, 91, 94–95, 159n25; *Cannery Row*, 3, 90, 98–100, 158n23; *The Grapes of Wrath*, 90, 93–94; "I am a Revolutionary," 94; *Log to the* Sea of Cortez, see *Sea of Cortez*; *Of Mice and Men*, 92–94; *Sea of Cortez*, 3, 91, 94–98, 157 n20; *Sweet Thursday*, 90, 98, 100, 158 n23; *To a God Unknown*, 90, 92–93, 100; *Tortilla Flat*, 93; *Travels with Charley*, 3, 91–92, 94, 158 n24, 159 n25
sublime, the, 24, 27, 87, 99

Taft, William Howard, 77–79, 151 n15, 155 n7
Taylor, Charles Vincent, 90
Tichi, Cecelia, 12, 42–43, 146 n6, 148 n2
Thoreau, Henry David, 4, 14, 16, 19–20, 28, 31–36, 41, 126–27, 130–31, 140 n1, 144 n8, 144–45 n9; legacy as environmental thinker, 144 n8; reception and publishing history, 144 n 8; works: *Walden*, 31–35, 130–31, 144 n8, 144–45 n9; "Walking," 32–35
Thurman, Wallace, 103, 107, 112, 159 n2
Tompkins, Jane, 39, 71
Toomer, Jean, 74, 102, 115, 117–19, 121, 163 n18
Twain, Mark, 14, 38, 41, 145 n2, 145 n3

Updike, John, 28–30, 143 n6
Urgo, Joseph, 86, 153 n3

Van Vetchen, Carl, 105, 114, 162 n15
Violence, 16, 23, 26, 41, 48–49, 51, 95, 104, 111–12, 119, 120–21, 127, 130, 161 n10
virgin land, idea of, 11, 12, 48–50, 53, 55, 65, 126, 132

Waggoner, Hyatt, 28
Wall, Cheryll, 107, 160 n6
Washington, Booker T., 115–17, 161 n10
Webster, Noah, 6
White, Walter, 161 n9, 162 n13
Whitman, Walt, 15, 28, 39–41, 70, 72–73, 152 n16
Whittier, John Greenleaf, 55, 71
Wilderness, 1, 16, 20, 31–32, 34–35, 43–44, 47, 52, 63, 103, 115, 130–32, 135 n1, 140 n2, 145 n9, 146 n6, 155 n9
Wilderness Act, 5
Wilson, Edmund, 138
Wilson, Woodrow, 77
Woodress, James, 80, 156 n10

Žižek, Slavoj, 137 n4